SOLIH LI

D1419051

the cinema of KATHRYN BIGELOW

DIRECTORS' CUTS

CHECKED   JUN 2008

the cinema of

KATHRYN BIGELOW

hollywood transgressor

edited by
DEBORAH JERMYN & SEAN REDMOND

✸ **WALLFLOWER PRESS** LONDON & NEW YORK

Rec **1 7 NOV 2003**
Stock no. 21865
Class
791.
43⅓
BIG/JER
Labels ✓
T

First published in Great Britain in 2003 by
Wallflower Press
5 Pond Street, London NW3 2PN
www.wallflowerpress.co.uk

Copyright © Deborah Jermyn & Sean Redmond 2003

The moral right of Deborah Jermyn & Sean Redmond to be identified as the editors of this work has been asserted in accordance with the Copyright, Designs and Patents Act of 1988

All rights reserved. No part of this publication may be reproduced, stored in a retrieval system, or transported in any form or by any means, electronic, mechanical, photocopying, recording or otherwise, without the prior permission of both the copyright owners and the above publisher of this book

A catalogue for this book is available from the British Library

ISBN 1-903364-42-6 (paperback)
ISBN 1-903364-43-4 (hardback)

Book design by Rob Bowden Design

Printed in Great Britain by Antony Rowe, Chippenham, Wiltshire

CONTENTS

ACKNOWLEDGEMENTS

Gavin Smith, 'Momentum and Design', was originally published in *Film Comment*, (Sept/Oct 1995), extract reproduced here by permission of the author. Robert T. Self, 'Redressing the Law in Kathryn Bigelow's *Blue Steel*', was originally published in the *Journal of Film and Video* (Summer 1994) and is reproduced here by permission of the author.

The editors wish to thank students, friends and colleagues at the Southampton Institute, in particular Cathy Fowler, Su Holmes and David Lusted; Conrad Withey from Momentum Pictures; the Stills Department at the British Film Institute; Simon Tomlinson for sharing his technical expertise; our contributors and Yoram Allon of Wallflower Press, for their enthusiasm and commitment to this project.

DJ – special thanks to Abigail Hanna, Abigail Kearley, Johnny Law, Nova Matthias and Steve Willmott who have indulged and tolerated discussion of Kathryn Bigelow with patience beyond the call of duty.

SR – special thanks to Carla, Joshua and Caitlin for their patience and burgeoning love of cinema.

NOTES ON CONTRIBUTORS

Will Brooker is Assistant Professor in Communication at Richmond, the American International University in London. His books include *Batman Unmasked* (Continuum, 2000), *Using the Force: Creativity, Community and Star Wars Fans* (Continuum, 2002) and, with Deborah Jermyn, *The Audience Studies Reader* (Routledge, 2002). He is currently researching discourses around Lewis Carroll's Alice in popular culture.

Deborah Jermyn is Senior Lecturer in Film Studies at the Southampton Institute, UK. She has published in *Screen* and *Feminist Media Studies* and is co-editor, with Will Brooker, of *The Audience Studies Reader* (Routledge, 2002). She is currently engaged in research into *Crimewatch UK*.

Sara Gwenllian Jones is Lecturer in Film, TV and Digital Media at Cardiff University and co-editor of *Intensities: the Journal of Cult Media* (www.cult-media.com). She is currently writing a book on cult television (Edward Arnold, forthcoming).

Christina Lane is Assistant Professor in the Motion Picture Program at the University of Miami. She is the author of *Feminist Hollywood: From Born in Flames to Point Break* (Wayne State University Press, 2000). She has published articles in *The Journal of Popular Film and Television* and *Cinema Journal* and has served as co-editor of *The Velvet Light Trap*.

Sean Redmond is Senior Lecturer in Film Studies at the Southampton Institute, UK. He is author of *Media Institutions* (Auteur Press, 2001) and editor of *Liquid Metal: The Science Fiction Reader* (Wallflower Press, forthcoming). He has research interests in the cultural representations of whiteness and cinematic transgression.

Steven Jay Schneider has contributed to such journals as *CineAction!*, *Post Script* and *The Journal of Popular Film and Television*. He is co-editor of *Underground U.S.A.: Filmmaking Beyond the Hollywood Canon* (Wallflower Press, 2002) and *Dark Thoughts: Philosophic Reflections on Cinematic Horror* (Scarecrow Press, forthcoming.)

Robert T. Self is Professor of English at Northern Illinois University. He is the author of *Barrett Wendell* (Twayne Publishers, 1976) and *Robert Altman's Subliminal Reality* (University of Minnesota Press, 2002), and his essays have appeared in *North American Review*, *The Velvet Light Trap*, *Film Quarterly* and *Cinema Journal*.

Steven Shaviro teaches in the Cinema Studies Program at the University of Washington. He is the author of *The Cinematic Body* (Minnesota, 1993), *Doom Patrols: A Theoretical Fiction About Postmodernism* (Serpent's Tail, 1997) and essays and forthcoming books on contemporary film, popular culture and cyberculture.

Gavin Smith is the editor of *Film Comment* and author of *Sayles on Sayles* (Faber and Faber, 1998). His interviews and film criticism have appeared in *Film Comment, Sight and Sound, The Village Voice* and *Frieze*. He is also a program associate at the Film Society of Lincoln Center's Walter Reade Theater and co-curator of the New York Film Festival's annual 'Views from the Avant-Garde' experimental film programme and the New York Video Festival.

Romi Stepovich is a PhD candidate in the Critical Studies Department of Film, Television and New Media at UCLA, a part-time lecturer at California State University, Los Angeles and a Teaching Fellow at UCLA. She has worked for a number of years in the film industry as a development executive and an Associate Producer.

Robynn J. Stilwell is a musicologist at Georgetown University. Her research is interdisciplinary, embracing both popular and art music traditions, and involves the interaction of music with other media, including film, dance, and television. She is the author of *Recontextualizing Music: The Use of Pre-Existing Music in Film* (University of California Press, forthcoming).

INTRODUCTION

Hollywood Transgressor: The Cinema of Kathryn Bigelow

Deborah Jermyn & Sean Redmond

Bigelow and the Romantic Tradition of Authorship

It could be argued that this is a romantic book, held together by a romantic idea, underpinned by a romantic conception. It could be said that any book that holds out for the sovereignty of an artist and the creativity and autonomy of the individual is bound to be full of romance, especially where the artist in question works within a commercialised industry such as American film.

The romantic idea of the very best painters, poets, writers and musicians as creative geniuses, misunderstood artists struggling to capture something unique, troubling or eternal about the human condition has been a long-standing part of socio-cultural discourses about the meaning and the place of art and artists within society (see Abrams 1981; Buscombe 1973). So, the romanticised myth runs, the 'outsider' artist works against the grain, against the prevailing artistic traditions and working practices of the day to capture the world, its places and people, its hopes and fears in epoch-changing ways. Romanticised artists not only transform their craft but the way spectators, readers, listeners and other artists see their craft and the social world itself.

Undoubtedly there is a degree of romance in this edited collection of essays on the cinema of Kathryn Bigelow. In fact, one of the key determinants of this book is to locate Bigelow as a film-making artist who is able to transcend the collective, industrial and commercial constraints of the Hollywood cinema machine to *individually author* her films in innovative and transgressive ways. In this study Bigelow is contextualised as a contemporary auteur, as a director with a distinct visual style who returns to the same themes and obsessions, and as a film-maker who pushes cinematic boundaries, both in terms of film form and the representation of gender. All of Bigelow's films are marked by a play with genre, and by ideological practices that question and undermine the formation of masculine and feminine identity.

On one level, then, the approach to Bigelow's film work that is taken here aligns itself with a particular tradition in film theory, a tradition that gives a privileged position to the role of the director. The origins of such a position lie with Alexandre Astruc's 1948 article, 'The Birth of a New Avant-Garde: La Camera-Stylo', in which he argues that the most creative directors use the film camera like a pen to write their worldview into the film. It is François Truffaut, however, in his seminal 1954 article, *La Politique des Auteurs*, who first makes the distinction between the 'auteur' or creative director and the 'metteur-en-scène', the director who merely reproduces the ideas of someone else (generally the scriptwriter). Andrew Sarris (1981) developed Truffaut's idea of the auteur film-maker into what he called a theory of authorship or 'the auteur theory' whereby the greatest directors were to be placed in a pantheon, and deemed worthy of study because of their position within this directorial premier league. Sarris's league of directors was a contentious one, since it drew heavily on film-makers working within Hollywood cinema. He argued that the very best film directors were to be found working in the American studio system and in American commercial cinema generally because of the production constraints that existed there.

In Sarris' romantic conception of the auteur, the most important films are the expression of the emotions, experiences and worldview of an individual director. This individual personality – the mark of a true 'auteur' – will be discovered through textual excavation across the body of their work regardless of and sometimes because of the constraints they find themselves working under. Hollywood's adherence to 'green lighting' genre pictures or films with formulaic scripts and the controlling power generally given to producers and studio executives right across the production processes work to constrain the artistic impulses of the auteur. However, according to Sarris, in this (entirely male) pantheon the auteur will wrestle with such constraints, will find *his* personal vision precisely because of and not in spite of such constraints, to produce something meaningful. Coherence and consistency of underlying theme and style becomes the signature of an authored cinema, Sarris argues:

The auteur critic is obsessed with the wholeness of art and the artist. He looks at film as a whole, a director as a whole. The parts, however entertaining individually, must cohere meaningfully. This meaningful coherence is more likely when the director dominates the proceedings with skill and purpose. (Sarris 1981: 65)

Bigelow, in one sense, clearly fits Sarris' conditions of entry into the pantheon of great American directors, both because she works within mainstream Hollywood cinema and because one can find or discover 'meaningful coherence' across the body of her film work. However, the transgresive nature of her authorship also connects her to the authorship traditions of European Art Cinema. Working in a different film-making context, it is often suggested that European auteurs are more able, have more freedom, to inscribe their films with radical and thought provoking messages; that they are able to test and push back the boundaries of film language and film representation in deliberate and often self-reflective ways. Steve Neale, for example, argues that European film directors are a 'conscious presence … directing audiences where to look' (1981: 11). One can look at Bigelow's films in the same way; her political play with genre and gender is self-conscious, and the signs of her authorship are a knowing presence in her film work, so that in much the same way that a Bresson or a Fellini film bears the corporeal traces of their authorship, a Bigelow film will bear the mark of her authorship throughout. Bigelow, in fact, is often written about as a film-maker who moves in and between the spaces of popular film conventions and art cinema traditions (Lane 1998) – as a European-inspired auteur working within the Hollywood cinema machine.

Bigelow's cinema of transgression, then, is a contradictory or paradoxical activity. On the one hand Bigelow subverts the codes and conventions of dominant film form, in part through employing a range of art-cinema devices (self-reflexivity, self-conscious camera work, the corporeal traces of her authorship), and on the other she accepts (and pays homage to) these codes and conventions by reveling in their exploration and execution. In short, by bestowing the moniker of 'Hollywood Transgressor' on Bigelow, the editors and contributors to this book are acknowledging how her work partly falls within *and* partly infringes the parameters of Hollywood cinema.

It could also be said, however, that this is a feminist book, driven by feminist principles and a feminist political agenda. It could be said that any book that attempts to foreground and contextualise the work of a female director is driven by a desire to question the male-centred and patriarchal-inspired tradition of authorship work which has, in the main, only canonised or valorised a 'pantheon' of great male directors. Authorship theory has marginalised or, much worse, effaced the great body of work by female directors so that in terms of film scholarship, classification and canonisation, women film-makers are nowhere, or only somewhere marginal, to be found. Writing in 1973, Claire Johnston was one of the first feminists to address this problem, suggesting that authorship theory produced a universal ideal of great cinema devoid of reference to cultural and historical context, and empty of references to women and gender.

> The idea that art is universal and thus potentially androgynous is basically idealist: art can only be defined as a discourse within a particular conjunction – for the purpose of women's cinema, the bourgeois, sexist ideology of male dominated capitalism. (Johnston in Kaplan 2000: 28)

This collection of essays clearly intends to situate Bigelow's film work within a guiding feminist perspective. By unpacking Bigelow's distinctive style of authorship, by foregrounding her visual artistry and her radical politics, by making a contextualised and progressive case for her innovative and challenging cinema, and by embedding and exploring the function of gender both textually and extra-textually across her film work, the editors and writers of this book are attempting to give Bigelow the critical and academic attention so often denied to female directors. If the editors were to play Ginette Vincendeau's (1998) 'game' of producing a pantheon of great female directors, then Bigelow would be in the canon.

However, to complicate matters, in numerous interviews Bigelow repeatedly denies the centrality of her gender to the style and radical politics of her films and to her position within Hollywood cinema. In fact, Bigelow attempts to represent herself as an author before or outside of gender, as a film-maker for whom the category or label of female is irrelevant. Bigelow herself plays on androgyny in the way she mixes feminine and masculine codes in her public appearances (for example, she is often photographed in a rather fetishised manner, wearing a trouser suit but with her long dark hair worn loose). Of course, the effect of Bigelow trying to efface her own gender from questions of authorship, and of her own carefully constructed media image, serve to actually underline the sense that in reading Bigelow one has to attend to her as an author who is at the very least immersed in gender politics. In fact, by attempting to *de-sex* her own authorship Bigelow implicitly connects herself to the radical androgyny of many of her central film protagonists, in effect providing a further motive for examining or exploring gender as part of her authorship.

It could also be said that this is a book driven by post-modernist, and (post-) auteur-structuralist concerns, concerns that take into account a number of key academic interventions that cracked open authorship studies in the 1980s. While authorship theory had always identified the director as the source and producer of meaning in a film, writers such as Roland Barthes (1977) turned this conception on its head by suggesting that meaning can never have this one point of origin (a sole creator), but rather must always be seen to emerge culturally, through a culture's shared language or sign system. Authors are not sovereign; rather, they are already written by the culture they exist in, and so any meaning that is produced is not singularly theirs. In this climate, authorship theory struggled to come to terms with a disintegrating sense of where meaning came from, how meaning was transmitted, and how meaning was received. Authors could no longer be seen as 'real' people, consciously reflecting free-thinking ideas through their texts, but either as unconscious structures with a set of meta-antinomies structuring their work (for example, the meta-antinomies of civilisation/wilderness in the work of John Ford: see Wollen 1998); or as constructed subjects themselves authored by the prevailing 'regimes of truth' (Foucault 1980: 131), so that what they spoke or saw or painted or filmed was culturally determined rather than the result of their unique, personalized vision.

However, in the 1980s auteur directors also become more definably commodified and branded, sold in the market place as guarantors of a certain type of film, and of a quantifiable box-office return (Corrigan 1991). In 'High Concept' Hollywood (Wyatt 1994) the auteur becomes a key ingredient in the pitch to green light a movie; a central component of the marketing campaign; the sign of cinematic quality on a film poster or trailer; and the mark of approval on a credit sequence. The words, *A film by Kathryn Bigelow*, brand the film like some high-status anchorage on an advert for a fast car.

This is a book that attempts to place an authorship study in terms of this *cultural turn* (Hall 1997) or the academic shift that took into account the impact of language and representation on meaning-making. A central part of this cultural turn is a recognition that meaning is never finally fixed and that interpretation (decoding) by spectators and audiences at the site of consumption is of central importance to understanding the different ways that texts can be read. In this final configuration the author becomes merely one of many representational signs or entry points into the cinema, no more significant or meaningful for audiences than the signs and codes of genre, or the cluster of signs that go into making a film star. In this final configuration the author is displaced from the centre of the cinema machine, so that by the end of the authorship journey at least part of the romance is dead.

Dead but not buried. Across the pages of this book, both implicitly and explicitly, we find all these versions of authorship present, underpinning argument, intellectualising illustration, contextualising analysis and point of view. We also find much of the history of authorship, and consequently some of the problems associated with it. *Bigelow: Hollywood Transgressor* – a romantic notion, an art-house auteur, a feminist icon, a representational sign and brand, but always, in one sense or another, ever-present as trace, structure or representation.

For two decades Kathryn Bigelow has been both confounding and (re-)defining what it is to be a director in post-classical Hollywood, demanding with every new film release that her audience reassess who and what 'Bigelow' is. She has demonstrated how the barriers and borders pertaining to gender, genre and film form in contemporary Hollywood are under constant negotiation. She has managed to straddle the presumed dichotomy between art-house predilections and commercial success. She has arguably become the most visible, enduring and accomplished woman film-maker yet to sustain a career in post-classical Hollywood. Having established a reputation as an experimental and provocative film-maker whose command of spectacle has manipulated and extended the capabilities of cinematic technology, and with a major new production, *K-19: The Widowmaker* (2002) starring Harrison Ford recently released, a reflective and investigative account of her work is now in order.

Before embarking on a journey through Bigelow's oeuvre some biographical contextualisation is necessary, since it is hard not to locate the seeds of much of her distinctiveness as a film-maker in the specifics of her background. Born in California, she was studying painting at the San Francisco Art Institute when in 1971, aged 19, she won a scholarship to the prestigious Whitney Museum in New York, where tutors included Susan Sontag and Richard Serra. Here she developed her interest and participation in the avant-garde art scene, becoming a member of Art and Language, a British-based group of conceptual artists, and working as an assistant to performance artist Vito Acconci. Throughout this time Bigelow was increasingly drawn to the more expansive communicative potential of film over art. She has said that she felt prompted to make the transition from painting to film because

> I felt painting was isolating and a little bit elitist, whereas film has the potential to become an incredible social tool with which you can reach a mass audience. Some painting requires a certain amount of knowledge or education on the part of the viewer to be appreciated. Film is not like that. It *must* be accessible to work within a cinematic context. (Bigelow in Bahiana 1992: 34)

Hence she next enrolled in Columbia University's Graduate School of Film where she worked with such notables as director Milos Forman and seminal film theorist Peter Wollen, committing herself to the medium that would allow her to explore her interests more expressly.

This intellectual background and training in 'high' art informs much of the weighty critical reception that has met Bigelow despite her penchant for the seemingly superficial allure of glossy action, and accounts for the ease with which she alludes to cultural theory in interview. In Bigelow, the taste for high-concept, visceral violence is tempered with a 'serious' critical engagement with associated issues; her first short film, *Set-Up* (1978), a twenty-minute experimental piece in which two men fight one another in an alley while two philosophers discuss the violence in voiceover, was an early indicator of some of the preoccupations which would go on to characterise her work. It pointed to what would become her recurrent fascination with the nature of 'masculinity', violence and the cinematic representation of violence, in narratives that seem to pander to these volatile themes while also taking a self-conscious and critical distance from them.

Set-Up enabled sufficient interest and confidence in Bigelow for her to move on to *The Loveless* (1982), her first feature film, co-written and co-directed with Monty Montgomery who had also been a film student at Columbia. Bigelow's art background is again evident here, though in different ways to *Set-Up*. This meditative snapshot of a gang of bikers passing through quintessential 1950s small-town America brings a loving, painterly eye to bear on the iconography of the era and the road-movie genre, with visual referents borrowed from Edward Hopper as much as *The Wild One* (László Benedek, 1953) and *Scorpio Rising* (Kenneth Anger, 1964). Despite the explosive events of the film, which culminate in the central female character, Telena, shooting her sexually-abusive father before committing suicide, it is marked by its leisurely pacing, fragmented exposition, performances and dialogue, all of which underline its low-budget, art-house origins. Furthermore, Augusta's sleazy but poignantly desperate striptease in the town's trashy bar was also an early example of Bigelow's characteristically ambivalent manipulation of the cinematic gaze and the power structures contained therein; the spectator is given the opportunity to pursue voyeuristic pleasure but in a context so discomforting that Bigelow seems to be exposing the tawdriness of the gaze as much as indulging it.

But it was *Near Dark* (1987) which really heralded Bigelow's arrival, quickly winning a cult status following among fans. As Sara Gwenllian Jones' essay in this collection points out, this modern-day fusing of the western and vampire genres has proved enduringly charismatic, with its evocative use of landscapes and light and oddly alluring depiction of the vampires' outlaw existence. Even at this early stage in her career, a fascination with sub- or counter-cultural lifestyles and a blurring of genre and gender distinctions were starting to emerge as signature preoccupations for

Bigelow. Themes that had already been set in motion by *The Loveless* are very much in evidence again. The 'outsiders' of *Near Dark* – its destructive but seductive vampire gang – are both feared and desired, just as *The Loveless'* bikers had been (and as the surfers of *Point Break* (1991) would go on to be). With her slight figure, cropped hair and command of traditionally 'male' spaces (the night, the road) *Near Dark*'s Mae seems both to mirror the androgyny of Telena and prefigure *Point Break*'s Tyler. In all three films we see a marked ambiguity around gender and desire, pursued not just through the films' androgynous casting but through their shared motif of latent homoeroticism.

Near Dark left Oliver Stone sufficiently impressed to produce Bigelow's next film, *Blue Steel* (1990). With Jamie Lee Curtis taking the lead role as Megan Turner, a rookie cop who finds herself the focus of an obsessive and deadly stalker who has witnessed her shooting an armed robber, *Blue Steel* represented another significant step up the Hollywood hierarchy for Bigelow. Co-scripted, like *Near Dark*, by Bigelow and Eric Red (whose later film *Undertow* (1996) stemmed from another writing collaboration between the two), *Blue Steel* received an enthusiastic popular and critical reception on a number of counts.

Firstly, it presented a complex and thoughtful depiction of a woman cop, positing another intriguingly androgynous articulation of gender and intervening in the conventions of the action genre. Secondly, it also featured some impressive cinematography, most notably perhaps the strikingly elegant exploratory movement in and around a Smith & Wesson gun in the opening sequence. With its haunting soundtrack, exquisite lighting and beguilingly fluid camerawork, the gun is disconcertingly and erotically transformed into an object of beauty as the camera manoeuvres its way around one intimate surface after another. It is a remarkable sequence that points, as *Set-Up* had, not just to Bigelow's cinematographic skill and inventiveness but to her (and our) fascination with the relationship between the cinematic audience, representations of violence and the mechanisms of cinema itself. Like *The Loveless*, *Near Dark* pointed again to Bigelow's interest in the melodramatic terrain and sordid secrets of the dysfunctional patriarchal family. Domestic violence lies at the core of Megan's family home just as incest pervaded that of Telena's relationship with her father in *The Loveless*. The largely unspoken tensions and resentments surrounding the families of Bigelow's first three features are returned to again in *The Weight of Water* (2000) where Jean's and Maren's families are both finally destroyed by sexual and emotional betrayal and jealousy. For Bigelow, the family is an inherently fraught and constricting institution, particularly for women.

Given the 'latent feminism' (Tasker 1999: 15) which seemed to inform *Blue Steel*, and indeed given Bigelow's performance in Lizzie Borden's *Born in Flames* (1983), 'a feminist utopian film in which radical feminists and lesbians attempt to take over the United States' (Lane 2000: 101), Bigelow's next film initially perhaps seemed something of a departure. Centring on the efforts of FBI agent Johnny Utah (Keanu Reeves) to infiltrate a gang of suspected bank-robbing surfers led by guru figure Bodhi (Patrick Swayze), *Point Break* was awash in a sea of testosterone. In it, Utah embarks on an Oedipal battle in which he desires approval and acceptance from two 'fathers', both Bodhi and his FBI boss, tellingly named 'Pappas' (Gary Busey).

However as Sean Redmond's essay in this collection argues, it is precisely in the excess with which Bigelow embarks on the action sequences and homoerotically charged male relationships of *Point Break* that its radical potential lies. While appearing to adhere to the rules of the action genre, Bigelow also exaggerated them in such an unrelenting fashion that she seemed to be toying with how far she could take both her characters and audience; witness the now-celebrated chase sequence where, along with Utah, 'we' the audience breathtakingly pursue Bodhi through a series of streets and houses seemingly without pause. Demonstrating her creative and innovative pursuit of the capabilities of camera technology again, this sequence was made possible through Bigelow's development of a specially lightweight Steadicam. Indeed the evident creativity and enthusiasm with which Bigelow takes on and experiments with cinematic technology is another way in which she undermines gendered discourses, within which women have traditionally been positioned as beyond or outside of the command of technology.

Bigelow's interest in groups of outsiders who elect to constitute a community as an alternative, or in opposition, to the conventional family unit and mainstream society is also evident here again in the surfers' radical group lifestyle. Like the vampires of *Near Dark*, they offer an enticing if ultimately untenable counter-cultural existence. The demise of these groups does not suggest that a conservative impulse lies behind Bigelow's work however, as Redmond's, Gwenllian Jones' and Steven Jay Schneider's essays argue, since all of these groups would rather give themselves up to annihilation than concede to conservative authority and dominant ideology.

With the success of *Point Break* Bigelow seemed to have secured her place on Hollywood's A-list but Hollywood is, of course, a fickle machine. Having directed an episode of cult television series *Wild Palms* in the intervening period in 1993, her next film, *Strange Days* (1995), knocked her from the top of the hierarchy just as soon as she had arrived. With its impressive cast, spectacular sci-fi setting and writing and producer credits from *Terminator* (1984) director James Cameron (who also executive produced *Point Break* and who Bigelow had married in 1989 and divorced in 1991), *Strange Days* seemed set for blockbuster success. However, as the essays that make up Part Two of this book detail at length, this thought-provoking but flawed film failed to fulfil its box-office promise. In a now familiar play with gender conventions, audiences seemed to respond well to Mace (Angela Bassett) as a commanding female action-hero, but not to Lenny (Ralph Fiennes) as a feminised anti-hero – another of Bigelow's 'rebel' males caught up in a crisis of masculinity.

Strange Days also demonstrated Bigelow's fascination with the objectifying cinematic gaze again, explored in post-modern fashion through the futuristic technology of the SQUID device – hi-tec headgear that enables individuals, and therefore the audience, to 'jack into' the physical and visual sensations experienced by others. The film's dazzling use of point-of-view shots again necessitated a specially adapted camera. In another virtuoso, spatially dislocating chase sequence, Bigelow shatters the confines of camera movement and mobility by pulling off a point-of-view shot from the perspective of a panic-stricken robber attempting to leap between two buildings. As with the opening sequence probing the gun in *Blue Steel* and Utah's robbery chase sequence in *Point Break*, Bigelow's camera here tenaciously enters and explores spaces which one would expect to thwart it. In this way the 'masculine' drive that often seems to underlie Bigelow's work is to be found not just in her penchant for 'male' genres and themes but also, in a more physical sense, in the relentless, penetrative action of her camera.

Controversially though, Bigelow also incorporated *Strange Days'* SQUID/point-of view device into a rape sequence where Lenny, and by extension the cinematic spectator, experiences the attack from the position of both female victim and male rapist. This led to horrified condemnations of her voyeurism, raising the question again of Bigelow's allegiance to/refusal of feminist principles in her work. Despite the fact that her films recurrently return to and play with the representation of gender, sexuality and androgyny, she has remained steadfastly equivocal on the subject of her own feminist politics, refusing to talk about herself as 'a female director'. As Christina Lane has noted:

> Her connections to feminism, as represented in public discourse, have always been ambiguous. She seems quite conscious of feminist politics and willing to engage with feminism, but she remains ambivalent about labelling her films in terms of gender or politics. (Lane 2000: 101)

Indeed Bigelow is of interest to feminist film criticism not just for her film-making, but for the representation of Bigelow herself in the popular and critical discourses that have constructed her persona and which return time and again to the subject of this one-time Gap model's striking good looks. By noting this discourse here this collection is of course contributing to it, yet its prevalence is too ubiquitous not to warrant observation and critique. As Deborah Jermyn's essay argues, there has proved to be something enduringly fascinating about a woman who, through her long, dark hair and willowy build, signifies desirable feminine attributes while simultaneously recurrently working in 'male' genres, and thus signifying a kind of female deviance through her preoccupation with action and violence. The apparent 'contradiction' contained within this conjunction is just one of the factors accounting for Bigelow's peculiar visibility in Hollywood. At this time though, under the cloud of both box-office failure and accusations of having rendered male sexual violence into objectifying spectacle, her career seemed to enter something of a wasteland. It would be five years before she made her next film, *The Weight of Water* (2000).

Bigelow: A Work in Progress

Nevertheless, Bigelow was still very active in this period, which included another foray into television when she directed episodes of *Homicide: Life on the Streets*. More significantly however, for some years she had been nurturing a project about fifteenth-century French heroine Joan of Arc, and to this end had undertaken research and writing (with Jay Cocks from *Strange Days*) for a film to be called *Company of Angels*. French director Luc Besson subsequently came on board to executive produce the project with the promise of securing funding. However, in 1996 Besson and Bigelow fell out when Besson insisted on casting his then-partner, Milla Jovovich, in the lead role, while Bigelow wanted Claire Danes. *Company of Angels* fell apart when Besson left to make his own Joan of Arc film starring Jovovich, *The Messenger: The Story of Joan of Arc* (1999), taking his funding with him. In June 1998 Bigelow filed a suit against Besson for breach of contract, alleging he had appropriated her historical research and numerous original script elements for his film (Ressner 1999; Anon 2001: 64). A settlement was eventually reached but the legal dispute nevertheless meant that Bigelow's cherished project remained unrealised.

At the same time she was also developing *The Weight of Water*, an adaptation of Anita Shreve's novel about a modern-day photojournalist who investigates a lurid nineteenth-century murder mystery. Despite the star-power of Sean Penn and Elizabeth Hurley, the film had only a limited release, for example failing to secure cinematic distribution in Britain, a state of affairs which points to the disappointing reception it has generally met to date. As Jermyn's essay details, with its fragmented interweaving of two narratives, contemplative pacing and unrelentingly bleak atmosphere, this character study does not lend itself to easy viewing and has proved particularly disappointing to those who still associate Bigelow overwhelmingly with the action genre. It remains to be seen if it will eventually garner more enthusiastic interest from audiences, but with two troubled and troubling female protagonists at its core it seems likely that this film will become a central one in the ongoing feminist academic interest in Bigelow's oeuvre.

The period since the box-office disappointment of *Strange Days* has clearly been a trying one for Bigelow. In an industry where the popular adage has it that you're only as big as your last movie, the pressure is clearly on for her to deliver another hit, and, with this in mind perhaps, Bigelow returned to a tense male adventure story with the release of *K-19: The Widowmaker*. Starring Liam Neeson along with Harrison Ford, the film is based on the true story of the 1961 maiden voyage of Russia's first nuclear ballistic submarine that suffered a reactor malfunction at the bottom of the North Sea, threatening to bring the world's superpowers to the brink of nuclear war. Given the epic status of its stars, narrative and budget, the eagerly anticipated *K-19* certainly promised to be the film that could put Bigelow back on the A-list map. It courted controversy in the American media following allegations that it depicted the Russian crew as a bunch of illiterate misfits. Bigelow has denied this strenuously however, commenting that 'From the moment I heard about this story, my motivation has been to make a film that shows the heroism, sacrifice and humanity of these men' (Bigelow 2001).

The sub-genre of the submarine picture enabled Bigelow to return to the kind of territory she had previously handled with consumate flair; it constitutes another 'masculine' genre where melodrama and action meet, centring on the construction of a male community set apart from the rest of society. Bigelow convincingly captures the claustrophobia and growing sense of dread onboard the doomed vessel. The agonising scene where the men wretchedly take turns to enter the reactor in an attempt to carry out repairs was widely praised by critics in the mixed reviews that met the film. But its celebration of the crew's heroism becomes increasingly heavy-handed and some of the characterisation is unsatisfactory. Some three months after its release, the film had recouped only $35 million of its estimated $100 million budget in the US. Reasons posited for its disappointing box-office have ranged from the miscasting of Harrison Ford to the inappropriateness of its summer release date in the US. What is certain is that *K-19*'s lukewarm reception means that Bigelow remains under more pressure than ever to serve up a film which again proves that 'Hollwood transgression' and Hollywood profit are not nutually exclusive.

The essays in this collection are organised in two sections. Part One, 'Bigelow's Moving Canvas', takes a largely chronological journey through Bigelow's oeuvre, exploring the aesthetic and thematic motifs and preoccupations that have marked her work and its reception. The analogy of the 'moving canvas' both positions the essays within the 'romantic tradition' of authorship studies and encapsulates a number of the features that characterise Bigelow's particular authorship style; the manner in which her fine art background – for example, her mastery of composition, framing and lighting – is transposed on to celluloid, and the way in which she has been conceptualised as a director who vividly captures action and spectacle through her bravura camerawork and *mise-en-scène*. However, the notion of the 'moving canvas' also indicates the parallels that can be more generally drawn between film-making and painting. Just as film authorship is embedded in the creative director's command of the camera, of every frame and movement that the audience see on screen, the artistry of painting is embedded in the painter's mastery of the form and content of the canvas.

Breaking with this chronological approach, Part Two, 'The Strange Gaze of Kathryn Bigelow', presents a detailed contextual and textual analysis of *Strange Days*. Such is the growing body of interest and debate over this film that the essays here form a case study exploring its making, reception and circulation from a variety of perspectives. While *Strange Days* was a relatively disappointing commercial failure and received poor reviews on its release, it has since been the subject of growing academic attention. It is now widely understood as a film that self-consciously explores the nature of the cinematic gaze, subjectivity and identification, while the attendant controversy that has dogged it also suggests the potent ways in which *Strange Days* exposes Bigelow's own troubling authorial signature.

Part One – Bigelow's Moving Canvas

This collection opens with an extract from a 1995 Gavin Smith interview with Kathryn Bigelow originally published in *Film Comment*. In the interview Bigelow discusses the aesthetics of a number of her key films and television work, including *Blue Steel*, *Point Break* and *Near Dark*, referring to every aspect of the film-making process. She eloquently explores the relationship between sound and vision in her films, the grammar of shooting and editing in her work and the technical choices that she makes. What clearly comes across in the interview is the 'painterly' way that Bigelow approaches all her work, from pre-production to post-production, and the way that she is involved in every area of a film shoot. From their discussion it is clear that Bigelow is also driven by a desire to experiment and innovate, to push back technological barriers and to re-imagine the very language of her cinema. There is a quantifiable energy and a sense of authorial direction that comes through when Bigelow is talking about Steadicam shots, long takes and cinematic spectacle. There is also a transgressive quality to the way that she describes her own film-making and the desires she has for making radical, progressive films; a notion that the rest of this collection attempts to explore.

Robynn Stilwell's essay makes an invaluable contribution to existing commentaries on Bigelow's work in her analysis of Bigelow's first three films' use of sound. As Stilwell notes, sound is all too often a neglected component of film-making, overlooked by film studies' common compulsion to prioritise the visual over the aural. As a director who has particularly earned a reputation as a 'spectacular' director, for her frenetic and innovative editing, cinematography and camerawork, Bigelow's use of sound has been all the more overlooked. Here, however, Stilwell argues that Bigelow's play with gender and genre in the visual and narrative fields of her films extends to her manipulation of the conventions of sound too. Just as her early films re-imagine familiar genres, 'the scores are not quite the normal fare. They interact with the sound design in unusual ways, crossing boundaries normally held fast in classical cinema'. The extensive jukebox scoring of *The Loveless*, the 'themeless, textural and tonal synth score' of *Near Dark* and the shifting 'point of audition' in *Blue Steel* are all used in ways which unsettle the image and bring another layer of irony and intervention to bear. Bigelow's soundscapes in these early films, then, are integral to the reconfiguration of gender and genre convention within them.

Sara Gwenllian Jones opens by exploring how the mise-en-scène of *Near Dark* immediately evokes the geography and mythos of the western and 'cowboy country'. Arguing that the vampires of *Near Dark* act as figures which echo the 'Otherness' of both homosexuality and the western's 'Indian', she suggests that Bigelow's film reworks the western genre through the incorporation of 'the fantastic', while maintaining an 'ideologically contrary and ambiguous' position. There are numerous parallels to be drawn between the vampires of *Near Dark* and the Indians of the western as primitive, instinct-driven, hostile, nomadic and, therefore, ultimately threatening to the 'white settlers' and their values. At the same time however, through their seductive eroticism, 'indetectability' and the homoerotic movement entailed in their stalking, violence and 'unnatural' breeding, they are marked as 'queer', underlining their transgressive position. This invasion of the fantastic into the territory of the western, in a kind of return of the repressed where darkness 'becomes as seductive as it is menacing', serves to expose 'white America's illusion of safety and control'. Adopting Jim Kitses' argument from his seminal study of the western, *Horizons West*, Gwenllian Jones finds that the apparent oppositions in values and lifestyle between the vampires and the settlers are not fixed in a binary structure. Rather the vampires represent, 'not just the threat of the other, but also its proximity, its glamour and allure'. In bringing the vampire into the domain of the West, then, Bigelow demonstrates how it is not merely genre boundaries which are fluid in *Near Dark*. In its vision of a transgressive culture that is simultaneously alluring and intimidating, social boundaries and hierarchies of knowledge and power are also revealed to be similarly precarious.

While adopting different methodologies, Gwenllian Jones and Steven Jay Schneider nevertheless reach some similar conclusions about the progressive potential of *Near Dark*. Both argue that it can be seen as a reflexive text in some ways, one that is often self-consciously interrogating conservative and patriarchal ideologies. Schneider however draws in part on a psychoanalytic reading of the text and argues that it 'places quotation marks' around its protagonist's apparent neoconservatism. Despite their different approaches, both suggest that reactionary readings of *Near Dark* are ultimately undermined by how its 'Others' – and the radical, alternative lifestyle they offer – may well appear more attractive to the viewer than, in Schneider's words, 'being human (which here means white, bourgeois male)'. Schneider suggests that Christopher Sharrett's 1993 essay, 'The Horror Film in Neoconservative Culture', which argued that *Near Dark* co-opts its radical potential into an ultimately reactionary text, neglects how the film 'thematises neoconservatism, revealing its operations and contextualising it within a larger, progressive ideological stance'. He suggests the film is better understood as a 'wish-fulfilling dream of liberation from repressive social, cultural and biological norms', however ambivalent the depiction of that dream and its protagonist may appear. The freedom from Oedipal anxieties enabled by the vampires' 'parenting' process, whereby each new addition to the 'family' is turned from humble human to immortal un-dead by just one progenitor, allows them to develop 'new and non-traditional lifestyle choices and family structures'. Their destruction at the end seems arbitrary in that much about the vampires remains resoundingly attractive; their mobility, their immortality and invulnerability, the excitement and vigour of a counter-cultural existence. These elements, in conjunction with a less than heroic 'hero' in Caleb, conspire to produce a text which celebrates its vampires as much as it punishes them, a fact underlined by the ambivalence and ambiguity of the 'happy' ending.

Writing originally in the *Journal of Film and Video* in 1994, Robert T. Self's largely psychoanalytical analysis of *Blue Steel* points to the 'crisis in sexual identity' at the centre of the film's narrative. Self argues that the central characters in the film – a rookie female cop, a psychopathic killer, and a male cop mentor/suitor – are all involved in a classic Oedipal scenario, involving feminine subjectivity, castration fears and images of lack. However, Self suggests that unlike 'other contemporary films with women cops in … that ultimately recuperate feminine subjectivity to Oedipal subject positions', the Oedipal trajectory in *Blue Steel* is so over-determined with a 'multiplicity of desires' that it both undermines and questions masculine authority, and draws attention to the inherent contradictions in gendered identification. Self identifies Megan (Jamie Lee Curtis), the rookie female cop, as the key agent of this instability; 'she is the subject of the narrative, the figure of the law, and the possessor of its power and authority; she is simultaneously the object of masculine investigation, desire, hostility and aggression'. Self goes on to suggest that the 'homicidal personality' of *Blue Steel* can be linked back to a general identity crisis that permeated culture at the time of the film's release. Drawing on work by Susan Faludi (1991), Self suggests that the independence that women had increasingly achieved in society around this time produced both a breakdown of 'ideological boundaries', and a corresponding 'misogynist backlash' in the way women were (mis)represented on screen. While *Blue Steel* taps into this identity crisis, Self argues that what marks it out as a radical text is its refusal to reaffirm the 'Oedipal trajectory of stable heterosexuality'.

Sean Redmond begins his discussion of *Point Break* by drawing attention to the simultaneous marginalisation and neglect of the film within discussions of the Bigelow canon, and to the dominant conservative readings of the film that have attempted to label it as both low-brow and retrograde. Taking up preliminary work by Tasker (1999) and Islam (1995), he suggests that not only is the film transgressive in its representation of the masculine and feminine but that its 'counter hegemonic' worldview marks the film out as a – if not the – seminal Kathryn Bigelow film. Furthermore, for Redmond, *Point Break* is a self-consciously politicised action film that takes on and parodies the excesses of the Hollywood cinema machine.

He argues that the film deliberately blurs normalised gender roles through the physical androgyny of the film's three principal characters and the intertextual/ extra-textual androgyny that the three stars – Keanu Reeves, Patrick Swayze and Lori Petty – bring with them. This is extended through what becomes a 'queer' love triangle between these characters because of the way they are constructed as desiring doubles, and through the use of a sexualised point-of-view that repeatedly captures men objectifying men. Redmond argues that this love affair takes place in a narrative that largely valorises a counter-culture lifestyle and demonises the regimes of a dominant culture regulated and primed by conformity. In this conception, *Point Break* mirrors but inverts the fascist ideology of *Dirty Harry* (Don Siegal, 1971). Finally, his essay argues that this is all largely shot and edited with a breathless sense of speed and spatial intoxication, so that by the end of the film, the viewer feels like they have got more than their money's worth or, more provocatively, that they have been asked to recognise the over-determining rollercoaster aesthetic of the contemporary film age.

Through analysis of *The Weight of Water* and its reception, Deborah Jermyn looks at how the notion of 'a Bigelow film' has become an increasingly troubling one over the course of her career. She argues that three key inter-related discourses circulate around Bigelow in the critical dissemination of her work; what it is to be a 'woman director', what it is to be an 'action director' and what it is to be an 'auteur'.

Bigelow, however, both fulfils and problematises all of these classifications. Through her reconfiguration of genres, her collaborative working relationships and her refusal to engage with questions about her gender (despite her films' fascination with that very subject) Bigelow points to the difficulty of ascribing simple authorial definitions in post-classical Hollywood. To date, *The Weight of Water* has been met with some unease and disappointment for its ponderous, complex shifting between two narratives. Jermyn argues that its strained reception parallels the tensions that have characterised the popular and critical construction of Bigelow herself, as a director who refuses to be easily compartmentalised in both professional and 'personal' terms. *The Weight of Water* upsets any straightforward labelling of Bigelow as an action director or woman director or auteur, yet also demonstrates why these questions continue to be so focal to our conceptualisation of her oeuvre.

Part Two – The Strange Gaze of Kathryn Bigelow

Romi Stepovich's introductory essay to this section on the production and distri-bution history of *Strange Days* contextualises the three academic essays by Steven Shaviro, Christina Lane and Will Brooker that follow. Her work tracks the making of the film, the key personnel involved in its production, and outlines a number of production moments that foregrounds Bigelow's determining role, and the production problems that led to it being a commercial failure. Stepovich's essay, then, provides an industrial or commercial context for understanding both how Hollywood films are generally produced, and for how creative directors, like Bigelow, work within these constraints.

Steven Shaviro's essay argues that through the SQUID device Bigelow produces a new regime of 'vision and affect', a 'kind of looking that is affective rather than cognitive, and that is not associated with a fully-formed phenomenological self or psychoanalytic ego'. Shaviro suggests that there is a cinematic layering to the way Bigelow produces this sense of textual dislocation and disorientation. For Shaviro it is the combination of different types of shots and editing strategies that produces a unique form of vision in the film. The non-established immediacy of the SQUID point-of-view shots, the unbroken long shots that mark out key moments of the action, and the dizzying, jarring camera work and montage cutting all open up new visual spaces. However, what particularly interests Shaviro is the play of complicity, distancing and dehumanisation that works through this regime of vision. Shaviro contextualises and politicises the oscillating looks of *Strange Days* in terms of Bigelow's own progressive politics and post-humanism.

Christina Lane's analysis seeks to contextually locate *Strange Days* in terms of its historical and authorial influences. She focuses on the film's intersection with postmodernism and the historical context of its making in 'The Year of the Angry White Male', how its themes are imbricated in the Bigelow/Cameron relationship, and more specifically how its racial ideologies relate to Bigelow's authorial influence. She finds that the film can be seen as a response to a series of cultural crises in the US in the early to mid-1990s, including the LAPD's attack on Rodney King and the Lorena Bobbitt trial. Each of these entailed marginalised perspectives 'coming into direct conflict with white, male hegemonic authority', an issue which makes itself partly felt in the film through Lenny Nero's identity crisis. Drawing on a Lacanian analysis, Lane argues that Lenny's relationship with the gaze shifts in the film, moving from complicity in victimisation and male aggression, to 'moral and feminist development'. Rather than neglecting authorial influences at the cost of attention to the contextual-historical, Lane suggests that the two are very much inter-linked. She argues that it is precisely in the different ways that Bigelow and Cameron responded to the cultural problems raised by the film that their different influences can be felt. This is particularly evident in the way Bigelow developed the character of Mace from Cameron's original script, using her to make 'valuable connections between female victimisation and racial oppression'. Lane suggests it is the concept of 'the loop', rather than 'the look', which offers an 'appropriate metaphor for Bigelow and Cameron's authorial contributions to the film's gender politics'. Ultimately, what the film's difficult articulation of looking actually suggests is 'two halves of a divided gaze', in a text that offers a radical and politicised understanding of the social unrest it details while paralleling real 'acts of resistance' occurring in the US in this period.

Will Brooker's essay moves the analysis of the film from textual and contextual issues to those of reception and consumption. His research looks at the *Strange Days* discussion boards on the Internet Movie Database through a textual analysis of 79 posts, in an analysis that can itself be located within the wider context of academic work on fandom and reception studies. Brooker looks at the relationship between the film's critical and commercial failure and the ways on-line fans of the film 'rescued' and appropriated it for 'cult', aesthetic and self-congratulatory reasons. Through the fans' appropriation of *Strange Days*, Brooker argues that there is a displacement of Bigelow as author or source of the text for generic foregrounding, a misrecognition of who the director was – with James Cameron often being cited as the 'creator' of *Strange Days* – and a desire to 'talk up' the stars and supporting cast. Brooker argues that responses generally 'serve to establish the reviewer's credentials almost as much as they encourage a reassessment of the movie'. Brooker also attempts to explain the responses in terms of gender: the discussion board is made up almost entirely of males and their denial of

Bigelow as source of the text, along with their reactions to key scenes within the film, suggest a particularised male way of rescuing a cult film text.

This, then, is the first collection dedicated solely to the work of Kathryn Bigelow. It reveals and constructs a film-maker whose presence and work within and around the margins of Hollywood cinema has proven contentious and innovative, perplexing and inspiring, travelling a number of tumultuous career highs and lows along the way. The deconstruction of Bigelow that is found here is one that involves an examination of her authorship, her politics, her gender and her status within Hollywood. As a consequence, the contributors draw on many different perspectives and areas of expertise, including feminism, psychoanalysis, queer theory, cultural studies and authorship, to produce a series of essays that offer the most detailed and expansive analysis yet of one of contemporary cinema's most important film-makers. In doing so the editors and contributors to this book do not intend to claim that this is to be 'the last word' on Bigelow; she is, after all, very much a work in progress. But this study makes major inroads towards demonstrating why, and ensuring that, Bigelow's oeuvre should be examined, celebrated and respected within and across the politics and the poetics of film studies.

PART ONE: BIGELOW'S MOVING CANVAS

CHAPTER ONE

'Momentum and Design': Interview with Kathryn Bigelow

Gavin Smith

Gavin Smith: When you design and execute a complex action sequence, how do you main-
tain a balance between elements and keep them alive? There's one in Point Break where
you have multiple areas of attention that have to be kept in motion…

Kathryn Bigelow: You're talking about the surf Nazi shootout. I think geography
is so important in action sequences. I see a lot of films in which geography is sacrificed,
it's just a lot of fast cutting, a lot of noise, a lot of impacts – and I have no idea where I
am, or who's coming from the left or right. So I start with story-boards. I usually have
a foam-core model built and work the pieces; sometimes I'll do video animatics to see
the angles and see how it works and then I keep compressing and compressing it in the
boards, pulling shots out to see how tight I can make it yet be completely oriented.

But it's also possible to use disorientation strategically.

Right, I cross lines; I'm not talking about keeping religiously to axes, but just keeping a fundamental sense of geography.

But when you cover a scene like that shootout, or the opening bank robbery, do you
cover each character's movements from start to finish so that you have all those options?

It depends what I need. At the end, in the big heist, the two cops lying on the floor – you don't cover them until you need them to figure in the story. So it's based on where you need the focus of attention to be at each particular moment. It's all about fragments. When push comes to shove, I'll always go for an additional setup as opposed to an additional take. I'll get another angle. You need coverage to make something like that work.

Are reverse angles more important in those scenes?

Reverses and tie-ins. There's nothing more golden than a tie-in. If you're shooting a gun at me, there's the obligatory single, then me, the reaction, getting shot. But what I think is as important – and I'll always have two or three cameras working simultaneously – is to get the tie-in, so I'll go behind the subject with another camera so you see the geography of the two people. Even if you just use it for six, eight frames, you have an instantaneous sense of, 'Oh, they're there'.

What about the camera movement in the chase at the end of that POV?

Basically it's a modified Steadicam that gives you the fluidity of Steadicam but the realism of handheld, without the limitations of either.

So you sort of retuned the Steadicam.

Right, there's a gyro-stabiliser you can trust or tune in, depending upon how much life you want in the camera. For when she runs into the train yard and in front of a speeding freight train, well, no insurance company or train yard would ever authorise that. Carrying a camera crew behind you with a train going at 80 miles an hour – I don't think so! So we did that backwards; the train was backing up and we reversed the footage. For all the POVs we tried to find ways of handling them so that it just looks like *that's what happened*. There's no real contaminating or adulterating the image so that it looks artificially created or too overly manipulated. Those are my favourite effects.

In the supermarket holdup in Blue Steel you intercut different moving camera styles: formal, distanced tracking, subjective handheld, and what I'd call sympathetic choreographed Steadicam movement somewhere in between.

I really only started to work compatibly with the Steadicam and trust it in *Point Break*. You can create an edit-free situation, yet it has the pace and sense of a quickly-cut sequence. People move in and out of their coverage, and the actor and camera can move counter to one another. I love the purity of an unbroken shot, and I love that juxtaposed with a sequence that has tremendous editorial intrusion.

It's musical.

Exactly, there are rest notes and then there are flurries. You need rest moments where the camera is simply covering two people in an unbroken wideshot and you see the body language. It's a cinematic exhale. That's why we have punctuation. Peak experience only exists in relation to something that is not. It's all context.

Figure 1 Bigelow on the set of *Blue Steel*: '*Blue Steel* is very stylised, intentionally so.'

Were the demands of the chase sequence in Point Break very different from the robbery sequences?

They're actually very similar. Both need a tremendous amount of coverage. The chase as scripted was this incredible, relentless piece and it's really what gave me the confidence that I could do these POVs in *Strange Days*. That was my first glimmer of an unbroken sequence: even though there are cuts, it was almost constructed as if there were none.

What were the most complicated shots technically in Strange Days?

The POVs, because they had to be continuous and unbroken. I shot all the POVs to be unbroken if I wanted them to be. We would choreograph for days in preproduction. In the opening POV, we're putting everybody into the refrigerator, and we realise the cops are there and we have to exit, so we look this way and we see the other robber going up the stairs, and we look behind us and see there are cops out the window… You have a whole crew that's equally choreographed: you pan and everybody drops, 18 people, then you pan back and they all pop up again.

What went into the visual style of the POV sequences?

We had to build a camera to do the POVs, a stripped-down Arri that weighed much less than even the smallest EYMO and yet would take all the prime lenses. And I also needed remote follow-focus capacity – your eye is so light and quick and mobile, whereas with a 40-pound Panaglide, everything is wiping and blurring because of the sheer weight of the camera; so we needed a lightness to give it the flexibility of the eye. Working with cameras that are that flexible, I think, is going to revolutionise action photography, because you can do so much more.

But these scenes required additional equipment, and we had to organise hidden cuts within the sequences to get in and out of the equipment. For instance, to do the jump across the roof: that's with a helmet camera, and you can't use that for the run up the stairs. I would go out with my Steadicam operator, Jimmy Muro, with a video camera and figure out where all the cuts would be; then I had to organise the action to enable me to make those cuts. To get into the helmet camera, I had to create a whip. You don't want to create an arbitrary whip, so: I hear the cops behind me, I look back, there they are, I come back and now I'm in the helmet rig, I jump. Now I'm on the other side, I look up and down, and then it's a descender fall with the helmet on. It has to make sense. It's fun – it's the ultimate chessgame.

What about the Jeriko clip?

It was logistically very complicated because Iris [Brigitte Bako] is witnessing this event, which had a lot of dialogue, no coverage, no outs, a 400-foot magazine so you have a little bit of latitude, and we could switch equipment when we needed to for the dialogue. You couldn't record dialogue with this little camera, it's too noisy, so we had to switch to Steadicam.

On Point Break, how hands-on was your directing of the surfing and skydiving scenes? Is that kind of thing usually left to a second-unit director/stunt coordinator?

With second unit it's all boarded and I make clear what the shots are, what the composition is, what time of day it is, what lens and stock are being used. Anything involving Patrick [Swayze] jumping out of a plane, I was there with a parachute on, strapped in.

But from an insurance point of view you couldn't jump.

No – and technically neither could he ... But he might have, yeah. For the water work, I was in the water, on a boat, as close as I could be without getting in the shot or making it logistically problematic for anybody. Sitting on a surfboard, yelling action and cut, then falling off the board.

I actually had many units on that working simultaneously. We had a stretch of beach on the North Shore of Oahu, and there were a lot of different breaks, and I just set up stages at each break, literally a hundred feet apart. I'd have an underwater unit at stage one, Keanu doubles for the learning-how-to-surf scene at stage two, a wipeout scene at stage three, and four surfers doing a Four-Horsemen-at-dawn shot on stage four, to which I added some optical fog afterwards. So you just work with [walkie-talkies] going back and forth. You gotta always be parallel-processing. I like to have at least two things going at once, one setup here, one setup there.

So your DP is always setting up the next shot while your operator executes the present one.

Always, always.

One of the best action sequences you've done is ironically very modest in scale and complexity – the final sequence of Wild Palms.

That's Jimmy Muro, my Steadicam guy. It's in the choreography, and I staged the action so that just as one event is starting to wind down, another one will be coming up in the corner of his frame that will stimulate the camera and it whips around. It goes back to painting. On that one, we're running to the door of the van, he is put in the back and we whip back up to the characters on the balcony getting shot, and they come down to the scene down below. And countermoves – moving the action and the camera in opposing ways. There's an organic quality that lends itself to those sequences *as* you're blocking it, and it's like you leapfrog the action one step ahead of the camera, and then the camera leads the next piece of action. That's what that piece was a perfect example of. We basically did that in only a few hours.

Was The Animals' 'House of the Rising Sun' already written in?

No, I put the music on.

The power of that conjunction of visuals and music rises to an almost transcendent emotional level, much the way Michael Mann sometimes does.

Kind of like a fugue state. I had fun. I did it really for Oliver [Stone, the executive producer]. It was an interesting challenge to work at that pace. We did 8–10 pages a day. There's something kind of freeing about it, once you break through to that other side.

On features like yours it's more like two- or two-and-a-half-page days.

Yeah. It sounds luxurious when compared to the other, but not when the level of complexity and the photographic requirements are so much greater. You just need to be constantly changing angles and images. You have to satisfy the appetite of the viewer's attention span and work within the dictates of that appetite, if you want to stay a step ahead of the viewer, constantly cycling images. Back to the old adage: material dictates. At a script stage you know how far you can sustain or suspend something. A narrative is a momentum in and of itself. It's like you're skiing down a hill and there's this avalanche behind you. How long do you want to pause? If the piece has inherent momentum, you have to be careful about your pauses. But you can't have momentum without pause. The value of cutting has been painfully abbreviated in some of the bigger contemporary films that are cut in six weeks. You can make a good film that way. You can't make a great film.

A great example of that control of momentum and suspension is the unusually long, ten-minute scene in the middle of Near Dark at the bar. I'm fascinated by how you structured it around four contrasting songs on the jukebox. It's a scene in four acts.

It's written that way, too. It's an entire reel. In a way it's a film within a film. With a beginning, middle and end. It's very lyrical in a way, its rhythm. Its strength is its patience. It's ultimately about turning a bar into an abattoir, but it's turning that process into a state of art. Hard to shoot. I always knew I was going to use the George Strait song at the end: I didn't know what the other material was going to be when I shot it but I knew I would find them. 'Fever' by The Cramps I just stumbled on, put it in and it was uncanny how it worked with Lance Henriksen's performance and the way the light and the fan above his head worked, and how evocative it was of how seductive that world might be. The real challenge in that film was that at a certain point you have to identify with the antagonists and want to take that ride.

That's true of all of your films.

I guess so. They become strange ad hoc heroes in a perverse way. At a fundamental level they are just alternate family structures struggling to stay intact, the two fathers fighting over the same son. There's always a sequence like that, like the surf Nazis shootout in *Point Break*. In both cases it's the moment where the main character goes through the looking glass and can never return. In *Strange Days* it's when Mace sees the Jeriko video, or Lenny witnesses the Iris kill. It's the end of innocence.

Just as there is an interplay of momentum and suspension in your films, there's also an interplay of visual control and visual abandon. Your most tightly controlled film visually is Blue Steel, yet certain moments don't follow customary visual patterns. I'm thinking of the scene in the deli when Megan sees the supermarket holdup across the street and you employ three shots that are emphatic interlocking pirouettes: 1) Turner spinning around to face the cash register, spilling the coffee; 2) her head turning; 3) a shaky 180-degree pan from the deli's toilet sign where her partner is, around through the window to the SLOAN supermarket sign across the street. It's an interesting formal repetition with variation. It has an odd freedom.

I know. I'd probably cut it very differently today. I had that pretty planned out. I don't want to give you the impression that everything is planned to within an inch of its life, but within that framework it's much more freeing than just arriving at a set and figuring out how you're going to do it. You can cover something an infinite number of ways, but I think if you're really intimate with the piece there's only one way it could ever be done. The best kind of photography and the best kind of film-making is when it seems like it's inevitable.

Blue Steel represents a kind of control I've tended to move away from. It's in a way too restrained. *Blue Steel* is very stylised, intentionally so, but I think I've been interested in a slightly less stylized approach to material. There is an elegance to *Blue Steel*, but it's like a series of still frames; there's a stillness in that film that seemed appropriate. When I wrote it I kept seeing it in a slightly removed state.

Its style has a very interiorized quality.

I was really just discovering long focal lengths, and that had a lot to do with it. Loving the compression, and the lack of depth of field, that had a tendency to create a kind of claustrophobia. I came through that and out the other side. *Point Break* is virtually the opposite. I'd still use long focal lengths at times, but I'd use an 85mm lens instead of a 300mm. 1 would do masters with a 300mm on *Blue Steel*. You had to find locations that could accommodate those focal lengths, and focus was really difficult. *Near Dark* had a lot of practical locations, and our longest lens was probably an 85mm. In *Point Break* I started to work with wider lenses and started discovering the 35mm, which is an extraordinary, beautiful focal length. And I moved the camera more. As you gravitate towards more camera movement, you tend to get wider because the sense of fluidity is magnified.

Your action sequences conform to classical principles of attenuation and elaboration of action, arresting or expanding time. In real life, violence is often over in the blink of an eye.

Yes and no. You can take the liberty of a moment of suspension, when something puts you in shock or is cathartic. Time stands still. It's perception, obviously. There's two ways of looking at a moment and they're both cinematic: either suspend it and examine it as if under a magnifying glass, with great detail, or have it be instantaneous, blink and you've missed it – which is more realistic, but in the *perception* of reality. Suspension of time for me is by cinematic choice and what I would imagine an event to be like.

I was in a tremendous near car accident once. The driver started to doze at the wheel at 5am on the freeway at 80 miles per hour. In seconds we went off the freeway, and we were heading for the side of an overpass, and I said something and then he over-corrected and we did a complete 360 across six lanes of traffic in one direction and down the meridian and across the oncoming six lanes, and ended up going straight ahead. You saw these semis going by you, they were just blurs of light and sound and horns. It seemed to me an eternity in what was fifteen seconds. There's just this sense of forever in a second. A collision of thoughts. I think it's because your system is flooded with adrenalin and everything is on hyper speed. So it's an aestheticization, a stylistic choice.

You've talked in the past about violence in terms of its inherent cinematic, kinetic qualities, and it's clear that it's useful to you as an expression of a certain kind of passion. But what kind of personal need does its representation satisfy in you?

It goes back to the voyeuristic need to watch and the Freudian idea that you want to view what you've been denied. You don't want to watch what you can always see – you want to see something that is transporting in some way, either frightening or some other reaction. And that's the idea of the SQUID in *Strange Days*. They're accessible fantasies and it's fundamentally human.

There's a very strong graphic quality to your compositions, but also a very tactile, sculpted dimensionality to them.

Probably because I love to shoot on location, which you pay the price for when you're mixing, because there's sound you can't get rid of and performance lines you're reluctant to loop. But I don't know – it could be in the sense that I'm interested in trying to make it replicate something to the extent that you humanly can, rather than go completely into a fantastic fictional space.

The shot in Point Break with the camera looking down on Keanu Reeves and Lori Petty lying in bed, with the contrast of black sheets and fleshtone combined with the very precise arrangement of limbs and shoulders, creates an almost sculpted image.

What you're commenting on is perhaps how it's lit, the kind of modelling of the light. If cinema is the artform of the twentieth century, lighting in some ways is your brush. That's how you create the tones and densities and dictate where your eye does and doesn't go and how it travels, how shape is defined and formed. And with that image, the starkness of it. If you were to overlight that, it would be much less interesting because it would just be a graphic silhouette. The challenge was trying to get the fleshtones to pop out from the sheets and not become one single shape.

Did you arrange the actors' physical postures?

Rather than have a preordained idea of how they should lie, what I love to do is see how an actor organically works a scene or works in a space, and then freeze it, shape it. So it isn't like you're imposing something that might not be organic to them or to that moment.

Where were you born?

Right below San Francisco, a town called San Carlos. My father managed a paint factory in South San Francisco, which I guess seems like an obvious influence. As long as I can remember, I was drawing and painting – not much imagination there! My mother was a librarian. It was a fairly normal environment. When I first started painting, I loved the Old Masters. When I was 13 or 14 I was doing details of Old Masters, blowing up a corner of a Raphael. I loved doing that, taking a detail and turning it into 12 by 12 feet.

It's interesting that you did something mediated.

I got very interested later on when I became more sophisticated about art, with Duchamp and the idea of found objects, which in a way is what film-making is. You're taking a lot of elements that already exist, and it's the context you're putting those preexistent elements into, the associations that you're creating.

Especially genre films.

When we wrote *Near Dark* we were very conscious of taking a genre and turning it upside down, subverting it in some way – taking the vampire mythology and putting it in the West. You could say the same with *Strange Days*: it's science fiction, but it's also total noir. I always thought of it as a film noir thriller that takes place on the eve of the millennium, the turn of the century, and perhaps the end of the world – in one sentence!

Before you made The Loveless you spent the 1970s in the New York art world.

I've sort of had many incarnations! I came to New York through the Whitney Museum in the early 1970s. At that time they gave fifteen people scholarships every year to come to New York and get your own studio. I had been going to school at the San Francisco Art Institute for a year and a half. I didn't realise that my teacher, Sam Tchakalian, had put me up for the Whitney. All of a sudden he came to me and said, 'If you want to go to New York and be matriculated at the Art Institute and work within the Whitney Museum where people like Susan Sontag and Richard Serra talk about your work with you, you can.' I was 19 and I was like, 'Excuse me?' So I did that for a year and a half. At the end you had a piece of your work shown in the Whitney. Which was amazing. The art world at the time became very politicised, conceptual art moved into a political arena, so the work was more and more aggressive. I started working with Art and Language, a British-based group of conceptual artists, and we had a piece at the Venice Biennale one year.

I read that you worked with [video and performance artist] Vito Acconci.

I was doing a million odd jobs just to stay alive. One of them was helping Vito Acconci on an installation he was doing. He did these great, very assaultive performance pieces, and needed these slogans and phrases on film loops that would play on the wall behind him during a performance piece he did at [the] Sonnabend [gallery] in a rubber bondage room he created. The job was to film these slogans. I'd never worked with a camera. I was starving to death. If I hadn't been at the brink of economic disaster, I think I never would have had all these detours.

Were you in one of his videos?

I was in a Richard Serra video for about five seconds, and a couple of Lawrence Weiner videos, *Done To* and *Green As Well As Red As Well As Blue*. I would by no means consider myself a performance artist, I'm too self conscious, its something I could never do. Lawrence's work is less about performance in a classical sense – it's kind of the gestalt of the moment. He puts you in a context and lets you run with the ball, and that's the piece. There's no script. They're very fascinating wordplay pieces. In one I was trying to talk Italian with somebody. It was such a community, almost like a repertory without any kind of structure whatsoever.

During that time I don't think I saw a movie that wasn't subtitled. I was really unaware of Hollywood per se, which may kind of protect me today. I think I'm still discovering it.

You were more associated with the New York underground film scene in the late 1970s. You also appeared in Lizzie Borden's Born in Flames.

You know, I've never seen it, although I'm very good friends with Lizzie. We always laugh about this. I played one of three somewhat militant girls in a scene. Art and film were not separated whatsoever – you were working in the same context using different mediums. It was never really thought of film-making per se, it was art.

At what point did you gravitate towards film?

I did this short film called *Set Up*. I shot it before I went to Columbia. I went to Columbia because I had run out of money and I needed a cutting room so I thought, Aha, Graduate School! I loved the process, it was intoxicating, so I just dived into film, all periods. I just opened up Pandora's Box. I'd see everything, from going to 42nd Street to see a Bruce Lee movie to *The Magnificent Ambersons* in Andrew Sarris's class to Fassbinder at the Lincoln Center. That would be a day. *Year of 13 Moons* – I thought I'd died and gone to heaven when I saw that film.

What was Set Up about?

This was the late 1970s when conceptual art mutated through a political phase into a French structuralist phase. There was a kind of natural evolution if I think back on it. It was really a very overtly political piece and a bit incendiary in its own small context. On the surface it's these two guys who beat each other up – maybe nothing's changed! *The Village Voice* called it the first skinhead movie. One guy was calling another a fascist, the other's calling him a commie. It was very politically *literal*. And then the same images are deconstructed in voiceover by these two philosophers, Sylvère Lotringer and Marshall Bronsky, both teaching at Columbia, discussing the material while you're watching it. So there's this kind of reflexive ideology thing going on. It sounds so kind of young and pretentious … but it's only 20 minutes, so it's pretty harmless. And the piece ends with Sylvère talking about the fact that in the 1960s you think of the enemy as outside yourself, in other words a police officer, the government, the system, but that's not really the case at all, fascism is very insidious, we reproduce it all the time.

That's part of what's going on inside Strange Days – an interrogation of the need for and dangers of spectacle.

The thing that's so interesting is that it's really a reflexive ideology, because you're trapped in the spectacle just as the characters are trapped with their own spectacles (SQUID). We're a watched society and a society of watchers. *Strange Days* [is linked to *Set Up*] in some ways more than [my other films], because it's really about understanding power structures.

Again, I wasn't really thinking about making a film, even though it was at night and beautifully lit. It was more of a text. But I drew it out, which is one thing that I still constantly go back to – I have to board a whole show. I have to see it and cut it first, every scene. And then I shoot it. Then it's all right, I've put it into my head. In *Set Up* I didn't know anything about stunt coordinators, and I needed different angles. It had a very strange, kind of crude sense of where the camera should be and how it should be constructed. I knew exactly what I wanted, but I didn't understand that you fake shots and fake hits and put sound effects in. I started shooting at about 9pm and finished at 7am, it was in an alley off White Street downtown, and it started to snow – and these guys were getting bloodier and bloodier. They were in bed for two weeks after, I almost killed them. And then on the soundtrack they talk about the fact that they felt kind of exploited in the piece. So the film is constantly folding in on itself like a Mobius strip.

What was the nature of your collaboration with Monty Montgomery who co-directed The Loveless with you?

Well, we wrote it together. Coming out of the art world, which is so ad hoc, I didn't really know what directing was. But it was a very easy, effortless process because we were really thinking on the same page and finishing each other's sentences, so the directing was very fluid. It wasn't like, 'You do camera and I'll do the actors.' There wasn't even any consultation. It was an interesting process, but I don't recommend it, because you become too solipsistic, too protective of the material. I hadn't embraced narrative at that point; I was still completely conceptual, and narrative was antithetical to *anything* in the art world. That was the big juncture, when you're thinking of plastic or visual arts you're using the non-narrative part of your brain. So the thinking behind *The Loveless* was to suspend the narrative and create this visual tapestry with enough narrative to give you the illusion of a story percolating, kind of there but not there, held by gossamer threads.

The whole film feels like one long interlude, like material left over from a larger narrative.

It was very perverse. That film has one foot in the art world and half a finger in the film world. It was neither fish nor fowl, and I had no idea of making this as a calling card for the industry. What I was really interested in was a Kenneth Anger–*Scorpio*

Rising kind of thing – images of power and a skewed perspective of it.

The Loveless is somewhere between a Warhol aesthetic and stylised narrative. The way the actors function...

I was very interested in his material. Some of the more aggressive pieces like *Vinyl,* which is wonderful. What I learned after *The Loveless* was that probably the greatest challenge was accessibility – with a conscience. I think of art as a somewhat elitist medium because it does require a little bit of understanding to appreciate a white-on-white square or Ad Reinhardt's black-on-black paintings. You can't come to it cold – but you can with a film. And in a way, Warhol's use of pop subjects – you could come to that completely cold, too. Everybody could have a different association. You would be mystified, but you wouldn't be completely alienated by it. There would be recognition.

I think my journey West, so to speak, has really been one that I think of as the pursuit of the Narrative. *The Loveless* was all about the rejection of it. I felt sort of sorry for the distributor, who tried to cut a trailer to make it seem like this action-packed motorcycle movie, and I just kept saying, 'You've got to use truth in advertising!' I remember going to the Beverly Center when it was released in L.A. and there weren't even posters on display. I went to the manager with a copy of the poster and said, 'My film's playing here, would you please put a poster up?'

CHAPTER TWO

Breaking Sound Barriers: Bigelow's Soundscapes from The Loveless to Blue Steel

Robynn J. Stilwell

It has become conventional when speaking of a film director to discuss matters of visual style and of narrative traits – two areas in which Kathryn Bigelow is especially distinctive and particularly intriguing.[1] One tenet of auteur theory holds that the director has authorial control over everything in his (usually his) film. Not surprisingly, the one element that film directors often have the least control over is also one which most film scholars either know little about, and therefore shy away from, or simply do not recognise as a part of a director's style. This element is the soundscape, or the entire sound field of a film including sound effects, dialogue, and music (see Stilwell 2001).

Most film directors usually have little control over the soundscape for the same reason film scholars ignore it – they don't really know anything about it. Intriguingly, however, some of the directors who have the most intensely individual visual styles – Alfred Hitchcock and Michael Mann are two other excellent examples – also create films that have equally distinctive soundscapes. Some directors form very strong bonds with their sound designers (Francis Ford Coppola and Walter Murch are the most obvious pairing) or composers (Alfred Hitchcock and Bernard Herrmann, Steven

Spielberg and John Williams, David Cronenberg and Howard Shore, and Kenneth Branagh and Patrick Doyle, for instance). When a director has collaborators in whom s/he has complete confidence, then the director can relax and let those collaborators do their work; the sound designers and/or composers are subject to less 'back-seat driving' and can perhaps be more adventurous. Bigelow – and Mann, with whom she shares some striking resemblances in terms of sound – is a different kind of auteur. With these directors, although the sound personnel change, there is a consistency of experiment and innovation in their soundscapes; whether or not this flows from the director or their collaborators is irrelevant in terms of the way the audience relates to their films. Enquiring scholarly minds might like to know, and a basic sense of fair play might insist that the right people get their due credit, but it is often very difficult to pinpoint actual authority, particularly in the case of sound because directors are so rarely asked about it in interviews and they are, of course, not always available to scholars. As a musicologist, I can propose a hypothesis that Bigelow depends on her collaborators and chooses them for their personal idiosyncrasies while Mann has a more controlling directorial ear, but I can do so only because Bigelow's early films are so different from one another while Mann's have a remarkable consistency, even though his collaborators are different.

Sound design is a relatively recent innovation and can cause friction in post-production. Depending on the division of labour on a particular production, the sound designer or the sound editor (but never the composer or the music editor) has power over the entire soundtrack and can manipulate the work of other contributors, including the composer, with unexpected and sometimes unwanted results. Industry lore is rife with tales of composers who found that their score was turned down to inaudibility, covered over with loud explosions, or even overlaid by sound effects which were out of key or out of tune with the music in particularly jarring ways that detracted from, rather than added to, narrative.[2] A sensitive sound designer, however, can create a soundscape that is richer, more integrated than a classical Hollywood soundtrack. It is ironically something which small films are, in a way, better placed to achieve.

'Film music' is largely a product of the studio system and one dependent upon the resources of a major production. For most people, both inside and outside the industry, 'film music' is not a technical term (music for a film) but a generic one, meaning an orchestral score written expressly for a particular film production. This is an expensive proposition, from hiring the composer to orchestrating and copying parts to engaging an orchestra. The studio system could sustain this expense by having an in-house music department; when the studios disintegrated, the orchestral film score was severely curtailed. By the early 1970s, the orchestral score was almost dead. Contributing also to this shift was the move to what was perceived as more 'realistic' film-making; music has always been vulnerable to visually-oriented film-makers who consider it 'less realistic' than editing, special effects, and the like.[3] John Williams has been credited for revitalising the genre with his scores to *Jaws* (Steven Spielberg, 1975), *Star Wars* (George Lucas, 1977) and *Close Encounters of the Third Kind* (Steven Spielberg, 1977), but the big orchestral score remains the province of relatively big-budget productions. Smaller-budget and independent productions are often forced to forego the familiar language of the orchestral score and two common solutions are the pop song score and the synth score.

The pop song, or jukebox, score relies on pre-existing recordings – though often huge mechanical production rights fees mean that they could be just as expensive as an orchestral score, sometimes requiring compromise on the part of the film-makers. The quintessential jukebox movie, *American Graffiti* (George Lucas, 1973), demonstrates how popular song is particularly good at evoking time and place (even if some of its songs are anachronistic by a few years). Another kind of jukebox movie appeared in the wake of *Saturday Night Fever* (John Badham, 1977) and *Urban Cowboy* (James Bridges, 1980), filled with songs that were cross-promoted with the film, creating another kind of cultural-historical text. These included the John Hughes comedies of the mid-1980s (*Sixteen Candles* (1984), *The Breakfast Club* (1985), *Ferris Bueller's Day Off* (1986)) and 'grew up' into the romantic comedies of the 1990s like *Pretty Woman* (Garry Marshall, 1990) and *Four Weddings and a Funeral* (Mike Newell, 1994).

In the late 1970s, synthesizers became both cheaper and more musically useful. One person could score an entire film – horror director John Carpenter (*Halloween*, 1978; *Escape from New York*, 1981) even composed his own film scores; Giorgio Moroder's pioneering scores for relatively high-profile films *Midnight Express* (Alan Parker, 1978) and *Cat People* (Paul Schrader, 1982) paved the way for a number of synth scores through the early 1980s, culminating in Maurice Jarre's score for *Witness* (Peter Weir, 1985). Post-*Witness*, most big-budget movies would use synthesizers, but only in conjunction with orchestral instruments. The extent to which the orchestral score is still seductive to film-makers and carries with it a certain cachet can be judged by the decision of Mark Snow to create an orchestral score for the film *X-Files: Fight the Future* (Rob Bowman, 1998), even though he had already created a unique synthesized sound world for the television series and using an orchestra violated that identity. The inexpensive synthesizer score is, however, still ideal for low-budget productions.

Kathryn Bigelow's first three films are all independent or low-budget productions and depend to a large degree on these scoring techniques: *The Loveless* (1981) has an extensive jukebox score; *Blue Steel* (1991) has a synth score; *Near Dark* (1987) falls between the two chronologically and in technique. They are also the most inventive – even subversive – regarding the relationship between sound, dialogue and music.

Just as these movies put a spin on familiar genres, the scores are not quite the normal fare. They interact with the sound design in unusual and effective ways, crossing boundaries normally held fast in classical cinema. Like Bigelow's narrative tropes, the scores often recast or reorient genre clichés, using them for their cultural punch while at times even questioning their validity, but using them in ironic and often unsettling ways. In a survey of her work, taking a closer look at the use of sound and music in these early films reveals that the traits of genre and gender play at work in the visual and narrative fields of her films are more often than not key in the soundscapes as well.

The Loveless

> *The Loveless* is a series of period tableaus; there are scenes where there's hardly any sound, certainly no dialogue. (Hultkrans 1995: 78)

> The summer air throbs and superheats with nonstop rockabilly rhythms, eerily suspended visual and emotional violence. (Murphy 1995: 51)

These quotes demonstrate an interesting dichotomy between the visual and the aural worlds of Kathryn Bigelow's first feature, *The Loveless*.[4] Both agree as to the static nature of the visuals, but one claims there is hardly any sound (certainly no dialogue, implicitly prioritising that part of the soundscape), whereas the other speaks of 'nonstop rockabilly rhythms'. These two statements would seem to be completely at odds with one another. How could both be true? In reality, of course, they cannot, exposing the extent to which music can be 'unheard' (to borrow from the title of Claudia Gorbman's seminal book on film music, *Unheard Melodies*) – Hultkrans clearly does not 'hear' the music which runs almost non-stop throughout the film. For Murphy, the music assumes primacy over the 'eerily suspended' image. Through rhythm, the music provides the movement in a film notable for its stasis.

Although *The Loveless* has a narrative, it is a very simple one, a riff on biker films of the 1950s, particularly *The Wild One* (László Benedek, 1953). A band of bikers descends on a rural diner, causes unease and sexual tension, the moody leader seduces a local maiden (though in the 1980s version, she is an abused child whose promiscuity is the recognisable psychological effect of incest), there is a fight between the gang and locals, and the bikers go on their way. The sketchy story is spun into a series of long, sometimes wholly eventless moments. Except for the music. The film coincides historically with the beginning of MTV, and some sequences could almost have been lifted out for airing on that fledgling channel. The oblique and fragmented quality of music-video narrative also coincides with – although, depending upon the director, may or may not be directly linked with – many of the principles of what Lane describes as 'counter cinema' (see Lane 2000: 18–29), an aesthetic in which Bigelow was well-versed through her background and education. One of the most significant traits is to invert classical Hollywood practice: techniques that were originally intended to create a seamless, 'naturalistic', even patriarchal text are thus exposed. For instance, Laura Rascaroli has examined the way that the oblique gaze of classical cinema is replaced, at least in some scenes, in *Blue Steel* and *Strange Days* by the direct gaze into the camera and fully subjective point-of-view shots. This conscious transgression of continuity editing is 'symbolic of her whole cinema: popular and classic on the surface, but deep down nonconformist and authorial' (1997: 242). But despite Rascaroli's assertion that 'Bigelow's cinema is essentially a discourse on vision (232), the gaze is only one element – some of them even more pervasive in the fabric of the film – with which the director toys.

Bigelow herself has said, 'I was still resisting narrative; [*The Loveless*] is more like a meditation' (Hultkrans 1995). She may well be unaware that she is using a term, meditation, which also has a musical meaning. Although it is not as firmly established a genre as 'symphonic poem' or 'opera aria', a meditation is a type of interlude found in some dramatic vocal works: the meditation from Jules Massenet's opera *Thaïs* is perhaps the most famous example, but there are also a series of meditations from Leonard Bernstein's theatre work *Mass*, for instance. As a moment of dramatic contemplation, a meditation comes with a shift of musical register or address; in these theatre works, they are instrumental passages of emotional intensity, not only without words but also without traditional musical structure, often building through repetition of a simple musical idea but increasing in orchestrational texture, force or figuration. While the analogy may be a little strained, *The Loveless* could be seen as a musical meditation within the context of normal narrative film. Its relative lack of narrative drive, the repetitive and fetishistic use of certain images which have historical, cultural and cinematic significance beyond the boundaries of the film itself, make it a contemplation of these images rather than any resolution or working out of them in a traditional storyline. Even the slender narrative threads have an iconic quality – the sexual encounter between gang leader Vance (Willem Dafoe) and Telena (Marin Kanter); the revelation of her father's abuse; the echo of her suicide with her mother's; the lonely widowed waitress Augusta's search for self-expression which culminates in humiliation through the striptease; even the disturbances engendered by Vance's lieutenant, the dangerous and dangerously sexy Davis (Robert Gordon), in his interactions with Augusta (Elizabeth Gans), his vampish girlfriend Debbie (Tina L'hotsky), and the youngest member of the gang, Ricky (Danny Rosen).

Homoeroticism is certainly itself a common trope in biker films, and a free-floating homoerotic atmosphere pervades *The Loveless*. Marin Kanter's Telena looks about fourteen; with her pixie haircut, lack of makeup, deep voice and slim hips in her shocking pink pedal pushers, she also looks more like a pretty boy than a woman, particularly compared to the other, more 'period'-looking women in the film (Debbie, Augusta, the woman with the flat) with their hourglass figures – the possible homoerotic implications of this pair is emphasised by the one scene in which we see Telena and Vance naked in bed; he is draped over her back, suggesting a sexual position more commonly associated with two men. Elsewhere, the garage owner's shy son watches gang member Hurley (Phillip Kimbrough) – whose jacket and jeans do not meet each other over the small of his back – work on his motorcycle and asks finally, ambiguously, 'Hey, okay if I sit on it?' There is also the sexual tension between Davis and Ricky, which eventually sparks off the film's climactic violence.

Christina Lane has convincingly argued that the film, although it seems to centre on Vance, is not about him at all; for Lane, it is Telena's story (2000: 106–9), and I would agree that it is Telena's story that provides the most emphatic narrative elements. But I would also argue that the other focus of the film is not Vance, but Davis, around whom most of the rest of the action centres and who provides the most aggressive and charismatic physical presence. Reversing the usual gender roles, Telena is the narrative agent, Davis is the sexual engine. After his initial, ambiguous act – white knight/molester of the woman with the flat tyre – Vance merely floats passively through the film: Telena picks *him* up (after initially eyeing Davis, who appears both interested and amused). Davis is the one whose nervous energy causes the real ructions among the locals.

Davis is both sidekick and villain in the film, and Robert Gordon's tough prettiness and sneering, swaggering performance hark back to the 1950s much more strongly than Defoe's rather blank Vance. Davis is a psychopath with the look of a teen-idol just a little too mature and knowing for his adoring audience – he really is 'The Leader of the Pack'[5] depicted in Jeff Barry and Ellie Greenwich's mini-melodrama recorded by the Shangri-Las (1964).[6] Gordon's own postmodern answer song, 'Too Fast to Live, Too Young to Die', is strangely absent from the soundtrack, but is there in spirit.

Gordon's look is classic 1950s – black pompadour, pouty mouth, big dark eyes with long eyelashes and lanky grace. He is ambiguous: androgynous, sleazy but glamorous, and sexually attractive/threatening in the best tradition of rock stars. This is hardly coincidental. Gordon himself never attained the heights of rock stardom, but for a time in the late 1970s and early 1980s, he was acclaimed by a small connoisseurship of music fans, including Bruce Springsteen, who penned the song 'Fire' – a

Figure 2 Davis (Robert Gordon) 'provides the most aggressive and physical presence' in the film.

disturbingly sensual evocation of date rape – especially for him. Gordon was admired for his deep knowledge and transformation of early rock styles, and for his undeniably spectacular baritone, an eerie combination of Elvis Presley and Roy Orbison. In addition to his pivotal role as Davis, Gordon was responsible for the music in the film, not just the original instrumental underscore, but also the selection of songs.[7]

The fetish character of the film reinforces the obsessive structure of the 'meditation' Bigelow suggests. Period images are isolated, lingered upon, from the bikers' jackets, shades, boots and bikes, to the waitress' white foundation underwear, to the clock and jukebox in the diner. Similarly, Vance's monotone voiceover is nothing but a string of clichés; and the exchange with which Davis enters the film echoes Brando's famous rejoinder in *The Wild One* ('What are you rebelling against?' 'Whadya got?'). Davis drives up on his Harley, bleached-blonde girlfriend Debbie riding pillion, and asks a man sitting on a porch for directions. 'Which a-way you comin' from?' asks the man; Davis replies, 'It don't matter which way I'm comin' from; it's which way I'm goin' to.'

The music has a similar fetish quality, concentrating on high-reverb guitar riffs, descending plucked walking basslines, rolling drums and growling saxophones. Although these traits are all certainly present in 1950s rock 'n' roll, the extent to and consistency with which they are used in the score of *The Loveless* is as excessive as the fire-engine red Coca-Cola machine outside the garage, which dominates several sequences more effectively than most of the actors do. The very fact that it is rock 'n' roll (and not jazz, as in *The Wild One*) draws attention to the symbolism of the musical style, as to a 1981 audience, rock would have connoted rebellion as jazz had in 1954.

The extensive use of period recordings as well as Gordon's own music blurs several lines that are normally taken to be distinct in the classical soundscape. One of the most basic distinctions is between underscore – that which only the audience hears – and source music – that which is heard by the characters as well as the audience and is normally located in the scene through the presence of a 'source' – a band, a radio, a record player or jukebox, or the like. These are distinguished as diegetic (source) and non-diegetic (underscore), and normally have two very different functions. The underscore (a word which has a dual meaning, as both the musical score 'under' the voices and images and as a kind of emotional underlining) colours the scene with musical-emotional coding. An effective underscore provides what sound theorist Michel Chion (1994: 5) terms 'added value' – it gives information which the audience assumes is already self-evident in the image, but in fact is indiscernible or indistinct without the music. The underscore can tell us truths of which the characters are unaware. Source music is frequently used to perform the diametrically opposed function – to make us aware that the music is *not* reflecting the characters' feelings. Chion calls it 'anempathetic'; it is the ironic use, for instance, of bright, upbeat music in stark contrast to a character who is unhappy.

Popular music in films is almost always cast as source music: when Tom Cruise dances around the living room in his underpants to Bob Seger's 'Old Time Rock and Roll' in *Risky Business* (Paul Brickman, 1983), we first see him push all the slides on his father's expensive equalizer to the top, establishing without doubt that the music is actually playing on the stereo in the room. Other times, the mere presence of a source can be assumed: we hear music in the interior of a car; most cars have radios, therefore we assume that the music is issuing from that source – but only if the music is pop;[8] if it is orchestral, we probably assume that it is underscore.[9]

In *The Loveless*, there is no real difference between the style of the source music and the style of the underscore. That easy distinction is suspended, and the film continually destabilises the diegetic/non-diegetic boundary. The opening three sequences manipulate the soundscape in different, but telling, ways.

The music over the opening credits is 'Relentless' by Eddie Dixon, and it displays many of the stylistic traits that are found throughout the score: a plucked, descending bassline forms the foundation, with a simple snare backbeat reinforcing the steady, sauntering rhythm; a clean, undistorted guitar with exaggerated reverb; and throaty vocals. As the credits end, the music continues over our discovery of Vance, sitting on his motorcycle in the middle of scrubby desert. This establishes two things: that the music is non-diegetic, for there is no possible source, and that the music is associated with Vance (this will be confirmed later in the film when the song reappears for the introduction of Telena, signalling her involvement with him and implicitly – perhaps falsely – drawing parallels between the two characters). In an unexpected highlighting gesture, the music stops as Vance preens in stereotypical biker fashion, combing his hair, buckling the waist of his jacket, and starting his bike. The camera pulls up and away to watch him ride onto the blacktop highway, and the music re-enters, linking into a larger association in many American road movies between travelling shots and rock music.

The second sequence is the only one in the film where we see Vance actually do anything. He comes upon an attractive woman of about forty in a snazzy car with a flat tyre. Despite his arrogant swagger, he is polite and changes the tyre for her; but then he kisses her (she seems attracted at first but – as it turns out, rightly – nervous about his intentions), fondles her breasts, and demands, then steals, money. Whether we want him to be a nice guy or a rebel, we will be probably be disappointed – he does a good deed but ultimately only to humiliate the woman, and even for a rebel, his behaviour is just petty and mean because a lone woman in distress represents no real power for him to rebel against.[10] The music likewise vacillates in an unsettling manner. When he first approaches the woman, we hear an uneasy and musically unstable gesture of dissonant piano and saxophone; this is mirrored at the end of the scene – a brief piano/saxophone cue (section of underscore) has the character of an opening gesture, but it disappears as he leans through the car window to manhandle and steal from her. Between these two non-diegetic moments, the music is diegetic.

As Vance approaches, she is putting on lipstick in the car's wing mirror and we hear a Spanish-speaking DJ, evidently coming from the car radio. As he changes the tyre, Vance demands, 'Crank that radio up.' The woman obliges, and we hear a fast swing number reminiscent of Benny Goodman's famous version of Louis Prima's 'Sing, Sing, Sing', heavy on tom-toms, riffing saxophones and brass stabs. The music is cut off mid-stream with an abrupt time jump, Vance closing the trunk of the car. It is the first of several awkward time- or place-jumps in the film; either the music editing was simply poorly done, or it was intentionally done to draw the audience's attention (one suspects the latter).

The third sequence is the most emphatically diegetic of the three, but a rare case in which the use of source music is deeply *un*ironic. Brenda Lee's 'I Want to Be Wanted', with its frequent refrain 'so alone', performs the underlining function usually given over to underscore. The scene is an obvious homage to Edward Hopper's famous painting 'Night Hawks', an almost motionless framing of the denizens of the diner, each of them sitting alone. The camera is elevated to take in the entire diner, including the glowing jukebox in the upper right hand corner of the frame, just so that we are absolutely sure the music is diegetic. In a reflecting scene later in the film, gang members, waitresses and diner patrons are all killing time in the diner while the jukebox is shown spinning 'The Stroll' by The Diamonds – although all this time, the call to movement *is* ironic, highlighting the indolence on display.

There is a gradual build-up of tempo and aggression in the music from the opening to Little Richard's 'Rip It Up', about a third of the way into the film, by which time the bikers have effectively taken over the diner. There is a noticeable drop back in musical intensity (tempo, rhythm and fullness of orchestration) as we move to a slower blues shuffle with slide guitar at the garage. Throughout the film, the recording level and sound quality help establish location, shifting between the diner, the garage and later the bar. Subtle variations within the overall style help define spaces and groups: the country blues of the garage; the hot swing in the flash car driven by the sexy older woman; the Nashville ballad style of Brenda Lee in the rural bar before the advent of the bikers, with harder r'n'b Little Richard and The Diamonds once they arrive. Other features persist across stylistic boundaries.

The saxophone is a staple of 1950s rock 'n' roll, but it has a long, jazz-induced association with illicit sex, a congruence exploited in the score of *The Loveless*. We hear a raunchy baritone sax solo over a close-up of Augusta's shapely posterior as she approaches Vance's table, a scene pointedly rhymed by a shot of Hurley's gyrating hips framed against the jukebox in the bar at the end of the movie. Sliding, discordant saxophone underlines Telena's disclosure of her father's abuse. And a sax-driven Latin number, reminiscent of The Champs' 'Tequila', plays in the garage during the sexually charged knife sequence between Debbie and Davis, then Davis and Ricky.

In the second third of the film, the garage (and that sexy Coca-Cola machine outside it) is the central location. A radio's presence is established through not only the sound quality but also by period commercials, an aural equivalent of the film's obsession with isolated images, which culminates in a languid sequence set to Gordon's ballad 'Dreaming of You'. Although the scene focuses primarily on Davis, the voices of Gordon and Davis are kept markedly separate. Davis and Debie are slow-dancing and kissing, intercut with close-ups of numerous period items, including Hurley's belt buckle and nudie shots from magazines on the walls of the garage. Sonically, Gordon's ballad 'Dreaming of You' is framed by commercials from the time, and young Ricky – an exceptionally pretty boy with a set of snapshots of his own severe scars, prefiguring the wound-fetishisation of *Crash* (David Cronenberg, 1996) – interrupts Davis and Debbie's kissing with an ad from a mercenary magazine, one of a series of transparent attempts to turn Davis' attention from Debbie onto him. In the next garage scene, Davis is caressing Debbie with his knife in a blatantly erotic manner. When Debbie refuses to play (and Davis reacts with a surprisingly tolerant, even pleased, laugh), Ricky again jumps in to grab Davis's attention, taking out his own knife and saying, 'Hey, Davis, come close to me.' This turns out not to be the seduction it first seems, but a challenge. They engage in a knife-throwing contest until Ricky protests, 'Hey, you nicked me again, Davis', and pouts off when things get too intense for him. Davis looks after him and grunts, 'Huh, he's just a joybang.' This apparently sexual but dismissively casual interest in Ricky may, however, be a misdirection, as we shall see.

Two other pairs of scenes demand attention for their exceptional use of sound. The first pair features groups of men peripheral to the main action, apparently there only to bolster the film's racial subtext (something also reflected in the television news sequence seen in the motel room). In one scene of the pair, white men in the bar watch news footage of a disastrous attempt to break the sound barrier on the Bonneville Salt Flats; the lack of music is explicable, even 'natural' here. However, in the rhyming scene of black men, sitting around talking and playing cards in the country store, the lack of music seems positively strange. It forces one to consider why we expect music in that scene. On a cultural level, one would merely expect music in this situation; on a cinematic level, one would expect country blues in such a scene. This expectation has a number of ramifications, including the stereotyping of Southern blacks in films as happy 'darkies', as Telena calls them; an even more unsettling reading exposes the uncomfortable underbelly of racism in rock 'n' roll. The garage where the white bikers are located is already staked out as a place of country blues; they have appropriated that style, leaving a vacuum for the representation of the men in the store.

The second pair of scenes oppose the first; where the first two are narratively static and musically silent, the second two are the action peaks of the film and music overwhelms the soundscape, reinforcing Lane's argument of Telena as central character as she is the focus of the sound manipulations. In the motel scene, as Telena sleeps, Vance turns on the television (which shows newsreel scenes apparently of a racist incident and the ensuing unrest). But we do not hear the broadcast; the soundscape is dominated by Gordon's singing 'So Young'. His powerful and precise baritone has an excessive quality that recalls the postmodern concept of the 'hyperreal', a kind of blank irony of exaggeration especially evident in this performance with its reiterated 'pretty baby' interjections from the breathy female background singer and the pointed references to 'my teenage love' and the impossibility of that love sung in a throbbing voice significantly deeper and richer than one would expect in this style. Two gunshots intrude, and Telena's father bursts into the hotel room and grabs her, dragging her out of the motel as she cries, 'Daddy, he ain't done nothin' you ain't done to me a hundred times before!' As the song ends on a sighed, 'Oh, baby', Vance closes the door and smiles vacantly in the mirror. He never does anything to help her, retaining his aloof, passive stance at all costs, including, eventually, Telena's life.

The matching scene of this pair is the final shootout in the bar, which also draws in the Davis/Ricky 'romance'. Telena's father eyes Ricky in the men's room, then there is a cut to him dragging Ricky out into the bar with his jeans around his ankles, inciting the mayhem that ensues. The ellipsis makes his motivation unclear: he has been bad-mouthing the bikers all along, but his sidelong glance at Ricky, his gaze lingering unmistakably below the waist at the urinal, is suggestive that perhaps he made an unwelcome advance on the boy. Davis is first to leap to Ricky's defence with a gun – perhaps suggesting that his earlier dismissal of Ricky as a 'joybang' was a cover for deeper feelings, or simply that he is fiercely loyal – but eventually the entire bar is caught up in the fight. The only sounds other than the music are inarticulate shrieks from the women, Davis' psychotic howl (bolstered by singer Gordon's prodigious lung-power), and the shooting. Telena also has a gun; her intention is much more focused. The soundtrack highlights this: when the camera cuts to her in the doorway, there is no sound. She drops her father with one shot, then returns to her father's car, and Vance watches (again, passively) as she turns the gun on herself, finally putting it in her mouth and pulling the trigger. The hesitance Telena shows in putting the gun in her mouth is ambiguous; it seems not only fear of the gun, but the sort of hesitance one might expect from a young girl with the erect penis the gun so obviously represents. Davis' 'knife' is also obviously sexualised, particularly in the knife-throwing scene, but also when he thrusts it into the cushion of the diner's booth; the colour of the vinyl covering is similar to the waitresses' uniform, creating an echo between the cushion and Augusta's bottom, which he had been ogling. This overt erotic imagery, long in use in patriarchal Hollywood, is something Bigelow toys with over and over, from Mae's teeth (phallic) and the victims' blood (feminine) in *Near Dark* (another gender flip) to the gun/phallus which Megan and Eugene struggle to possess in *Blue Steel*.

'Relentless' fades back up on a flashback shot of Telena, her childish giggle the only diegetic sound. Not only her voice, but her subjectivity controls the soundtrack in the end. Vance's ineffectualness is exposed; Telena is the one who is 'relentless'.

Near Dark

Bigelow's first solo directorial feature, *Near Dark*, is a vampire-western-film noir with elements of counter-culture road movies like *Easy Rider* (Dennis Hopper, 1969). The film is often spoken of as a 'one-off', unlike any other film, but actually it bears some noticeable resemblances to Michael Mann's techno-gothic-vampire-World War Two film *The Keep* (1983).[11] This is ironic on one level, because Bigelow is usually considered a 'feminist' director, or at least one with feminist sensibilities, whereas Mann seems incapable of creating female characters with any depth or narrative purpose. However, both of them have a wildly hybrid approach to genre, a balletic approach to violence, and a distinctive visual style marked by striking shot composition and a surreal combination of gritty realism and glamour. In *The Keep* and *Near Dark*, both also adopted a neo-Gothic look heavy on nighttime scenes with blue filters, fog and piercing light sources, an aesthetic similar to that of early music video (the green laser lights in the fog at the climax of *The Keep* were already a video cliché in 1983, although Mann has a better narrative 'excuse' for it than most videos). Between *The Keep* and *Near Dark*, of course, Michael Mann's television series *Miami Vice* revolutionised the use of current popular songs not just as source music, but as non-diegetic and participating actively in the narrative.

The Keep and *Near Dark* also share a composer: the German electronica/progressive rock band Tangerine Dream, spearheaded by Edgar Froese, provides the synth score for both films. Although all kinds of films had synth scores in the 1980s, the fantasy genre exploited the literally 'unnatural' sound of the synthesizer to greatest effect in films like *Cat People* (scored by Giorgio Moroder, 1982), *Blade Runner* (Vangelis, 1982), *Legend* (Tangerine Dream, 1985),[12] and even *The Natural* (Randy Newman, 1984). The eerily pure tone and floating attack of the synthesizer eased audiences into these unreal worlds, often gathering rhythmic momentum as vague images gradually coalesced on the screen. In *The Keep*, the obviously artificial synthesizer and Caribbean rhythms create a dissonance with the shockingly beautiful images of rusty Nazi tanks rolling into a picturesque Romanian mountain village, the flare of a match lighting a cigarette, a close-up of Jürgen Prochnow's famously blue eyes. Just the dissonance between the geographical and historical sources of sound and image let us know we are in for some serious dislocation; conversely, the close-up of a mosquito (and we know only female mosquitoes draw blood) at the beginning of *Near Dark* has resonance rather than dissonance, recalling the pseudo-documentary *The Hellstrom Chronicle* (Walon Green and Ed Spiegel, 1971) with its award-winning close-up insect photography and eerie electronic score by Lalo Schifrin.

Both directors also rely on the energy and drive of rock music, particularly to spectacularise violence, and make excellent use of actors who were dancers (Edward James Olmos, *Miami Vice*; Patrick Swayze, *Point Break*), athletes (William L. Petersen, *Manhunter*), or simply unusually graceful (Scott Glenn, *The Keep*; Lance Henriksen, *Near Dark*) to create sequences that approach the musical number in their melding of music and movement. The use of popular music in *Near Dark* is especially pointed, not only in how it is used but how it is *not* used.

The soundscape of *Near Dark* is dominated by the themeless, textural and timbral synth score. There are no distinctive melodies and the rhythms are often vague, creating a sense of suspension, an effective reversal of the static images and driving rhythms of *The Loveless*. But a hint of the power of popular music occurs twice in the early part of the film. In his attempts to woo Mae, Caleb tries to find a station on his truck radio; the moment he finds one he likes, the scene cuts away; and in a brief cut back, the radio is playing so softly it is hard to determine anything about the music other than it is playing. In a rhyming scene, the vampire tribe's leader Jesse (Lance Henriksen) and his consort Diamondback (Jenette Goldstein) are driving along a road, reminiscing lovingly about how they met. Unlike the obnoxious Severen (Bill Paxton) or the impatient Homer (Joshua Miller), Jesse and Diamondback are confident, stealthy hunters; one can almost read their relationship, as Lane has done with Telena in *The Loveless*, as an important alternate possibility showing through the texture of the film like the pattern on the back of a tapestry. For all the violence of the way they live, there is a great tenderness between them, although as is typical with Bigelow, there is play with gender expectations. Diamondback has the name of a lethal snake (an obvious phallic symbol), and she seems physically the more imposing of the two; she also wields a knife. Jesse is taller and most definitely the leader, but he is also almost delicately built, and it is he who uses sex to lure his victim in the bar siege before offering her up to Diamondback for the kill and the sustenance.

Jesse and Diamondback pick up a couple of hitchhikers who think they are going to rape and rob the couple, who merely smile knowingly. When it becomes clear that the hapless hitchhikers are about to become victims themselves, Jesse reaches over and turns up the radio. The scene cuts away immediately after the first burst of guitar, but we are primed with the association of loud music and vampires killing. But again, the sound of popular music is held back. The pay off is the bar siege, the only sequence in which the music is really heard, emphasised by the contrast of the synth score in the rest of the film.

This action climax of the film conflates two striking moments from *The Loveless* – the final blow-out in the bar, and a fleeting but viscerally exciting confluence of sound effect, motion and music – a striking audio/visual cut to one of the bikers playing a table bowling game. The strike of the ball kicks off Little Richard's 'Rip It Up'. This effect is made even more powerful in *Near Dark* to open the bar siege, in part by framing it more deliberately.

A soft synthesizer wash forms an auditory analogy to a lovely shot of the vampire tribe cresting the hill outside the bar, silhouetted against a bright white backlight between the dark earth and the deep blue sky. It is a moment of stasis, shattered by a cut to a pool break and the door slamming open to admit the vampires, set to the odd synthesizer introduction of John Parr's contemporary hit 'Naughty, Naughty'. The jumpy phrases are played on a wooden-sounding synth patch, similar to the sound of the pool balls striking one another. The vampires take up a symmetrical position, just made for the movie posters, and the few denizens of the bar sit up and take notice, right on the beats of the music. One of the bar patrons is standing over a jukebox, making a strong visual connection to the source of the music.

The action 'catches' beats in the music to such an extent that it seems necessary for the music to have been playing on set rather than laid on in post-production, although the sensitivity of the actors toward the music varies greatly. The scene unfolds in a series of seduction/attacks by members of the vampire tribe, attempting to show Caleb 'how it's done'. The aggressive macho swagger of 'Naughty, Naughty' seems most appropriate to the cocky Severen, but he is the least sensitive to the music. The music is faded down to its lowest level in the entire sequence as he takes the lead, harassing the bartender and provoking a fight with a hunter.

When the attention shifts to the waitress nervously serving Jesse, Mae, Homer and Diamondback at a booth, the music becomes more prominent under Jesse's come-on line to the waitress, just as his sexuality seems to 'turn on' – his entire *mien* changes, and he delivers his line in pauses between the singer's lines, making the music more noticeable because he is working with, not over, it. He rises gracefully to take the terrified waitress in his arms, then draws her back down onto his lap as he sits down, all in time to the music. This is not the same kind of correlation as the editing at the beginning, but a deeper, dancer's awareness of the rhythms of the music which is inseparable from his change from leader to sexual predator,[13] reinforcing the long-standing association between musicality and sexuality that predates rock 'n' roll by centuries. But the odd violent tenderness that exists between Jesse and Diamondback once again emerges as he offers the waitress to his consort; as Diamondback slits the woman's throat and Jesse catches her blood in a beer glass for Diamondback. Homer rocks his head and shoulders, singing along with the music, creating a kind of family resemblance between him and Jesse.

When Severen comes to the fore again, moving and acting straight through the beat of the music (a blues shuffle called 'Morse Code' performed by Jools Holland), a question of characterisation arises. Was this intentional, accentuating Severen's obnoxious personality? It has been stressed throughout the film that he is oblivious to anything but his own desires (literally marching to a different drummer?). Or is it just that the actor, Bill Paxton, is far less sensitive to music than Henriksen, Miller and Wright? In effect, it does not matter, for his abrasive nature is well represented by his bulldozing right through the music.

'Fever' is next, a song made famous in a sultry version by the lushly feminine jazz siren Peggy Lee; this version is by The Cramps, a punk band known for its toying with gender expectations and drag, extratextually connecting with Bigelow's gender play. 'Fever' has a double significance in the scene, as Caleb's 'fever' is reaching its highest intensity – he needs to feed, or he will die; Severen is also reaching a fever pitch of destruction. He revels in it in a way the others do not, slashing the bartender's throat extravagantly with the spur on his boot. The song dies away to the phrase, 'What a lovely way to burn', prefiguring the fiery end to the siege, as well as the final fate of the vampire family. Caleb is shot (though it has little effect on him) and is still unable to kill. With a jerk of his head, Jesse signals for the lessons – and the music – to continue.

Mae takes over to a sweet country ballad, 'The Cowboy Rides Away', performed by George Strait. Mae (Jenny Wright) is almost an anomaly among Bigelow women. With a blonde pixie haircut and dressed in jeans and a sleeveless chambray shirt, she looks like a cross between Peter Pan and Tinkerbell. The boyish look is consistent with Telena, Megan (Blue Steel), Tyler (Point Break) and even Mace (Strange Days), but for all her physical strength, and even the emotional strength she shows in protecting Caleb, Mae still seems the most fragile and vulnerable of Bigelow's women, possibly just because of Wright's delicate, elfin beauty. Although she makes a come-on to the handsome young cowboy (James LeGros) in the bar, she still acts within the norms of the confident but sweet country girl going after her shy beau. Mae moves lightly with the beat, dancing more obviously to the music than Jesse did, but moving in a far more innocent, less sexual way. 'The cowboy rides away' by jumping out the window; Mae sends Caleb after him as the others set fire to the bar to facilitate their escape.

So we have three different approaches to music, to killing, and one could even say to sex: the aggressive, the sensual, and the romantic – represented in these three 'lessons' that the vampires give to Caleb. But we also have the clearest set piece of violence in the film, tightly (or not) choreographed to the music. Music is an integral part of spectacle in cinema: whether a John Ford landscape or a violent ballet such as we have here, music adds depth, focus, rhythm and what Michel Chion terms 'vectorization' (1994: 12), an orientation toward a future; along the way, it also organises smaller fluctuations of intensity.

On the larger narrative scale, this siege set piece is Caleb's rite of passage – albeit one in which he fails. He is shown 'the way' and is unable to follow through, one of the key ways in which Bigelow subverts the narrative, as in the end he redeems/domesticates Mae in the usual manner of the 'good woman' in a western.[14] In the texture of the film, the music is as important as lighting and shot composition in establishing style: rock music in the wash of the Tangerine Dream synth score is the aural equivalent of the bar burning orange-bright in the centre of the blue-washed frame as the vampires torch it and continue on their way.

Blue Steel

Blue Steel is Bigelow's first major feature and is the most mainstream, both in narrative and soundscape, of these early films. Traces of Bigelow's genre/gender play remain, however. The Hitchockian 'wrong man' – in this case, 'wrong woman' – suspense narrative has the dark, mythical undertones of a fairytale. As the gender roles are inverted in the narrative, many of the traditional principles of scoring are inverted in Brad Fiedel's synth score – the lower the pitch, the higher the tension, for instance. The boundary between score and sound design is significantly eroded, and thematic material is idiosyncratically deployed, as the 'point of audition' of the score shifts among the human characters until it finally seems to reside in the title character of the gun.

In many respects, Blue Steel is a typical police action thriller of the late 1980s, with similarities to movies like Lethal Weapon (Richard Donner, 1987) and Sea of Love (Harold Becker, 1989). The lead character is often a maverick officer under some sort of censure from the police hierarchy; unlike most police characters in this kind of film, however, Megan (Jamie Lee Curtis) is a rookie, inexperienced and vulnerable; her character profile is more that of the usual sidekick. Megan's desire to be a police officer is a means of exerting the control she did not have in her family situation (her father beats her mother), a psychology widely recognised in real-life police officers, but one not usually explored in mainstream police fiction because of its emotional fragility.[15]

Despite the central female lead, *Blue Steel* is, like almost all examples of the action-thriller genre, essentially a conservative text. For instance, why does Megan fall in love with Nick? Apparently because movies have to have a 'happy ending' love interest, although Nick has been objectionable, patronising and domineering throughout the film and never seems to respect Megan in any significant way. There is even a disturbing fascistic element in the juxtaposition of tall, curly-haired, blonde, blue-eyed Nick Mann (Clancy Brown), with his Aryan looks and strong, monosyllabic name which literally reinforces his masculinity, and shorter, stockier, dark Eugene Hunt (played by Jewish actor Ron Silver), lumbered with a name redolent of childhood taunts of 'nerd' and 'sissy'.[16]

Congruent with this disturbing remnant of German Romanticism is the more poetic trace of fairytale and horror.[17] Megan is a child at the beginning – even, as in all good fairytales, an orphan, or at least motherless: first she is a student who fails; unlike others at her graduation, she is not pictured with a spouse or mother. Her 'family' is represented as her childhood friend Tracy and Tracy's family; Megan is abandoned by her parents, who did not come to the ceremony (although one can also see her as Tracy's 'child').

This childlike presentation is complemented by the contradictory and ambiguous way her sexuality is constructed in the famous opening sequence – traditionally masculine attire (her police uniform) over the lacy accoutrements of femininity. Probably the greatest amount of the literature on Bigelow is based on this opening sequence, most of it from a psychoanalytical (or less commonly, sociological) point of view (see Mizejewski 1993; Tasker 1993; Powell 1994; Self 1994; Rascaroli 1997). Bigelow is undoubtedly familiar with the tenets of psychoanalytic film theory (one can see her playing with that just as she does with the classical cinematic apparatus – the fetishisation of the male body and of Gordon's voice in *The Loveless* is indicative of that), so those interpretations are perfectly valid (although I would hesitate to use the word 'correct' as Rascaroli does (1997: 238)); there are other angles from which this can be approached which, while not invalidating the Freudian interpretation, do not rely upon it. Certainly a simple one is that Megan at the beginning is immature, gender-fluid, on the brink of 'awakening' sexually, like the heroine of a fairytale.

Megan is checked out by women as well as men as she walks home, a strut of self-confidence given to her by her costume of authority. But the self-confidence seems to be a surprise, as if this is the first time she is experiencing the desiring gaze of others. The colour scheme is particularly indicative: at the beginning of the film, Megan is dressed in her light-blue uniform, the same tone as the dominant blue-filtered set, costume and lighting design. But once she develops a sexual interest in Eugene, she is marked by red, like Snow White's apple or Sleeping Beauty's pricked finger, a colour associated with blood, the onset of puberty and sexuality. She wears a dark red silk blouse on their first dinner date, and then is seen in a watermelon-coloured t-shirt throughout the bulk of the film. It is her little red riding hood to Eugene's big bad wolf; the image of him as a wolf, as an animal, makes an anti-Semitic reading of the film uncomfortably easy, but it is also possible to make a less distasteful werewolf reading. Eugene hunts at night in the light of the moon; when he kills the prostitute and wallows in her blood, he practically howls at the moon; and Megan finally kills him with the 'silver bullet' he has been desiring throughout the film.

This fantastical element, as in *Near Dark*, allies the film with a number of fantasy films of the 1980s with pervasive synth scores – in other words, the score is coded as fantasy, whereas the dominant narrative signals 'thriller'. The sounds that make up the musical score by Brad Fiedel (who also scored *The Terminator* and *Terminator 2* (James Cameron, 1984; 1992)) are created by synthesizers and/or electronic manipulation of acoustic instrumental means, and evoke the cold, smooth blue steel of the title.

The title sequence is dominated by extreme close-up shots moving along the gun, some of them so close as to be almost abstract images of the textured handgrip, the barrel, the muzzle; the shots of the bullets being loaded foreshadow the theme of penetration that runs through the narrative. And here the music – such as it is – is first mated to the image of the gun, and perhaps more importantly, to a highly eroticised image of the gun.

The basic sound is a deep, reverberant, clearly synthetic one, deployed in a series of drones. The drone has long been used in dramatic music as a tension-building device: it is a telling exercise in musical perception. When one first encounters a drone, one waits for a change; when it does not come, one of two things happens, sometimes in succession – the listener becomes inured to the tension-inducing quality of the drone and becomes complacent, bored, or merely 'tunes out'; or the sense of tension increases through an elevation of irritation with the lack of movement or anticipation of change.

Some harmony is created through voice leading, but there is only the barest hint of 'melody', and it might be better described simply as linear motion. Mixed into this are percussive sounds, like snare hits, cymbal splashes and nail scratches across the ridges of cymbals. Some of these percussive sounds are slowed down so that they are both lower in pitch and more sustained (and more immediately unrecognisable, rather like the extreme close-up images of the gun in the title sequence). A third major component of the music-cum-sound effect track is a breathy sound, like that produced by someone blowing across a hollow pipe – or the barrel of a gun? While producing a sound that has a recognisably metallic source, this effect also brings an element of life to the largely cool, astringent soundscape, for it does sound like breath and not merely wind.[18]

In the title sequence, the music's material connection with the gun is firmly established, almost investing the gun with a personality of its own. But this association is soon split into something much more subjective, representing two separate characters' different, but equally obsessive, emotional states connected with the gun: Megan's anxiety about performing her police duties bolstered by her reassurance in having the gun, and Eugene's fascination with Megan, mediated by his fetishising of the gun (or vice versa). The phallic potential of the gun is played upon by both characters: Megan takes on a traditional male role, the police officer with the gun, and displaces her father as head of the family; Eugene is dysfunctionally masculine, needing the gun for rape and murder; but when they are making love, Eugene is aroused by Megan's handling of the gun, shifting the focus of his phallic desire. In the end, when Megan finally shoots him, there is a moment of eye contact between the two characters in which he seems to desire the shooting, fulfilling the moment he had placed the muzzle against his forehead during their foreplay.

The music's association with Megan's state of mind is established early on, a drone underlies the opening training exercises which ends in Megan's 'death'. When she arrives home from the commencement exercise to find a message from her mother, the drone enters as she listens to the playback and looks at her uniform hat. A little later, as she is riding in a prowl car, the lightly pulsed drone seems more ominous than the situation might suggest, but this is the first appearance of a recurring joke in the film – several times, when people ask her why she wants to be a policeman, Megan replies deadpan, 'Because I wanted to shoot people.' She always defuses the moment with a grin and a 'Just kidding', but the audience is left with little doubt that there is a grain of truth in her initial reply. Firmly connecting the music to Megan's state of mind, rather than the situation, is the fact that the music is not present when the actual hold-up takes place; it only enters when she reacts. After the event, the music fades down and we become more aware of other sounds, the alarm going off, the street noises. It is a classic example of 'subjective sound', as we hear things from Megan's point of audition: the music is like the adrenalin-soaked blood rushing in her ears, deafening her to sounds not immediately pertinent to her situation; in a constrasting scene, the street noises outside her apartment deafen Megan to Eugene shooting Nick in her bathroom.

The sound design in this sequence is remarkable. The sounds of Megan and Nick making love are almost uncomfortably exposed: the creaks of the bed, their breathing, their kissing. In films, we are used to music cushioning such intimate sounds. The high-pitched drones which enter with an insert of Eugene in the bathroom with the gun (an exception to the norm in the film, where low drones indicate suspense) create a sense of unease that builds as the drones grow louder and higher through the sequence.[19] We hear Eugene loading the gun before we actually see the bullets going into the gun, and the sound of metal sliding against metal is unnaturally loud. When Nick leaves the bed to go to the bathroom, the street sounds rise from imperceptible to natural to too loud as Megan sits up in bed and lights a cigarette, deafening her to the sound of Eugene shooting Nick with the gun, wrapped in a muffling towel. After Nick is shot, the street sounds, most unrealistically, subside again. The roles of sound effect and music effectively reverse in this sequence.

The music's connection with Eugene is effected through the gun: a mickey-mousing-type swishing sound as he takes the gun in the supermarket inserts him into the musical texture; the synthesized breath sound is almost like the gun sighing in pleasure or relief as he takes it (the gun is projecting on Eugene, or Eugene is projecting onto the gun through the sound). This is reinforced by scenes of him taking the gun home to examine and caress, playing with the gun in the bathroom at the stock exchange, engraving Megan's name on the bullets, and finally committing murder, all to similar sounds. Synthesized voices are heard in the score only once, when Eugene hears the voices that urge him to kill; these voices are wordless, they do not actually speak the words Eugene hears. In effect, Fiedel underscores what we do not hear, what is going on inside Eugene's head.

An unusually subtle sort of resolution is achieved in the end credit sequence. Megan sits, exhausted, physically and emotionally, in a squad car as police and onlookers mill around the scene of Eugene's death. Rascaroli speaks of her being 'totally shattered, her gaze is absent, darkened, completely catatonic. It is a long, opaque instant in which life is suspended...' (1997: 246). We have no idea whether she will survive this devastating incident intact; yet over the synthesizer drone rises an electric violin. The bluesy phrasing of the violin brings an individuation of the musical structure, a first perceptible melody, something so much more familiar that becomes a point of rest. That it is done in such extreme terms – a single voice of piercing timbre in a style easily recognised by the general movie audience – emphasises a sense of arrival. The gaze is broken, but the music is still subjective; it gives Megan a strength, a continuation, even if also a resignation, that the image does not – a perfect example of Chion's 'added value'.

Conclusion

The three elements of Kathryn Bigelow's films that normally draw the most comment are all interconnected: genre, gender and violence. Her gender surprises people because of the violence of the films; she works in genres that are violent and therefore more normally associated with men; but her approach to genre is to blend and twist

– usually subverting or inverting them by playing on patriarchal expectations of gender and sexuality, though occasionally putting forward a puzzle as to whether this is recapitulation to or comment on conventions.

The soundscapes of her cinematic worlds vary significantly in her early films. Yet just as the images and narrative toy with genre, so do the soundscapes. In *The Loveless*, the rebellious sound of rock 'n' roll is both narrative symbol and historical fetish; within the context of the film, music provides rhythm and drive to a notably static set of images. The diegetic/non-diegetic boundary is established and then transgressed. Rock music, with its strong associations with aggression and sex, is crucial in the pivotal and violent 'scene of instruction' in *Near Dark*, and this is highlighted by the contrast to the score in the rest of the film. In both *Near Dark* and *Blue Steel*, the relatively amorphous synth score ties the films to the fantasy genre, elements of which are there in the image and narrative but not as foregrounded as in the scores (one could imagine *Near Dark* with a Coplandesque neo-western score, for instance, or *Blue Steel* with a late-1980s action-film score by Michael Kamen or a neo-noir score Jerry Goldsmith, but this would reinforce different and perhaps more obvious generic elements).

For Bigelow, as for most film-makers, music is important for violent scenes. In most films, however, music is there for rhythm, for visceral excitement, as part of the spectacularisation of the image; in Bigelow's films, the music does that at the same time questioning that use. In most films, the violent action sequences are the least interesting musically; in Bigelow's films, they are almost always the most interesting sequences.

The soundscapes of Bigelow's films have become more polished, less contradictory, as her films have become more mainstream. Neither *Point Break* nor *The Weight of Water* use music in such inventive or ambiguous ways; even if the scores themselves are interesting as film music (and both of them do have interesting elements), the kind of border transgressions so evident in the earlier films are not there, or at least are highly attenuated – Marc Shaiman depicts water sounds evocatively in his score of *Point Break*, but it does not have the same narrative power as the breath sounds associated with the gun in *Blue Steel*. Music obviously plays a very important role in *Strange Days*, interacting with the narrative, but in doing that, it is following already common models like the musical or the jukebox movie. In jukebox films like *American Graffiti* (George Lucas, 1973) and *The Big Chill* (Lawrence Kasdan, 1983), popular music is used lyrically to reflect on the narrative – like a musical – and also to set a sense of historical time, and producer Steven Charles Jaffe even said, 'instead of … building absurd cars and designing bizarre costumes … we realized that one of the things that would help define the future in a subtle way was the music' (quoted in Parisi 1995 in Romi Stepovich's article in this volume; see Stepovich for more information about the music, particularly its adjunct as a marketing tool, in *Strange Days*). Again, although the music might be intriguing in itself, its deployment in the film is along traditional lines.

To some degree, this 'mainstreaming' may be the inevitable conservatism that comes from the division of labour necessary on such a large production, dealing with people who have established their way of working. One could also argue that the mainstream itself has shifted; techniques that were radical or experimental in the 1980s, such as the narrative use of a non-diegetic popular song or the synth score, become resolutely ordinary in the 1990s. Ironically, the pure synth score is probably still the more unusual, as the artificial sound has as yet not become 'normal' to most audiences; it still signifies the unreal or the supernatural.

Sound seems to speak more directly to the audience. There is an assumption that it is either more realistic than the image or 'unheard', therefore unimportant. However, the soundscape is just as constructed as any other part of a film, and can be more or less 'realistic' than any image or visual effect. And even if it is 'unheard' – that is, not apprehended with the same awareness or semantic precision as speech or image – it still communicates to an audience, often with an effect all the more visceral because it bypasses conscious intellectual processing.

Glossary of musical and scoring terms

Cue – a section of underscore from the music's entry (cue) to its exit.

Drone – a sustained musical tone, usually one underpinning other musical activity; bagpipes drone beneath the melody, for instance.

Patch – a synthesizer sample that produces a particular timbre.

Timbre – sound quality or colour, often described in visual or tactile terms (bright, velvety, wooden and so on).

Notes

1   Christina Lane's introduction to *Feminist Hollywood* explores the problem of 'authorship', and I subscribe to her principle of implicit quotation marks around a director's name. An already problematic idea in film because of the intensely collaborative nature of film-making, using unexamined feminism and/or auteurism to approach her work is made even more problematic in Bigelow's case: first, her key collaborators – co-writers, co-directors, producers – are men (not to mention her high-profile marriage to director James Cameron), and she works in genres more commonly associated with men (action, westerns, horror); but second, she herself has a film theory background and is quite aware of the 'authorial presence' of a director, so is therefore more likely to foster the creation, or appearance, of such a presence.

2   On a 2002 edition of the Trio TV series The Score, composer Marc Shaiman performed a telling (and hilarious) song, 'Printmaster' – to the tune of 'Goldfinger' – about the travails of having the music at the mercy of an unsympathetic sound editor at the printmastering stage.

3   A Hollywood urban legend relates an exchange between Alfred Hitchcock and composer David Raksin during the filming of Lifeboat (1944): Hitchcock reportedly asked, 'But they're in a lifeboat out in the middle of the ocean – where's the orchestra?' Raksin shot back, 'Right behind the camera.' (In an alternative telling of the fable, Raksin replies, 'Where's the camera?') This reminder of the cinematic apparatus of the camera exposes the extent to which people will delude themselves about the 'reality' of the visual over the aural.

4   In a reversal of the usual marginalisation of women, the auteurist/feminist approach to Bigelow often minimises or ignores the fact that The Loveless was co-written and co-directed by Monty Montgomery and Eric Red co-wrote Near Dark and Blue Steel. Only her links with the high-profile James Cameron are normally acknowledged.

5   It is not actually clear that Davis is meant to be the sidekick at all – just because the film places him in a peripheral position vis-à-vis Vance does not necessarily mean that he holds that position in the gang. In fact, he seems to exert the most control over the other members, stays with the group while Vance goes off on his own, has the only girlfriend (like the alpha male in a wolf-pack), and is clearly idolised by Ricky (although that could simply be physical attraction, Ricky's puppy-like need for his attention would also seem to indicate he holds considerable power within the group dynamic).

6   To belabour a point that may or may not be obvious, 1964 is after the period of the film, but the song's operatic excesses already speak to a nostalgic (therefore historical) position.

7   In his musical style and his contributions both behind and in front of the camera, Gordon prefigures the much more high-profile career of Chris Isaak, who emerged just about the same time Gordon left the scene in the mid-1980s. However, Isaak's sunny, at times rather goofy, persona is a far cry from Gordon's twitchy screen presence, and even Isaak's own haunting musical style. These differences reflect the stereotypical difference between the California (Isaak) and New York (Gordon) scenes. Both Gordon and Isaak are more serious, musically, than the wave of rockabilly pop that hit in the early 1980s with groups like The Stray Cats.

8   The non-diegetic use of pop music increased during the 1980s in the wake of MTV and the ground-breaking Miami Vice, but The Loveless predates this development. Music-video style is more obvious in Near Dark.

9   An obvious third possibility would be classical music on the car radio, but other clues, including recognisability of the piece, sound quality, and the response or lack of response to the music from the characters will probably resolve that ambiguity.

10 Lane (2000: 106) argues that Vance is selective in his misogynistic behaviour, disapproving of Davis's leer at Augusta, 'Are you on the menu?' Davis, however, does not physically force himself on her the way Vance does on the woman in the car. At the least, this makes Vance hypocritical. Perhaps this decentring of Vance's character is part of a larger attempt to destabilise the narrative (maybe it is just bad character development!).

11 I am not trying to argue that Bigelow was necessarily influenced by Michael Mann but that they are working along similar lines. Ridley Scott's Blade Runner (1982) and Terry Gilliam's Brazil (1985) have similar visual styles, but although Blade Runner also has a synth score, their soundscapes are not as similar.

12 The European version of the film, ironically, had an orchestral score by American composer

Jerry Goldsmith.

13 This is not the only time when Henriksen's unusual grace is exploited in films: his dance-like movement is used to great effect as a gunfighter in *The Quick and the Dead* (Sam Raimi, 1995) and *Gunfighter's Moon* (Larry Ferguson, 1996), his ability to move smoothly but oddly helps create the ethereal quality of the android Bishop in *Aliens* (James Cameron, 1985), though his appearance in *Aliens³* (David Fincher, 1992) as the 'real' Bishop has much of the threatening sexuality of his performance as Jesse Hooker, and his unnerving stillness makes him one of the reliable bad guys in contemporary cinema (see especially *Hard Target* (John Woo, 1992)). This latter quality inspired James Cameron to write *The Terminator* for him, though the exigencies of funding meant that the part eventually went to the much less ambiguous Arnold Schwarzenegger and Henriksen instead played the wise-cracking detective Hal Vukovich. The physical presence of an actor, especially his or her quality of movement, is something not normally discussed, but I would argue that it has a profound subliminal impact on an audience, a visual analogy to the power of music.

14 Another reading, following the alternate pairing of Jesse and Diamondback, would see the film as tragic, their 'family' and age-old way of life torn apart by the new, in the guise of Caleb.

15 The only other example I can think of is Det. Raymond Vecchio (David Marciano) in the Canadian-American TV series *Due South* (1994–96), a comedy-drama with unexpected emotional depths (another genre-bending example, ranging from farce to Shakespearean tragedy, sometimes in the same episode). Ray was a brutalised child, and his psychological motivations in being a police officer are, like Megan's, strongly marked by his ambivalent desire to prove himself to – and be better than – his abusive (dead) father.

16 This does not preclude the sort of name-play discussed in Self (1994), for instance Me(gan) and Eu(gene).

17 Nazi anti-Semitism was at least in part the decadent culmination of the desire to recapture/construct a German Volk past, which had earlier, in the nineteenth century, manifested itself in the enshrinement of folk culture, including songs and tales, as in the collected stories of the Brothers Grimm. A common culture was necessary in order to justify politically the formation of a German state from a collection of formerly separate principalities, and one way of uniting peoples is, of course, giving them a common enemy.

18 In an interview on *The Terminator* DVD (MGM 15917DVD Z1, 2001), Fiedel speaks of integrating the sound of a heartbeat into the synthesizer score, so 'humanising' another mechanical character with a biological sound would seem to be within Fiedel's personal style.

19 This could also be a playful homage to the infamous shower sequence in *Psycho* (Alfred Hitchcock, 1960) with its screeching strings, resonating not only through Hitchcock but intertextually through Curtis, who is Janet Leigh's daughter. It need not be an intentional reference, however, to be effective on a visceral level.

CHAPTER THREE

Vampires, Indians and the Queer Fantastic: Kathryn Bigelow's Near Dark

Sara Gwenllian Jones

Daylight

By day, the landscape of Kathryn Bigelow's *Near Dark* (1987) is a flat, featureless geography of sepia and burned orange and yellow ochres stretching to a far horizon. The scorched sky is variously an aching blue, or ash-white, or a searing blaze of copper and gold; the air is choked with dust; tumbleweed bowls across deserted roads. The human population is thinly distributed among isolated farmsteads and quiet backwater towns; people and buildings alike are dwarfed tenants of a rugged, impartial wilderness. The cultural presence of this raw terrain is saturated with romantic histories of pioneers, cowboys, outlaws, marauding Indian war bands, gunfights at noon and lynchings at dusk, cattle drives, rodeos, ghost towns, the railroad revolution. It is a land that seems custom-made for tough snake-eyed white men with ropey muscles knotted under wind-burned skin: cowboy country. This is the American Midwest, a dense semantic domain constructed and reconstructed in the pages of thousands of dime novels, in a cinematic tradition that begins in 1898 with Thomas Edison's one-minute westerns *Cripple Creek Bar-room* and *Poker at Dawson City*, in television series, theme parks and on dude ranches.

Like cinema itself, the classic western has played a central role in white America's narrativisation of its history and its imaginative construction of its national identity. Unlike most genres (but, I will suggest, very much like the gothic horror), the western is wedded to a specific geography. The magnificent landscapes of the frontier are its inspiration, fabric and essence, rough-textured topographies that shape and infuse the genre's iconography, stories and ideological import. The basic story components and themes of the classic western are more or less universal collisions encoded in terms of good and evil, civilisation and nature. Like European historical narratives and mythology, the western has its lone heroes, its intrepid explorers, its 'kings', warriors, profiteers, rebels and renegades. But the western renders these elements and themes specific to an American context, drawing its iconography and narrative detail from the history, culture and geography of the Wild West. This is the America of an imagined golden age, nostalgically recalled, a time of wagon trains winding across vast prairies, of edgy frontier towns, of homesteads where hard-working Christian settlers sweat out an honest living, of roaming cowboys, gunslingers, fortune-hunters and assorted ruffians.

Steven Neale, drawing on Ed Buscombe's work, notes that the relationships between the western and American geography and history are 'not only generically unique' but also 'blend, focus and participate ... in what is often termed a "mythology", a mythology that has itself been uniquely central to US history, US culture and US identity' (2000: 134). For critic Peter Flynn, also, the movement into and colonisation of the American west is at the heart of America's myth of becoming, the inspirational foundation and organising principal of its idealistic understanding of itself:

Manifest destiny; rugged individualism; a pre-modern Eden of moral simplicity; a future built on the harmonious union of man and nature – all four cornerstones of the American psyche, each with their locus on the single moment of expansion and creation. No other period in American history has so frequently been called upon to define and solidify national identity. For this reason alone, the migration West is the single most important event in American history – an event that is replayed over and over in an affirmation of all that is American, all that is good, bad and ugly. (Flynn, n.d.)

The mythic idea of the frontier is an idea of an epic destiny, of the movement of hundreds of thousands of settlers into a territory perceived – wrongly, of course – as *terra nulls*. The mythic West is a cipher for the final conquest of a continent and for the deliberated, hugely ambitious project of constructing a new civilisation almost from scratch. Cinema, as André Bazin has argued, is perhaps 'the only language capable not only of expressing this [myth], but above all of giving it the true aesthetic dimension' (1974: 148). The frontier rolls across the big screen in technicolor panoramas of untamed wildernesses, unfurling the mystery and promise of uncharted territories and unreachable horizons, the merciless and multiple dramas of discovery and subjection. These majestic settings are ideally suited to the sagas of migration, heroic action and expansive gestures of freedom. Part travelogue and part odyssey, the western requires distant horizons for its narratives of movement and colonisation. Inevitably, the landscape itself takes centre stage, functioning as setting, catalyst and 'character' all at once. What happens when a semantic domain so profoundly invested with a particular ideology, so multiply imagined and yet so consistent, is disrupted by the intrusion of the fantastic and the other? This chapter will examine how *Near Dark*'s transgressive reconfigurations of genre and discourse unsettle the mythic, ideologically saturated geography of the Midwest, replacing certainties with ambiguities that refuse any final reading of the film's meaning.

Nightfall

The sunlit and solid world of the western is not where one expects to find vampires. Just as the western belongs to America's geographical west, so do vampires and the gothic horror belong to the ancient landscapes of central and Eastern Europe. Gothic horror is concerned with a haunted and emphatically Old World realm of mist-shrouded mountains, deep dark forests, hovels, tilted ivy-grown tombstones, gloomy taverns and bat-infested castles perched high above wooded valleys. Its human inhabitants are surly peasants and cruel aristocrats. Its folklore engages with the sinister, the entropic and the supernatural rather than with the dynamic and the heroic. It is a mythology of nightmares, madness and evil portent, not of ideals and glorious destinies. Its demonised others are monstrous and magical: werewolves, witches, ghosts and, of course, vampires. Aesthetically, too, the chiaroscuro of gothic horror is a world away from the broadly realist and doggedly bright visual style of the western. Drawing upon the influence of German Expressionist cinema – a film style that Andrew Tudor describes as 'capable of infecting almost any subject matter with its eerie tone' (1974: 208) – gothic horror invests its representations of the material world with the insensible, menacing forms of the supernatural. As in German Expressionist cinema, perspectives are skewed and disorientating; extreme high and low camera angles menace protagonists and emphasise the threat of predators lurking in the obscuring dark; jagged shadows stab across frames. Again like German Expressionism, the gothic horror is concerned with dark moods, psychosis and emotional extremes, with hallucinatory projections of hellish interior visions upon the surfaces of actuality, with nightmares that escape the dreamer's mind and become manifest and lethal in the world at large.

Tudor notes that, of all film genres, gothic horror is perhaps the one that has the *least* connection with American culture and tradition (1974). Its shadowy world speaks of different inspirations, influences and concerns than do the sunshine and open spaces of the western. Where the western celebrates America's confident, striving and glorious dream of itself (and, sometimes, its faltering and uncertainties), the gothic horror is Europe's sepulchral vision of decay, chaos, madness and death. *Near Dark* brings together elements from each of these very different traditions and weaves them together in a semantically rich, complex and unsettling tableau. The film's hybridity constitutes it as, to use Bigelow's own term, a 'vampire-western' (Anon. 1988). Bazin describes such hybrids as 'superwesterns'; films which are still essentially westerns, but which are supplemented by elements taken from other genres which add 'aesthetic, social, moral, psychological, political or erotic interest, in short some quality extrinsic to the [western] genre and which is supposed to enrich it' (1971b: 151). *Near Dark* is neither the first nor the last film to introduce dark supernatural elements to the western genre; other examples include Clint Eastwood's mysterious 'man from nowhere' in *High Plains Drifter* (1972) and *Pale Rider* (1985) and the dark, hallucinatory mystique of Jim Jarmusch's *Dead Man* (1996).

Where *Near Dark* differs from these 'supernatural westerns' is in its explicit invocation of the gothic through the medium of the vampire – an iconic motif with an attendant folklore powerfully linked not just to the uncanny but also, and specifically, to the gothic horror genre. Nevertheless, *Near Dark*'s primary generic allegiance is to the western rather than to gothic horror, a primacy arising from the mythic weight of the film's setting and iconography. Upon this familiar semantic domain, *Near Dark*'s gothic elements function like dark prisms, casting warped shadows across the western's bright geography, disrupting and shattering its comfortable nirvana of home, family, community and security. The diurnal world of the western is consumed by the monster-populated night.

Near Dark's introduction of vampires into the Midwest resembles the disjuncture central to Todorov's definition of the fantastic:

Into a world which is indeed our world, the one we know, a world without devils, sylphides, or vampires, there occurs an event which cannot be explained by the laws of this same familiar world. The person who experiences the event must opt for one of two possible solutions: either he is the victim of an illusion of the senses, of a product of the imagination – and the laws of the world remain as they are; or else the event has indeed taken place, it is an integral part of reality – but this reality is controlled by laws unknown to us. (1973: 25)

Todorov, then, locates the fantastic in the experience of an event that confounds the ordinary logics of everyday actuality; into the world that we inhabit and which we imagine that we understand erupts something unfamiliar that cannot be explained by means of the usual epistemological mechanisms. Into the midst of normality comes something that should not exist, that should not be present, which cannot be accounted for except through a radical adjustment of the knowledge systems that exclude and deny it. The occurrence of fantastic events or elements reverberates through the entire structure of the naturalised equilibrium state, calling into question the efficacy of existing knowledge structures and, by further implication, the power relations that they uphold. Rosemary Jackson notes how the fantastic…

> …points to or suggests the basis upon which the cultural order rests, for it opens up, for a brief moment, on disorder, on to illegality, on to that which is outside dominant value systems. The fantastic traces the unsaid and the unseen of culture: that which has been silenced, made invisible, covered over and made absent. (1981: 4)

Robin Wood makes a similar point about horror, arguing that the genre's 'true project' is 'the struggle for recognition of all that our society *re*presses and *op*presses' (1979: 10). Society's excluded and dispossessed return in monstrous form, filled with its terrors, uncertainties, and guilt. Uncontrollable forces that refuse a condition of banishment and suppression burst through fault lines, exposing the illusory nature of the existing social order's security and permanency. Fixity is replaced with fluidity; boundaries dissolve.

Near Dark's naturalised equilibrium is the contemporary Midwest – a Midwest where the Indians have long since been vanquished, the land has been settled and tamed, and the resident rural white middle-class population lives a secure and comfortable existence. The film opens with a humorous clue to what will follow: a close-up of a mosquito settled on human skin, swatted just as it starts to suck blood. A lazy sequence of scene-setting shots follows. Caleb (Adrian Pasdar), the film's corn-fed all-American farm boy protagonist, reclines with his booted feet propped up and silhouetted against a fiery sunset as he waits for nightfall. As well as cowboy boots, he wears blue jeans, a brown suede jacket and a black Stetson that is tipped forward over his eyes. A cigarette dangles from his lips, Clint Eastwood-style. As he drives from his father's farm into town, his pick-up kicks up a dust trail that churns along parallel to the darkening horizon. Already the country road and the one-storey buildings strung along its length are dissolving into night. The sun sinks in a hot metallic sky, the bright and substantial world of daylight yielding to the shadow-realm of the gothic, a pervasive and thick darkness that begins the gradual transformation of this familiar western geography into a zone of night and blood where vampires rule. As Jeff Karnicky observes, '*Near Dark* defines the difference between the human and the non-human (vampire) as the difference between night and day' (1998). Dusk and dawn are especially dangerous – liminal temporal zones, between-times where one jurisdiction slides into another. Caleb's migration from home and daylight into the enclosing night is also (though he doesn't know it yet) a journey between worlds, and so the ordinary act of a young man going to meet his friends to spend a night on the town is presented through an evolving aesthetic of threat. As darkness colonises the screen, the camera shows Caleb in profile as he drives; he lights a cigarette, the brief and tiny circle of light from his Zippo dwarfed by the night that fills and surrounds the cabin of the pick-up. In town, the streets are glossy with rain and the pick-up slides through an oily darkness cut with neon and textured with starlight. Reflected in the ellipse of the rear-view mirror, Caleb seems isolated and exposed, already marked out as a victim.

Caleb encounters Mae (Jenny Wright) outside a liquor store in town. Childlike and pale, she stands by herself a short distance away from a gathering of rowdy young men. She appears lost and vulnerable, a fragile girl alone in the night. From the outset, it is Mae's apartness and otherworldliness that attracts Caleb; she has a silvery luminosity and seems herself almost a thing of starlight, soft and ethereal against a backdrop of blazing neon. Caleb's approach is part bravado and part fascination, a fascination that increases as the night progresses and she describes its wonder to him using an evocative mix of cross-connected sensations and trivia: 'It's dark … it's all so bright, it'll blind you … listen! Do you hear it? … the night, it's deafening … the light that's leaving that star now will take a billion years to get down here.' Mae is tuned to the night's poetry and seductive beauty and Caleb's responses to her eerie receptivity veer between gentle romance, awe and clumsy sexual aggression. He drives Mae to his father's farm to show her his horse, proudly lassoing it in a display of masculine control that fails to impress because the horse rears and frets in Mae's presence. In the first of a number of gender role reversals hinged on relations of domination and submission, Mae instead lassos Caleb, roping him in towards her. Later, as the early morning light leeches the darkness from the sky, Caleb stops his truck in the middle of nowhere and refuses to drive on until Mae kisses him. Again Mae suddenly but subtly assumes the role of aggressor: the vampire's kiss draws blood. Mae penetrates Caleb, her teeth tearing into his soft flesh, an invasion that begins his possession.

So begins a tale of boy meets girl, girl bites boy.

Caleb's 'infection' with vampirism decisively introduces the alien gothic fantastic into the familiar world of the western. Once bitten by Mae, Caleb belongs to the feral night. The ordinary, everyday world of home and family becomes a sanctuary to which he cannot return. No matter how much he yearns and strives to get back to the sensible world of daylight, his infected physiology ensures that he remains chained to the night. His new craving for human blood is overwhelming and mirrors the symptoms of drug addiction; he shivers and sweats and suffers cramps, a cold turkey experience extended because of his refusal to kill. 'What are you on?' asks the suspicious cop that Caleb encounters at the bus station in a later scene. 'You wouldn't believe me if I told you', answers Caleb. It is Mae – deadly seductress, mother figure and saviour – who alleviates his 'withdrawal' symptoms by biting open a vein in her wrist and allowing him to feed upon her blood. In this strange new world of darkness, Caleb the newborn vampire is helpless, kneeling on the ground and suckling from Mae like an infant. Though Caleb's suckling alleviates his sickness, it offers no comfort; the act is choreographed not as succour at the maternal breast but rather as a mechanical intimacy emptied of nurture. It underlines Caleb's abjection and loss of agency; once bitten, he has little control over events and is instead caught up in a succession of reactions to his new and uninvited situation.

Like the other vampires, Caleb cannot tolerate the acid burn of sunlight. As he returns home after Mae has bitten him, confused and still unaware that he has become a vampire, he staggers across a ploughed field at dawn and starts to smoulder and smoke as the first rays of morning catch him. From a distance, his helpless and uncomprehending father and sister Sarah watch. Just as they work out that he needs help, the vampires arrive and wrench him into the sunless interior of their carefully screened Winnebago. A lingering shot from the rear of the vehicle as it drives away shows the farm, partially obscured by a cloud of dust thrown up by the tyres, shrinking into the distance. For Caleb, as for the other vampires, going home is no longer an option. His choices now are limited by the demands of his contaminated blood. He is presented with two ways of being: that represented by the farm, and that of the lawless, nocturnal vampire tribe. His vampire-infected physiology dictates which of these he belongs to. It is the blood in his veins that determines his destiny.

The notion that blood, socio-cultural belonging and lifestyle are inextricably linked has a powerful resonance with concepts of racial identity and with the fear of racial mixing that underlies depictions of Indians in many westerns. In its linking of blood and belonging *Near Dark* echoes some of the themes and plot devices of *The Searchers*, John Ford's classic western of 1956. Both films present an idealised equilibrium centred upon the farmstead and the white 'settler' family. Mildly dysfunctional families are represented in both films: *The Searchers* suggests an attraction between Ethan Edwards (John Wayne) and his sister-in-law, while Caleb's mother is absent from the family home in *Near Dark*. At the same time, both films invoke the *ideal* of a strong family unit – loving, protective, secure. In both, the family – as actuality and as ideal – is shattered by the intrusion of a hostile other (vampires, Indians) and the abduction of children or young adults. In *The Searchers*, Ethan's young nieces Lucy and Deborah are taken by a Comanche war band; in *Near Dark*, Caleb is taken by the vampires. In each case, a male family member attempts rescue and restoration (Caleb's father in *Near Dark*, Ethan in *The Searchers*). Ethan's seven-year search for the Comanche who abducted his nieces is an embittered quest, soured by his deep racist hatred of Indians – a hatred which leads him to vow that he will kill his oldest niece if it turns out that she has been 'defiled' by a brave. His mission is not just about rescue and vengeance; it is also a matter of maintaining racial purity. 'Blood' is of central importance, a cipher both of family (Ethan's blood relation to the girls) and of racial difference (his revulsion at the notion of miscegenation, the mixing of blood). In each film, predation, abduction, assimilation and contamination combine to threaten not just the physical existence but also the racially inscribed integrity of the white settler family.

Set against the morality and orderliness of God-fearing middle-class white rural America, the lifestyle of *Near Dark*'s vampires seems – like that of the Comanche in *The Searchers* – to be primitive and instinct-driven. Repeatedly, the film represents these characteristics in ways that recall cinema's traditional constructions of hostile Indians as uncivilised savages and white settlers as rational, peaceable and decent. Like Indians, the vampires live as a tribe rather than in atomised family units within a wider social structure. They are nomadic and therefore unaccountable and ungovernable. They lead anarchic, unstructured lives, surviving through predation (that might also be considered parasitism) rather than by productive labour; they do only what pleases them and what they must do to survive. 'What do we do now?' Caleb asks Mae. 'Anything we want until the end of time', Mae replies. Immortal, they live in the moment, like animals, without apparent regard for the past or ambition for the future; theirs is a 'now' stretching into eternity. Again, like conscienceless animals or 'savage primitives', they are without mercy and cannot be reasoned with. Their invasion of a roadside bar and relentless terrorising of its staff and customers strongly recalls countless portrayals of Indian attacks upon white homesteads. In a move gesturally reminiscent of a scalping, one-time Confederate soldier Jesse, now the vampires' leader, runs a blade across the throat of a pretty blond waitress. The act is rendered doubly cold and darkly comic when, instead of drinking from the wound in conventional vampire style, Jesse drains her blood into a beer glass. The bloody scenes that follow are, in Anna Powell's words, 'orgiastic, with sexual aggression leading to death and blood trickling spurting orgasmically as the vampires get their kicks' (1994: 153). The vampires literally 'play with their food'; they take pleasure from terrifying, torturing and killing their victims. Some of Caleb's reluctance ebbs away; when he discovers that his new vampire self has the strength to knock a man clear across the room, the power that he now enjoys excites him. Mae, who despite her tender relationship with Caleb shows no revulsion for the murderous parade that is vampire life, slow-dances with a petrified youth who has just watched the vampires slaughter everyone else in the bar and has every reason to believe that he will be killed next. When they have satisfied their bloodlust, the vampires torch the bar and watch excitedly as it burns – just as Indians in so many westerns torch white homesteads after having slaughtered their inhabitants.

Near Dark's Americanised version of vampirism is entirely situated within the conventions of the western, a position that is reinforced over and over in the film's reworkings of incidents and details from the western tradition. The first clear indication that there is something not just unusual but also unnatural about Mae occurs when her presence spooks Caleb's horse, the emblematic animal of the western unsettled by the presence of the emblematic beast of gothic horror. Caleb's 'first kill', which he fails to go through with, is set up for him by the vampires as a ritual of tribal initiation, a rite of passage. They present him with an allotted victim and watch and wait for him to bite and drain the youth of blood; at first, he goes along with it but, at the last moment, he cannot bring himself to kill the boy. Later, after Caleb rescues the vampires from a classic western style shoot-out, Severen – a particularly psychotic vampire who dresses all in black like any self-respecting western bad guy – ritualistically removes one of his spurs and presents it to Caleb in a grudging gesture of acceptance and brotherhood; Caleb has 'won his spurs'. The climactic confrontation between Caleb and his abductors near the end of the film is staged like any western showdown. Caleb rides his horse into the deserted town, takes off the spur that Severen has given him and throws it to the ground, a rejection of and a challenge to the vampire clan.

This constant resonance with the conflicts and lore of the western is deepened by the absence in the film of most of the usual signifiers of vampirism. Interviewed in *Cinefantastique*, Kathryn Bigelow explains the film's generic influences and mechanisms:

In an effort to sort of modernize the material, to update it and make it contemporary, we got rid of all the gothic aspects of the vampire mythology – the teeth, the bats, holy water, crosses, mirrors, all of that. We just kept the most salient aspects – they burn up in sunshine, they must drink blood to live, they live forever, bullets don't hurt them, and they're very strong. Then as we set them in the mid-west and used aspects of the western – shootouts, shadows at high-noon, only in this case it's high midnight. (Anon. 1988)

These, then, are vampires substantially redesigned for a contemporary American setting, killer punks in black leather and ripped jeans. The signifiers of traditional affiliations of vampires with the folklore of the Old World are stripped away, with the effect that the model of otherness they present takes many of its characteristics and inflections from the film's generically informed geography and socio-cultural context. As if to underline this, a recurring image in the film is of lines of cruciform telegraph poles leading away into the distance, visual reminders of vampire lore rewritten for this western landscape. *Near Dark*'s vampires seem to erupt not from the European past but from nature itself, from the unruly wilderness that lies just beneath the surface of the farmed and settled American Midwest.

The intrusion of the fantastic into this seemingly domesticated territory is in many respects a return of the repressed wilderness, which reasserts itself in hostile form to expose and rip apart white America's illusion of safety and control. Predatory, living from moment to moment, unrestrained by empathy or remorse, the vampires are pure hunters who relish both the chase and the kill. Their relation to their environment centres upon their adaptation to its cycles; they live *within* nature rather than by dominating and manipulating it as humans do. At night, their extraordinary physical strength and in-built immunity to humanity's arsenal of weapons makes them invincible lords of their nocturnal world, at one with a darkness that is as seductive as it is menacing. As Karnicky notes, '*Near Dark* continually offers glimpses of the beauty of the night: Mae's hair gleams brightly in the moonlight; the camera captures gradients of lights, from black to light shades of blue; stars glitter in the sky, reflected by rain-slicked streets' (1998). The cinematography sculpts the vampires' domain from rich shadow and diffused starlight, inviting the audience to experience its beauty and mystery as well as to fear the horrors that may lurk in its fathomless depths.

As much as the night belongs to the vampires, so too do they belong to it. Sunset and sunrise are temporal boundaries that restrict them to a nocturnal existence. During the daylight hours, they must hide themselves away; the sunlight that nurtures nearly all other earthly life is lethal to them. If they stray into its radiance, they will ignite, burn and die. Sunlight is the only danger the world holds for them, and they evade rather than overcome it. Their attempts to extend their activities beyond sunrise are shaky and inadequate; shrouding themselves in clothes and blankets slows down but does not prevent their inevitable combustion. When they are caught outside at daybreak, travelling in an inadequately screened car, they frantically attempt to block out the sunlight, using whatever is to hand. During the shoot-out with the police at the motel, it is not the bullets that menace the vampires but the searing bolts of sunlight that thrust through the bullet holes in the walls to criss-cross the room like a spreading grid of lethal laser beams. In *Near Dark*, territory is something that is temporal as well as spatial, entailing occupations that are never complete because the occupiers must always retreat with the shift of day into night or of night into day. Space as territory is a contest between two antagonistic cultures, each becoming vulnerable when it trespasses outside its allotted temporal domain.

In *Horizons West*, his seminal study of the western, James Kitses outlines a grid which maps many of the oppositions that organise the mythology of the western, arranging them under ideologically opposed umbrella headings of 'wilderness' and 'civilization' (1969: 11). This binary structure maps comfortably on to *Near Dark*, which is built around a number of apparent oppositions: vampire versus human, night versus day, predator versus prey, hunting versus farming, chaos versus order and so on. But such oppositions, as Kitses suggests, are not fixed and absolute but rather constitute a volatile array of ideological collisions, alliances and potential transgressions that make the western genre dynamic, flexible and, in some important respects, ideologically contrary and ambiguous. Thus, *Near Dark*'s vampires represent not just the threat of the other but also its proximity, its glamour and its allure. While their lifestyle is antithetical to some centrally important aspects of the American dream, it also represents its fulfilment in other ways – perhaps most strikingly in the freefall of the vampires' absolute freedom from any socio-political constraints, a freedom that has its vertiginous exhilarations as well as its attendant horrors. At night, the vampires go wherever they want and do whatever they feel like doing; they are untroubled by pangs of conscience, beyond the reach of any human law, physically stronger than their victims, invulnerable to bullets. Between sunset and sunrise, they are unstoppable. While human life is restricted by social, economic and moral obligations, the vampires recognise only the basic, amoral imperatives of survival and thrill seeking. Like the outlaws of the old Wild West, they are a teen-dream of absolute liberation and non-stop adventure, of invincibility, of superhuman physical powers, of peer-group rather than familial allegiance, of an extreme and highly romanticised outsider status.

Twilight

The deeper threat of the 'other' lies not in its otherness as such, which constitutes the necessary 'them' against which 'us' is defined and upheld, nor even in the perceived or actual hostility of the other, but rather in the other's inevitable epistemological proximity and potential to erupt across or dissolve the category boundaries which structure and maintain hierarchised relations of power and knowledge. *Near Dark's* 'return of the repressed' in the form of the intimate vampire others, who transgress both by being able to pass as human and by their alchemical ability to transform humans into vampires, invokes the fantastic in ways that undermine categories through slippery refusals to be contained by them. All that transgresses is not fantastic, but all that is fantastic entails transgressions. But transgression, as Foucault suggests, is a paradoxical process; it defines, illuminates and announces its dependence upon category boundaries in the same instant that it defies their efficacy:

> Perhaps it is like a flash of lightning in the night which, from the beginning of time, gives a dense and black intensity to the night it denies, which lights up the night from the inside, from top to bottom, and yet which owes to the dark the stark clarity of its manifestation, its harrowing and poised singularity; the flash loses itself in the space it marks with its sovereignty and becomes silent now that it has given a name to obscurity. (1977: 35)

The threat of the other lies in its capacity to move across boundaries, to bring the outside into the centre and, by the very act of crossing over, to disrupt and expose the artifice of naturalised power relations that define themselves in terms in inclusion and exclusion. 'Race' represents one important crisis zone of opposed categories and transgression in *Near Dark*, and intersects with another: that of the heterosexual nuclear family.

Although they sport neither capes nor fangs, with their pale skin and dark grungy clothing *Near Dark's* vampires look out of place among the rugged citizens of the Midwest, like a gang of urban street punks on an unlikely outdoors adventure experience (echoing the bikers of *The Loveless* (1982) who are equally at odds with the community they visit). But, while their difference to the locals is visually marked, they nevertheless fall comfortably within the parameters of the recognisably human. They do not look like monsters; their vampirism is invisible to the naked eye. Their monstrous otherness is subtle and the threat it presents is allied to proximity, intimacy and violation; by the time you recognise them as monsters, it's already too late. Like the monstrous aliens of 1950s science fiction films such as *Invasion of the Bodysnatchers* (1956), their horror resides in their indetectability; they could be anyone, and anyone could be one of *them*. As Harry M. Benshoff comments of 1950s 'communist infiltration' science fiction cinema, the 'narrative formula for most of these films was surprisingly similar: 'normal' small-town USA (usually represented by an actively heterosexualised couple) is menaced by something unknown, something queer' (1997: 128–9). Aliens which look human, which can 'pass', can be read both in terms of fears about communist infiltration and 'as allegories about the invisible homosexual' (1997: 130) – the homosexual that looks exactly like one of 'us' but is, to use that telling term once more, really one of *them*.

The seductive assault of the vampire has an innate and emphatically queer eroticism that works across all possible gender combinations. The vampire's attack entails close physical contact, skin against skin, the bowed head and questing lips of the predatory vampire, the exposed throat of the victim darkly reminiscent of sexual abandon. The intense intimacy and need of the vampire's deadly kiss and feeding blurs together codes of violence and desire. Teeth penetrate yielding flesh, drawing blood, feeding on the juices of human prey, reversing the trajectory of ejaculation. In a humorous acknowledgement of the homoerotic connotations of vampirism, Severen, crouching to feed upon a hairy biker, echoes heterosexual women's complaints about male facial stubble: 'I hate it when they haven't shaved.' As Anna Powell points out, 'the male-on-male violence, particularly, bears a homoerotic charge' (1994: 193). The man set up to be Caleb's first victim is, like Caleb himself, handsome, young and naïve-looking; the vampires instill terror in him, and when he runs away, panicking and stumbling in the dark, the predator's pursuit is suggestive of other cinematic chases that conclude with rape. Caleb's refusal or inability to feed upon and kill the boy may be interpreted as an act of pity or revulsion, or both.

Alexander Doty argues that queerness is integral to invocations of the fantastic: '*everyone*'s pleasure in [fantastic] genres is 'perverse', is queer, as much of it takes places in the contra-heterosexual and the contra-straight' (1993: 15). It is always 'normality' that is disrupted by the fantastic and white heterosexuality is usually American cinema's shorthand for normality. The terrorising of young heterosexual couples and of families by monsters is the staple narrative device of horror cinema, and monstrousness is coded not just by monstrous actions but also in biological and social codes which situate their perpetrators outside heterosexuality, as either icily sexless or sexually and reproductively weird. In keeping with the 'queer' reproductive methods of science fiction aliens (pods, eggs, cloning, 'cuckoo' impregnations of humans who act as hosts to monstrous alien offspring), the vampires of *Near Dark* reproduce themselves not through sexual intercourse but through contagion, the viral transmission of vampirism from saliva to blood. Their method of reproduction bypasses heterosexuality altogether. Both sexes are equally capable of reproducing and do so in exactly the same way; the male vampire Jess begets the female Diamondback; Diamondback begets Mae; Mae begets Caleb. The relationship between vampire and convert is unique – part parental, part sexual – but the naturalised biology and structures of heterosexual parenthood (sexual intercourse, romance, marriage, home, nuclear family) are absent. Caleb's human family is valorised in opposition to the unruly bad object of the vampire tribe, which threatens it on all fronts. Caleb himself becomes a contested trophy in a war between different social units, abducted, partially assimilated, reclaimed. When he escapes the clutches of the vampires, they instead take his sister, thus maintaining their threat to the integrity of the family.

Near Dark's release in 1987, at the height of the AIDS epidemic, inevitably lends a particular resonance to the film's fusion of queer sexualities, virally transmitted vampirism and the notions of 'clean' and 'infected' blood that structure its play with both racial and queer metaphors. Like vampirism, AIDS is a disease of proximity, of intimacy and fluid exchanges, of invisible menace. The vampire, neither living nor dead but 'undead', occupies a liminal zone like that of an AIDS sufferer who is alive but marked with and for death. From this perspective, the film may be read as a reactionary text which, through the metaphor of vampirism, allies a 'degenerate' contra-straight lifestyle with a deadly disease, and cure or redemption with a return to the heterosexual family effected through a transfusion of 'clean' blood. But, while there is much in the film that would seem to support such a reading, there is also much that does not. Far from being debilitating or fatal, vampirism bestows superhuman strength and immortality. The vampires' bloodlust, sadism and allegiance to the night are sensual and hedonistic, riven with moments of dark beauty. Their 'disease', like their otherness, is ambiguous; it both repels and seduces, and calls both responses into question.

Dawn

The horror represented by *Near Dark*'s queer fantastic ends with a restoration of the heterosexual family unit. Again, blood and belonging are fore-grounded. Caleb's father restores his son to humanity by giving him a blood transfusion; although the source of the blood is not made clear in the film, we are invited to assume that it is an infusion of the father's own blood that saves the son. This act of biological recolonisation brings together a set of values and knowledges that underpin the idealised rural 'American way of life' presented in the film: family values, patriarchal protection, racial integrity, the basic science of the transfusion, pragmatism and commonsense combine as an effective counter to the dark forces of the supernatural. As if to underline the triumph of normality, Caleb subsequently uses the same approach and techniques to 'save' Mae. By the end of the film, the family unit is restored and the heterosexual couple is rescued from its deviant origin and resituated within the acceptable parameters of normality. The threat of the other is banished from the daylit, heterosexualised world of contemporary rural America.

Or is it? The film leaves doubts and questions. The mythologised landscape of the western has been indelibly inscribed with the dark fantastic, its assumptions and certainties cast awry. Mae wakes to morning and the discovery that she is no longer a vampire. Her reaction is ambiguous:

Mae:	Caleb, what's happening?
Caleb:	I've brought you home.
Mae:	I'm afraid.
Caleb:	Don't be. It's just the sun.

Caleb embraces her. But Mae's body is tense; she gazes, with what might be wonder but could equally be fear, at her hand, miraculously unburned by the sunlight streaming in through the open barn door. Caleb's last words linger, more hope than certainty. Beyond, an irredeemably unsettled daylight world awaits them.

CHAPTER FOUR

'Suck ... don't suck': Framing Ideology in Kathryn Bigelow's Near Dark

Steven Jay Schneider

The look of the film, where the night appears very seductive, was intentional. I wanted the lifestyle of these people to seem attractive. But I don't think this is a straight violence movie, nor is it a straight romance. There's a bittersweet quality here, because Caleb and his girlfriend have been tainted by their experience. And they have to decide whether to give up immortality for a 'normal' life. At the very least, we could say, they have a lot to talk about. (Bigelow in Coburn 1987)

In his oft-cited 1993 essay, 'The Horror Film in Neoconservative Culture', Christopher Sharrett puts forward the sophisticated and largely convincing argument that, despite their progressive trappings, a great many post-1970 horror movies in America actually operate so as to subtly/sneakily reinforce conservative capitalist ideology. One of the films Sharrett picks out as particularly egregious along these lines is Kathryn Bigelow's 1987 vampire love story, Near Dark.[1] An initial viewing of the film would seem to confirm this interpretation, as it appears to manifest all four of the themes Sharrett identifies as evidence of 'neoconservatism':

(a) a dominant order that is simultaneously discredited and affirmed, (b) an atmosphere of apparently unfettered sexual expression that offers status to women insofar as they are incorporated into the dominant order, (c) a recognition of a carnivalesque, diverse, chaotic universe that is celebrated at the same time that it is subdued, and (d) a recognition and lionization of the Other only as a preface to its total destruction or incorporation into dominant ideology. (Sharrett 1996: 257)

A closer, more detailed look at *Near Dark*, however, reveals a quite different agenda than the one Sharrett claims for it. Rather than working to co-opt radical discourses for ultimately reactionary ends, Bigelow (and Eric Red, with whom she co-wrote the script)[2] are more concerned with exposing the limitations of, and on, a fully-indoctrinated subject's ability even to conceive or fantasise a sustainable alternative form of life. If, as I hope to show, *Near Dark*'s narrative is best read as a wish-fulfilling dream of liberation from repressive social, cultural and biological norms, it is nevertheless one that is comprised by the dreamer's own hypocrisy and ambivalence, an ambivalence which may well explain the dream's manifestly nightmarish qualities. Perhaps this is not all that surprising, considering the dreamer's status in reality as a young, handsome white male with relative freedom to do as he pleases. Despite the fact that the events in the narrative are heavily focalised through the film's protagonist, Caleb Colton (Adrian Pasda), key moments of directorial intervention provide additional information which effectively undermines Caleb's reliability as an intra-diegetic narrator. In short, while the fantasy 'produced and directed by' Caleb's unconscious, and with himself in the role of hero, may well signal this character's own neoconservative inclinations, *Near Dark* is a film which *thematises* neoconservatism, revealing its operations and contextualising it within a larger, progressive ideological stance.

The alternative interpretation of *Near Dark* to be presented here is supported by a critique of the specific claims Sharrett makes about the film. It will be shown, for example, that *Near Dark*'s 'linchpin' is *not* 'the "rescue" of the idealised, redeemable May (*sic*) from … her savage family, concurrent with the restoration of Caleb's Norman Rockwell family', nor that 'the malevolence of clan patriarch Jesse … is sufficient to make the image of the clan itself discredit the alternative model of the family caricatured in the clan's rapacious nihilism' (1996: 260). Also problematic are Sharrett's contentions that 'the free-form, gratuitous slaughter carried out by the clan partakes of media notions of punk and other youth formations as merely symptomatic of social decay', and that 'the operatics of the vampires' demise are unwarranted, since there is virtually nothing in the narrative to motivate sympathy for them' (1996: 261). Sharrett is certainly right to call attention to the 'particular tendencies of the consciousness industry to reabsorb culture's adversarial impulses' mainly via a 'restoration of the Other' (1996: 254–5), and his identification of the neoconservative strategies at work in such films as *The Silence of the Lambs* (Jonathan Demme, 1991) and *Bram Stoker's Dracula* (Francis Ford Coppola, 1992) stands as a welcome corrective to those analyses which place undue emphasis on the liberal leanings of these films' respective directors. But *Near Dark* is redeemable from a progressive political perspective, insofar as Bigelow succeeds in getting viewers – even if not Caleb – to seriously question at the film's end whether being part of a family of immortal, nearly indestructible vampires is really worse than being human (which here means white, bourgeois male).

Before turning to *Near Dark*, a few words about methodology. At the beginning of his essay, Sharrett acknowledges his theoretical debt to Robin Wood, whose work on American horror in the late 1970s has proven enormously influential for subsequent investigations of the genre. Adopting Marcuse's elaboration and extension of Freudian thought, Wood analyses the monsters of cinematic horror as a hyberbolic 'return' to consciousness of that which dominant American society must systematically repress or deny in order to maintain its existing ideological and institutional structures. As he puts it, 'the true subject of the horror genre is the struggle for recognition of all that our civilization represses or oppresses, its re-emergence dramatized, as in our nightmares, as an object of horror, a matter for terror, and the happy ending (when it exists) typically signifying the restoration of repression' (1986: 75).

Although Sharrett takes Wood as arguing the 'essential political progressiveness of the genre for the questions it raises about the social construction of "evil" in western society' (1996: 253), he is aware of the fact that Wood allowed for the political conservatism of particular horror films and cycles.[3] According to Wood,

> The genre carries within itself the capability of reactionary inflection, and perhaps no horror film is entirely immune from its operations. It need not surprise us that a powerful reactionary tradition exists – so powerful it may under certain social conditions become the dominant one. (1986: 191)

Accepting Wood's explanation of the horror film monster as a return of the 'surplus repressed' – that which 'makes us into monogamous heterosexual bourgeois patriarchal capitalists ("bourgeois" even if we are born into the proletariat, for we are talking here of ideological norms rather than material status)' (Wood 1986: 71) – Sharrett proposes a reading of *Near Dark* and other recent horror fare according to which the 'return' in question offers a vision of change while at the same time undermining this vision in order to support and strengthen the status quo. According to Sharrett, such a strategy is 'emblematic of capital's ongoing attempts at refurbishing its democratic façade by acknowledging the cynicism of the population while simultaneously emphasizing an ersatz liberalism, and by making use of a variety of progressive discourses current in academe that inevitably appear transmuted within the commercial entertainment industry' (1996: 255).

David Bordwell characterises the type of symptomatic interpretation practiced by Sharrett as 'demystifying' in nature: '"Demystification" aims to show up artworks as covert propaganda, sugar-coated pills. Whatever explicit meanings can be ascribed to the work, the demystifying critic constructs reactionary implicit ones that undercut them' (1989: 88).[4] Wood's earlier look at reactionary horror in the 1980s, in contrast, is not demystifying so much as straightforwardly reflectionist, concerned with 'demonstrating culture's reflection of capitalism's various political cycles' (Sharrett 1996: 254). By arguing that the diegesis of *Near Dark* contains both textual and meta-textual elements, the latter in the form of non-focalised 'directorial commentary' interspersed throughout the narrative, I hope to show that Bigelow makes it possible for the film *itself* to engage in a demystifying critique; and that she does this by carefully framing the conflicting ideological impulses at work within the context of Caleb's dream/nightmare, as well as by providing the viewer with privileged visual information which undermines Caleb's neoconservative impulses.

In a sense, my own method is one of 'progressive interpretation', according to which the critic attempts to 'save' a film by 'showing how it either contains progressive elements or embodies in its very incompatibilities some instructive indications of how fiercely ideology must struggle in order to maintain its authority' (Bordwell 1989: 88–9). As opposed to symptomatic (and psychoanalytic) interpretation more generally, however – practices which typically purport to reveal the 'hidden' meanings concealed by a film's manifest content – and in keeping with the tenets of New Criticism (without subscribing to the latter's ahistorical and anti-intentionalist biases), I claim for myself none of the 'insight that rightly belongs to the text itself' (Allen 1999: 142).[5] Rather, I believe that close textual analysis of *Near Dark* along the lines suggested above lends support to those arguments in favor of Bigelow's status as an auteur director, one whose films consistently invoke the romantic, phantasmatic, perhaps inherently (neo)conservative elements of generic popular cinema while still finding ways of critiquing and presenting alternatives to existing racial, sexual and political/ideological norms.[6] Finally, I would just note that the validity of my own, psychoanalytically-inflected reading of *Near Dark* is not dependent upon the truth (whatever that might mean) of psychoanalytic theory more generally. As I have recently argued, a great many horror films, cycles and subgenres have been plausibly and productively interpreted as 'thematizing, narrativizing, and embodying ideas and constructs similar to those found in orthodox psychoanalytic theory and its revisions. … What really matters is whether these ideas can be shown to be present in the text' (Schneider 2002).[7]

The next section of this essay will focus on the first few scenes of *Near Dark*, examining how dialogue and cinematography in particular serve to facilitate Caleb's entrance into a self-generated world of simultaneous dream and horror. If Bigelow had made this 'entrance' too literal or unambiguous – for example by showing Caleb asleep in bed, high on drugs, or deathly ill – much of the film's emotional impact would have been lost, as the viewer's ability to identify with Caleb would be severely compromised due to a fixed epistemological asymmetry. Then, I will look at how the biologically and socially non-traditional family structure of *Near Dark*'s outlaw vampire clan offers Caleb the opportunity to fulfil an unsatisfiable (in reality) psychic wish:[8] oral-erotic intercourse with a mother figure, absent the threat of castration at the hands of a jealous and vengeful husband/father. In short, becoming a vampire allows for the dispelling of those Oedipal fears which typically result in the successful socialisation of male subjects, when they come to realise that they are better off investing libidinally in a more 'appropriate' – i.e. non-incestuous – object choice. Finally, I will identify the ways in which Bigelow in effect places quotation marks around her protagonist's neoconservatism (evident above all in his decision to give up vampire status and return to the 'light' of normal existence, taking Mae with him), thereby maintaining the film's progressive edge.

Near Dark's opening shot is a carefully framed close-up of a mosquito perched upon someone's out-of-focus arm. There is a notable elegance about this precariously positioned and nearly transparent insect, whose life is ungraciously snuffed out by a hard slap immediately preceded by the gravel-voiced command, 'Don't suck'. Cut to Caleb lying on his back outside his father's farm, a bored expression on his face that gives way to a satisfied and slightly malevolent smile. If the mosquito stands as an all-too-obvious forerunner of the vampires soon to invade Caleb's small-town universe, then this opening sequence establishes the young man's mastery over all such nocturnal bloodsuckers: he grants initial access to the mosquito, even lets it penetrate his skin, but kills it as soon as the pleasure of this admittedly small-scale violation becomes too uncomfortable. From our privileged vantage point, however, and despite any pre-existing dislike we might have for mosquitoes, we see this one as beautiful, even statuesque in its stillness and grace, and so are encouraged to view Caleb's action as cruel and somewhat gratuitous. There is a mean streak in Caleb, one that runs parallel to his naïveté and charm, and contrary to his ostensible purity and 'heroic' status in the embedded narrative.

The next scene can be read fairly straightforwardly as facilitating Caleb's entrance into a fantasy or dreamworld of his own making. As the sun sets and the sky becomes dark, Caleb drives his truck into town, a lit cigarette dangling from his mouth (early sign of the oral fixation which serves as the boy's signature character trait, and which will continue to be highlighted through dialogue as well as action). Parking outside a nondescript convenience store, Caleb gets out and for no apparent reason shoves the young man standing next to his truck. From the surprised look which registers on the young man's face, Caleb and he are obviously friends. 'What's eatin' you?' he asks, thereby articulating Caleb's own desire – to consume, and to be consumed – in the form of a question. 'Your mama', Caleb replies, intentionally misinterpreting a line which makes eating a metaphor for being troubled or upset as a slang expression for oral sex. By implying, in the form of a nasty remark, that it is fellatio from a mother figure that is responsible for his unprovoked display of aggression, Caleb effectively reiterates his earlier command, 'don't suck' – but once again, only *after* allowing some sucking to occur in the first place.

According to the chain of visual and verbal associations being established here, mosquitoes and mothers are both capable of providing Caleb a degree of pleasure (if only imaginary) by their sucking, albeit a pleasure that Caleb deems unacceptable and ultimately renounces in violent fashion. In the case of mosquitoes – and, of course, vampires – sucking serves to deplete the victim/subject of blood, a fluid necessary for life; therefore, any resistance can be plausibly explained as stemming from the victim/subject's biological imperative for survival. In the case of mothers, however, the sucking in question is actually *productive* of fluid (semen), and so the reason for Caleb's resistance in all likelihood psychological and socio-cultural – stemming from awareness on some level of the prohibition against incest, and indicative of Oedipal anxieties concerning retaliation from a jealous and angry (because displaced) husband/father figure.[9]

James B. Twitchell, in his study *Dreadful Pleasures: An Anatomy of Modern Horror*, argues that 'incest has always been embedded in the vampire folklore; after all, the vampire (like the werewolf) is supposed to return to attack first those whom he most loved in life' (1985: 120). Twitchell even goes so far as to assert that the 'main contribution' of Bram Stoker's *Dracula* is its 'projection of interfamilial sexual fantasies' (1985: 125). Bigelow, who has admitted in interviews to having read only *Dracula* and Anne Rice's *Interview With the Vampire* in preparation for co-writing the *Near Dark* screenplay with Red, takes up and twists for her own purposes Stoker's contribution, by establishing the fact of Caleb's incestuous desires while he is still fully human, and by making vampirism a practical solution to the problem of how to satisfy (or at least fulfil) such desires without fear of reprisal.[10]

In response to Caleb's insult, and presumably without having any idea just how right he is, the boy can only think to say 'You wish'. This elicits from Caleb the unexpected – and unexpectedly self-directed – reply, 'Wish I may, wish I might, wish I were a thousand miles away from here tonight,' This line does more than simply add to *Near Dark*'s fairytale quality. As we soon come to realise, Caleb's mother is either dead or else living somewhere far away from her husband and two children; whatever the case, she is quite literally 'out of the picture'. Her absence from the narrative is glaring, yet is never once commented on by any of the characters, not even Caleb's father or little sister. It makes sense that Caleb would have 'mama' on his mind, and his remark to the young man reveals an unsatisfiable, regressive wish for the return to a time in which obtaining oral-erotic pleasure from a maternal figure is not only possible, but socially acceptable. From this manifest (if unconscious) expression of an Oedipal desire, the seeming non sequitur Caleb free associates to – 'wish I were a thousand miles away from here tonight' – can easily be read as a metaphorical acknowledgement (in terms of travel and great physical distance) of the realistic impossibility of ever returning to this infantile stage of development.

But there is even more here worth commenting on. 'Wish I may, wish I might, wish I were a thousand miles away from here tonight.' This spontaneous rhyme, which sounds almost like a mystical prayer or invocation, calls to mind the famous line uttered by the gypsy Maleva (Maria Ouspenskaya) to near-werewolf Larry Talbot (Lon Chaney, Jr.) in Universal's 1941 horror classic *The Wolf Man*: 'Even a man that is pure in heart, and says his prayers by night, may become a wolf when the wolfbane blooms and the autumn moon is bright.' The key difference being that Caleb, near-vampire that he is, undergoes monstrous transformation *because* of (and not despite) the prayers he says 'by night'.[11] If we refrain from interpreting the latter clause metaphorically, then Caleb's prayer would seem to be for an erotic (sucking) mother figure, namely Mae (Jenny Wright) – homonym of 'may' in 'Wish I may…' – to grant him temporary freedom from his mundane existence as an Oklahoma farm boy.

As if on cue, another young man standing outside the convenience store advises Caleb to 'feast your eyes', on the ethereal, waif-like girl standing by herself midway up the block licking an ice cream cone. 'I'm dreaming', gushes Caleb's antagonist, and in order to provide visual support for this claim, Bigelow treats the viewer to an eyeline match of Mae, who is bathed in a radiant blue light coming from the cheap neon signs behind her, and whose movements are aestheticised, rendered all the more graceful via slow-motion camerawork. As one reviewer wrote around the time of *Near Dark*'s release, 'when Caleb first sees Mae … it's as if the world has slipped into another gear' (Hinson 1988). We have here what looks like a paradigmatic example in support of Laura Mulvey's contention that, in mainstream (i.e. dominant, patriarchal, conservative) Hollywood film, one of the two strategies employed to protect male viewers from the threat of castration (absence and lack) posed by the female form is the representation of 'woman as icon, displayed for the gaze and enjoyment of men' (Mulvey 1999: 840). The psychoanalytic terminology Mulvey uses to characterise this strategy is 'fetishistic scopophilia', whereby the represented figure is turned into a fetish 'so that it becomes reassuring rather than dangerous', its physical beauty built up, thus 'transforming it into something satisfying in itself' (Ibid.).[12]

However, if we stop to think about the action Mae performs during this slow-motion sequence, then it is possible to construct an alternative reading according to which the male impulse towards fetishistic scopophilia is actually *exploited* by Mae. As we learn a little bit later, during a scene in which Caleb gags while trying unsuccessfully to eat a candy bar, vampires have no stomach for human food. Blood is their only source of sustenance. Thus, Mae's licking of an ice cream cone can be retrospectively interpreted as a *ploy* on her part, a way of making herself even more appealing to the red-blooded (and hot-blooded) young men in town. This interpretation is supported by another scene later in the film, a well-crafted montage sequence in which each of the vampires is shown making use of their particular 'talents' – really just their particular physical characteristics – to attract potential victims. For example, Homer (Joshua John Miller), a vampire trapped in the body of a small boy, feigns a bike accident in order to get a concerned motorist to stop and check on his well-being. Mae's ploy certainly works on Caleb, who, for his own reasons, cannot resist the promise of oral-erotic satisfaction implicit in her licking of the ice cream cone; and it works as well on those in the audience who identify with him. Thus, as befits her distinctive status as a 'feminist' director working within the Hollywood studio system, Bigelow here finds a way of undermining patriarchal viewing structures through the creative use of established generic conventions – both thematic and cinematographic – instead of resorting to such radical, avant-garde techniques as those hinted at by Mulvey in her 'Visual Pleasures and Narrative Cinema' essay, and in contrast to those employed in Bigelow's first two films, *The Set-Up* (1978) and *The Loveless* (1982).[13]

At least as mesmerised by this vision of Mae as his dumber and dumbstruck peers, Caleb replies 'You can go ahead and keep on dreaming, son', the suggestion being that he alone will be the one to approach the girl and make their collective fantasy a reality. But what we really have here is Caleb signalling his desire to *participate* in a dream of his own making, albeit one which, as we have just seen, is not entirely under his control. And lest we overlook this seemingly insignificant detail, by referring to his antagonist as 'son', Caleb assumes for himself (at least implicitly) the role of the boy's father. This, of course, would make him the appropriate sexual object choice for 'mama', with nothing to fear from being 'eaten' by her. Constance Penley, in a fascinating discussion of *The Terminator* (James Cameron, 1984), argues persuasively that

> within the structure of fantasy that shapes the film, John Conner is the child who orchestrates his own primal scene, one inflected by a family romance, moreover, because he is able to choose his own father, singling out Kyle [Michael Biehn] from the other soldiers. That such a fantasy is an attempted end-run around Oedipus is also obvious: John Conner can identify with his father, can even *be* his father in the scene of parental intercourse, and also conveniently dispose of him in order to go off with (in) his mother. (1991: 69)

As Penley explains it, a primal-scene fantasy is 'the name Freud gave to the fantasy of overhearing or observing parental intercourse, of being on the scene, so to speak, of one's own conception. The desire represented in the time-travel story, of both witnessing one's own conception and being one's own mother and father, is similar to the primal-scene fantasy, in which one can be both observer or one of the participants' (1991: 68).[14]

Penley's observations are very relevant to a consideration of *Near Dark*, in which Caleb Colton – much like John Conner in *The Terminator* – 'orchestrates his own primal scene', one that is also 'inflected by a family romance' (whereby the subject dreams up an ideal parent to compensate for the perceived shortcomings of the real one) in order to attempt an 'end-run around Oedipus'. For Caleb, travelling back in time is not an option. Instead, he fantasises a situation in which his absent mother is replaced by a beautiful, immortal female vampire who will give birth to him anew, and who treats him simultaneously as sexual partner and infant son. In the latter role, Caleb requires from Mae the vampiric equivalent of breast feeding, which amounts to sucking blood directly from the veins in her wrist. All differences aside, however, the underlying motive operative in *The Terminator* (and if Penley is right, other time-travel films) and *Near Dark* (and if Twitchell is right, other vampire films) is the same: 'the work of fantasy allows the fact of incest to be both stated and dissimulated. It is only in fantasy, finally, that we can have our cake and eat it too' (Penley 1991: 70).[15]

Confidently striding up beside the girl, Caleb asks, 'Can I have a bite...? I'm just dyin' for a cone'. The double entendres in these lines are obviously inserted for comedic effect, but it is worth noting that here, as throughout the film, the trouble Caleb gets into comes as a direct result of his inviting it. Mae asks Caleb to drive her home, and when she insists that he make it back before dawn, he takes her fear to be evidence of a strict father: 'it's your Daddy, right? If I don't get you home on time he's gonna give you a whipping, right?' In fact, although Mae does have something of a

'Daddy' at home (though not in the traditional sense; more on this below), her fear is not of paternal punishment, but of being destroyed by the sun's rays. The real truth of Caleb's remark can be seen in the way he projects on to Mae his own, Oedipal fears of Daddy's jealous rage, due to his attempted seduction of Daughter (soon to be his Mommy).

On the road back to Mae's place, the couple stop a couple of times. First, at her behest, to walk around outside and look at the stars. This scene establishes Mae's heightened perceptual abilities, as she exhorts Caleb to look at the night, as well as Caleb's relative blindness/impotence: 'I can't see!' '– Well, listen!'. Mae comments that when the light from the stars above reaches earth millions of years from now, she will be still be around to see it. 'Sounds like fun … I'd like to be there too', Caleb replies, referring not just to the prospect of immortality, but of spending eternity with Mae (Mom). She hints that this is possible, but when Caleb asks how, she shrugs, 'Who knows?' She also refuses to make out with Caleb, causing the surprised stud to declare: 'I sure haven't met any girls like you.'

Later, after Mae realises how close it is to sunrise, Caleb stops the truck in the middle of the road, hides the keys, and demands a kiss before driving any further. Although innocent enough in the context of what the first-time viewer of *Near Dark* has seen thus far, the fact that Mae will die a horrible death – burnt to a crisp by the sun's rays – unless she makes it indoors before dawn, means that Caleb's cheeky request is not so different from an attempted rape. In a subversion of traditional Hollywood love scenes, as well as the 'natural' human reproductive process, the long, slow (and slow-motion) kiss that follows is interrupted by a disconcerting popping noise on the soundtrack when Mae's teeth puncture Caleb's neck. In this primal scene fantasy, with its family romance elements, not only does Caleb occupy Father's place at the moment of his own (re)birth; *he* is the one to be penetrated, not Mae/ Mother. The fact that Caleb is only *metaphorically* de-virginised, however, renders his immediate re-conception as a vampire 'immaculate' (in the Biblical sense), with the result that Mae now stands as a sort of Mary figure – the ultimate Mother, especially for boys suffering extreme Oedipal anxiety. The wisdom of Penley's insightful remark, 'It is only in fantasy, finally, that we can have our cake and eat it too', becomes even more apparent.

In the final scene before he is picked up and transported off (in a boarded-up motor home, no less) to a new existence by the clan of outlaw vampires, Caleb limps back to the family farm, in obvious agony from his recent birth trauma as well as from the brutal sun, which has just become the enemy. Finally making it home, smoke escaping from his very pores, little sister Sarah (Marcie Leeds) catches sight of him in the distance and exclaims 'Hey Dad, there's Caleb!' Instead of lifting his head up to catch a glimpse of his out-all-night son, Loy Colton (Tim Thomerson) continues to focus on giving an injection to one of the cows in the stable. He just grumbles, more to himself than to Sarah, 'About time he came home.'

This is only the first indication we are given that the relationship between Caleb and his father is less than 'Norman Rockwell'-esque, despite Sharrett's contention (quoted above), and despite Loy's efforts at 'rescuing' a son who, at the time, does not seem especially eager to be rescued. The tension between the two is also apparent near the end of the film, the evening following Caleb's successful conversion/reversion back to human form, thanks to an emergency blood transfusion from Dad. This transfusion (the idea for which Bigelow claims to have lifted from Stoker's novel)[16] stands as a restoration – at once biological, cultural and symbolic – of paternal authority, as Caleb once again owes his life, and his identity, to the senior Mr Colton. (It is reasonable to assume that Caleb's Oedipal anxieties will be back in force now as well.) After Sarah excuses herself from dinner, and father and son are left by themselves at the table, an awkward silence ensues. Their obvious unease is as much a sign of the fragility of their relationship as it is evidence of the social code of masculinity which makes it so difficult for fathers and sons to express their emotions in each other's presence. 'Days are getting shorter', Loy finally mutters. Caleb, still preoccupied with thoughts of Mae, weighing the pros and cons of a life(style) decision that has effectively been made *for* him, corrects his father, 'Nights are getting longer.' With that, he gets up to go outside, leaving Loy alone at the head of the table. Unlike those who, after being rudely awakened from a pleasurable (even if intense and at times terrifying) dream, immediately try to fall back asleep in order to re-enter the world they left behind, Caleb will have another opportunity to engage with the creatures of the night.

If Caleb's encounter with Mae can be read as the initiation of a dream or fantasy on the part of the former, albeit one with nightmarish qualities (shortly after being picked up by the vampire clan, Caleb demands that one of them 'slap me if I'm dreaming'; he gets slapped – draw your own conclusions), then a key question remains to be answered. What is it about this angelic-looking vampire and her-less-than angelic clan – described by Sharrett in such terms as 'savage', 'barbaric', 'repugnant', 'destructive', 'nihilistic' and 'post-punk' (1996: 104) – that would make them so appealing in his eyes? Well for one thing, they are mobile. Although their primary motivation for staying on the road is practical rather than philosophical, a matter of survival rather than choice, the fact is that their constant movement and refusal to settle down in any one place for too long makes them counter-cultural figures, grants them a freedom from many of the constraints (social and behavioural) operating on American families in the latter half of the twentieth century and beyond. Bigelow's comment about *Near Dark*, that 'at … heart, it's a road movie' (Anon. 1988), reveals the importance of the journey trope – both literally and metaphorically – for an understanding of Caleb's liminal experience.

For another thing, they are immortal, and nearly invulnerable besides. The benefits of eternal life and imperviousness to harm are fairly obvious – the wishes of many a frustrated and powerless youth – and are frequently alluded to by the vampires themselves. It is clear that they get a lot of pleasure from invoking their supernatural abilities. One evening, for example, Severen (Bill Paxton) suggests that they play a game of poker in which the loser of each hand performs a round of 'Russian Roulette'; everyone laughs, since it is not as if getting shot in the head poses any real threat to a vampire. Interestingly, Bigelow and Red choose not to thematise the existential angst that contemplating the prospect of eternal life might engender in vampires, a familiar character trait of those populating the novels of Anne Rice. In *Near Dark*, the only real negatives of vampirehood – and these come across as relatively insignificant when compared to the positives – are an inability to walk around in the sun, and (in Homer's case, since he is the only prepubescent member of the clan) being stuck in a body that will never grow or change.

Like other formerly or still-sometimes human monsters, e.g., werewolves, Bigelow's vampires are closer to nature, more in touch with their pre-socialised selves, and less subject to surplus repression than their mortal counterparts.[17] After discovering that what he used to call food is now indigestible matter for him, and feeling the insatiable urge for blood, Caleb inquires of Mae, 'What do we do now?' Her reply, 'Anything we want, till the end of time', perfectly encapsulates the sense of freedom and empowerment that being a vampire allows. And when Caleb complains that he doesn't want to have to kill in order to survive, Mae instructs him not to think of it as killing. 'Don't think at all', she tells him, 'Just use your instincts.' *Contra* Sharrett, the true 'linchpin' of *Near Dark* is Caleb's refusal to kill a potential victim following the memorable ten-and-a-half-minute set-piece at a roadside bar, where the other vampires stage a gory massacre to intra-diegetic music playing on a jukebox.[18] Tackling a young man who has escaped certain death inside the bar by jumping out a window, Caleb somehow manages to resist his overwhelming desire for blood, and lets the boy go free. This display of compassion and manifest 'morality' on Caleb's part may seem like evidence in favor of the film's neoconservatism. However, what appears to be a denial of instinct and refusal to give in to temptation is in fact nothing more than proof of Caleb's hypocrisy, since he never hesitates to drink the blood of freshly-killed humans when it is Mae who does the killing and allows him to feed off of her. Caleb is not much different from a person who abhors the inhuman treatment of animals bred for purposes of food, but who has no problem at all eating those same animals in processed and packaged form.

By far the most appealing aspect of the vampire clan, at least to Caleb, is the 'alternate family structure' (Bigelow, quoted in Smith 1995: 56) that it represents. Because vampires reproduce asexually, by biting and then nursing (instead of bleeding to death) their once-human offspring, each new vampire only has one sire. This means that there is no Oedipal triangulation, and perhaps as a (psychological) result of this fact, the vampires seem to have no problem with incestuous activity taking place between a 'parent' and his or her 'children'. The generational structure of the clan is as follows: Jesse (Lance Henriksen) is the oldest vampire, and this more than anything else is what positions him as leader. He was responsible for 'turning' Diamondback (Jenette Goldstein) – with whom he subsequently formed a couple – and possibly Severen as well, although the latter's origins are left unclear in the narrative. Diamondback turned Homer, who eventually turned Mae. And as we have seen, Mae was put in a position where she basically had no choice but to turn Caleb; her only other option would have been to let him die. It is only *after* parenting Caleb that Mae gives herself to him freely, becoming both his mother and his lover at one and the same time. Thus, despite Bigelow's contention that 'at a fundamental level', Jesse and Loy are 'two fathers fighting over the same son' (Ibid.), it is evident that, fundamentally-speaking, Caleb is a son fighting to gain freedom from his one, real-life father.

That a special bond holds between vampires and their individual parents is made clear in Diamondback's treatment of Homer. She looks out for him, and is fiercely protective of his well-being, constantly reminding him to heed the sunlight. And although members of the clan grant a token parental respect to anyone above them on the family tree, they do so in a manner that seems to suggests a mockery of traditional etiquette. During a Western-style shootout with the local police, for example, Caleb tells Jesse to 'Gimme the keys, grandpa' (when really, Jesse is his great-great-grandfather). Jesse replies sarcastically, 'Go ahead. We'll cover you, *son*'. Later, after being chided by Diamondback for not killing the young man at the bar, Severen bullies Caleb, 'that's your mamma talking, boy' (when really, she is his great-grandmother).

There is no doubting the fact that Caleb's true vampire mamma is Mae. Confirmation comes early on via a point-of-view sequence from Caleb's perspective, when, close to death, he stumbles towards Mae in the dark. Dropping on his knees before her, putting his head in her lap, she bites her wrist and lets him suck(le) the blood from the wound. As Mae's fluid begins coursing its way through Caleb's body, we hear a heart beating progressively louder on the soundtrack. Soon (and predictably) enough, this nursing session turns erotic, as the two begin making out as Caleb's strength returns. In his 1908 essay, 'Family Romances', Freud describes a stage of development in which the male child (his focus when theorising about sexual development) begins to feel slighted, especially by his father, with whom he particularly identifies – as if he is not receiving all of his parents' love and his own affection is not being reciprocated. This is when the child begins to daydream or fantasise, to use the imagination as a vehicle for the 'fulfillment of wishes and as a correction of actual life' (1959: 238). The hostility a male child develops towards his father, coupled with an intense desire to bring his mother – the object of intense sexual curiosity – into 'situations of secret infidelity' (239) with him, is what motivates the wishful fantasy of an artificial family. We have noted the emotional distance between Loy Colton and his son, as well as the total absence of Mrs Colton from the narrative. It is hardly an interpretive stretch to read Caleb's dream/fantasy of incest with a vampire mother as the construction of a gothicised family romance.

The nearest thing Caleb has to a father once he becomes a vampire is not Jesse, but Homer, his closest male progenitor. In a perverse inversion of the typical Oedipal scenario, the 'father' (really, the grandfather) is jealous of the 'son' for entering into a sexual relationship with the 'mother' (Mae). Threatening to make a vampire out of Sarah Colton in revenge for the perceived wrong done to him by Caleb, Homer proffers the illogical argument, 'I turned Mae. She went off and turned you. Now I'm turning your little sister. I'd say that makes us Even Steven.' Homer's unsuitability as a replacement father figure for Caleb is highlighted earlier in the film, when he introduces himself by grabbing the latter's crotch and commanding him not to forget his name (spelling it out, 'H-O-M-E-R', thus attempting to shift his status from Real to Symbolic father via a linguistic articulation of the Lacanian *nom-du-père*). This thinly-veiled castration threat is more laughable than frightening, since Homer is trapped in the body of a little boy and poses no real danger whatsoever. Thus, to the limited extent that Caleb has made room for Daddy in his family romance, he does so by switching things around, turning his *father* into the powerless one.

I have been assuming that the psycho-sexual motives behind Caleb's dream/fantasy can be aligned fairly straightforwardly with a progressive ideological stance. This because the wish being fulfilled – freedom from Oedipal anxieties – allows for the development of new and non-traditional lifestyle choices and family structures. There is in addition the vampire clan's mobility, outlaw/outsider/rebel status, and the pleasure they take from breaking all manner of taboos and conventions. None of this is to deny the neoconservative elements in *Near Dark* identified by Sharrett (minus the narrative framing), and highlighted by Caleb's defeat of the clan and subsequent 'liberation' of Mae. But to get the whole picture, so to speak, it is necessary to acknowledge the various strategies employed by Bigelow to comment critically on Caleb's character, and to make the viewer seriously question the choices he winds up making.

First are scenes in which Bigelow undermines Caleb's position as ostensible hero of the narrative, revealing him to be hypocritical and possessed of a sadistic quality that exists as an unrepressed personality trait. The second time Caleb sucks blood directly from Mae's wrist (instead of killing the human victim for himself), mutually-felt sexual urges give way to an ugly greed and selfishness on his part. Refusing to stop sucking – the irony here should be obvious, considering the film's opening line – Mae finally has to push him away, crying out 'Caleb, you can kill me if you drink too much.' Completely unmoved by the threat he just posed to Mae's well-being, Caleb offers no apology; he simply sits on the ground a few feet away, a mess of blood on his face and a cruel smile on his lips.

Another instance of Caleb's hypocrisy and mean streak comes when he takes control of an eighteen-wheeler and smashes it into Severen in an effort at destroying him. This is a somewhat gory and frankly over-the-top sequence, something straight out of *Terminator* or a post-George Romero zombie movie. The designation of Severen as 'simply evil', 'totally nonhuman' (Wood 1986: 192), and therefore eminently deserving of annihilation (i.e. re-repression), probably constitutes the film's most reactionary moment. But it is hard to miss the designation of Caleb *too* as something less than fully human here. Hooting and hollering with pleasure at the prospect of killing Severen, he pleads for his enemy's death (really, Severen is the character in *Near Dark* most like an older brother to Caleb) and quite clearly has an interest in finishing him off that goes far beyond a desire to rescue the kidnapped Sarah.

Bigelow also includes a number of scenes which are not focalised through Caleb at all, and which provide the viewer with information to which Caleb himself is not privy. These moments of directorial intervention function to mitigate the malevolence of clan patriarch Jesse, and to render unstable the dividing line between human and monster (Self and Other). In one such moment, we travel by car with Jesse and Diamondback as they scour the road one evening looking for hitchhikers to victimise. Eventually spotting a gentle-looking young man, they pull over and invite him to get in. The hitchhiker promptly puts a knife to Diamondback's throat, threatens to rape her, and is joined by a friend who pulls a gun on Jesse. The joke, of course, is that these criminals (definitely rapists, possibly murderers) have no idea what they are in for, as Jesse and Diamondback laugh at the harmless threats coming their way. But at another level, Bigelow seems concerned to contrast her vampires – who kill because they need to, and who enjoy the hunt besides – with the many anonymous, nondescript humans whose motives for killing are far less justifiable.

Another non-focalised scene occurs near the end of the film. Having just witnessed the destruction of Severen, the betrayal of Mae and the death of Homer (his desire to make Sarah a vampire partner so intense that he runs after her in broad daylight, leading to his implosion), the last two members of the clan set their sights on Caleb. Although Sharrett considers the 'operatics of the vampires' demise … unwarranted' (1996: 261), Bigelow manages to generate a fair amount of sympathy for Jesse and Diamondback as their car veers slowly off the side of the road, where it explodes in flames a moment later. Numerous close-ups of their burnt and blackened faces inside the car give viewers ample time to contemplate the fact that their offspring have all either died or disowned them. Rather than live a life without family, one in which they are sure to be constantly hunted by people who will never understand or respect them, they seem content to commit an act of sure suicide. An insert of Jesse's smoking hands on the wheel is followed by a shot of Diamondback placing hers on top of his. A small smile creeps across her face as she utters her last words – 'Fun times' – evidently thinking back and harbouring no regrets about her life as a vampire, as the couple proceed together to their fiery demise.

Finally, it is worth considering the static shot at the end of *Near Dark*, in which Caleb is shown hugging Mae in the Colton barn the morning after her successful blood transfusion. This shot is followed by a slow zoom-in, which freezes on a medium close-up of the pair. At first glance, what we have here may seem like irrefutable proof of the film's neoconservatism; Yvonne Tasker, for example, writes that '*Near Dark* ends with a blood transfusion by which vampire Mae is reclaimed to embrace hero Caleb' (2000: 199). However, the *mise-en-scène* of this frozen image suggests something quite different. As Jeff Karnicky astutely points out

> the film cannot return so wholeheartedly to the world of the sun. The shot of Caleb and Mae embracing stays unchangingly on the screen, like a photograph. Scrutinizing the image, the spectator can see that while Mae's face is in the light, Caleb's face is in complete darkness … something lurks underneath the complacent human joy that *Near Dark* ends on. … Caleb and Mae have rejected the power of the night, the transformative abilities of darkness, of the vampire, of cinema. (Karnicky 1998)

I would only note that Mae's choice to 'reject the power of the night' has really been made *for her*, by Caleb. Not once has Mae suggested that, given the option, she would prefer to give up her vampire status – with all of its attendant gifts – for the constraints (biological, psychological, social) of mortality. Her love for Caleb and concern for Sarah is what prompted her to renounce the clan, *not* a desire to be human and part of a 'normal' American family. The more one focuses on this final image, with its somber atmosphere, dark undercurrents and wistful score, the more one gets the distinct impression that *Near Dark*'s supposedly 'happy' ending is really anything but.[19]

Notes

1   A true experiment in mixed genre conventions, *Near Dark* has been called, among other
     things, a 'vampire-noir-western' (Tasker 2000: 198) and 'an erotic vampire thriller'
     (Coburn 1987). Bigelow herself has called it a 'road movie' (Anon. 1988).

2   Bigelow was introduced to Red by a mutual friend, who suggested that they collaborate on
     a script. Red's previous work included the screenplay for *The Hitcher*, an intelligent and
     gripping cult horror/thriller directed by Robert Harmon in 1986. Bigelow and Red ended
     up writing three scripts together. The first was entitled *Undertow*, which Red finally got
     the chance to direct in 1996. The second was *Near Dark*, which found a backer almost
     immediately and so was released first. The third script was *Blue Steel*, directed by Bigelow in
     1990. As reported in *Cinefantastique*, 'just as things seemed to be happening for the writing
     team, Red mysteriously departed the *Near Dark* project during preproduction. Red never
     explained his sudden pull-out, according to Bigelow (he's credited as co-producer as well
     as screenwriter). She denied having any romantic involvement with Red and would not
     speculate on his reasons for leaving' (Anon. 1988).

3   See Sharrett 1996: 273.

4   Bordwell defines explicit meanings as what the viewer or critic constructs when he or she
     'takes the film to be, in one way or another "stating" abstract meanings' (1989: 8). Implicit
     meanings are assigned by the viewer or critic when 'the film is now assumed to "speak indi-
     rectly". Units of implicit meaning are commonly called "themes", though they may also be
     identified as "problems", "issues", or "questions"' (1989: 8–9).

5   Cf. Bordwell: 'Despite the many changes which it created in the social role of film study,
     symptomatic criticism as an approach was less innovative than is generally recognized.
     Standard versions of its history stress the break with New Criticism, here conceived as an
     asocial and ahistorical "intrinsic" criticism. Yet in a broader senses – that which takes the
     critical task to be interpretation of one or more texts – symptomatic criticism is the newest
     avatar of the New Critical practice of close reading' (1989: 97).

6   Hannah Ransley, for example, writes that 'Bigelow's films ... consistently explore themes
     of violence, voyeurism and sexual politics. ... Bigelow is significant, not just as an all too
     rare successful female director working within Hollywood, but as a director who manages
     to combine thematic complexity, technological experimentation and a sophisticated visual
     style with a more populist approach' (2002: 50–1).

7   The question whether or not, or the extent to which (since she is certainly familiar with
     the debates and discourses), Bigelow deliberately invites a psychoanalytic interpretation of
     Near Dark is an interesting but ultimately less-than-vital line of inquiry. As Noël Carroll
     points out, such interpretation may be plausibly warranted with regard to unselfconscious
     filmmakers as well as fully conscious ones: 'in addition to being a medical practice, psy-
     choanalysis has also become a common idiom of thought throughout Western culture; its
     concepts, scenarios and metaphors have seeped into everyday language. Just as ordinary
     speakers may employ psychoanalytic frameworks without being aware of doing so, so may
     artists' (2002).

8   As James Hopkins explains it, the difference (according to Freud) between *satisfying* a wish/
     desire and merely fulfilling one is that, 'In the case of desire and action, transmission and
     satisfaction go together. ... In the case of wish and dream this is not so. The satisfaction of
     a wish to drink cool water would be an actual drink, not a dream; and in fact the dreamer's

real underlying thirst remains unslaked. The process of wishful imagining generally produces only representations of satisfaction, and not real satisfaction. ... Indeed, wish-fulfillment can be seen as a paradigm of irrationality. To the dreamer, it seems as if he is active and satisfying his thirst; in reality, he is supine, and (so to speak) merely fobbing himself off, with an hallucination which, however pleasant, can at best bring temporary relief. So in a sense the dreamer is self-deceived, both about how things are with him (his motives and their gratification), and about how things are in the world (what he is actually doing)' (1991: 97–8).

9   Although I am here emphasising a crucial difference between them, the associative *link* between blood and semen has been frequently remarked upon in the psychoanalytic literature. Ernest Jones (1971), discussing the vampire myth as it relates to adolescent sexual fantasy, writes: 'The explanation of these phantasies is surely not hard. A nightly visit from a beautiful or frightful being, who first exhausts the sleeper with passionate embraces and then withdraws from him a vital fluid; all this can point only to a natural and common process, namely to nocturnal emissions accompanied with dreams of a more or less erotic nature. In the unconscious mind blood is commonly an equivalent for semen.' It should also be noted that the prohibition against incest might ultimately have a foundation in biology as well. The 'moral' of all horror stories, according to Twitchell, is 'biological efficiency, repression in the service of protecting established reproductive patterns. Such sagas articulate the best way to ensure the generative safety, not so much of the individual, but of society. From such stories adolescents learn what is sexually permissible and what is sexually damaging ... to the species' (1985: 139).

10 See note 8, above.

11 *Near Dark*'s numerous full moon shots serve to reinforce the film's connection between vampire and werewolf mythology.

12 The other 'protective strategy' defined and described by Mulvey in her seminal 1975 essay is sadistic voyeurism, according to which the represented woman is investigated (and thereby demystified) and eventually punished and/or forgiven.

13 *Set Up*, a 20-minute experimental short completed while Bigelow was attending graduate film school at Columbia University, consists of two men beating each other up, calling each other 'fascist' and 'commie' respectively, while a pair of philosophers critique the spectacle in voiceover. According to Bigelow, 'It was really a very overtly political piece and a bit incendiary in its own small context. ... There's this kind of reflexive ideology thing going on' (Smith 1995). *The Loveless*, a 'postmodern nostalgia movie' (Osgerby 2002) co-directed by Monty Montgomery, echoes such classic biker films as *The Wild One* (1954) and especially Kenneth Anger's *Scorpio Rising* (1964) in playing up the homoeroticism implicit in America's hypermasculine motorcycle culture of the 1950s. Largely eschewing dialogue and narrative in favor of stunning visuals and a rockabilly score, the film ends with an eruption of female violence which 'leaves Willem Dafoe's Vance powerless to prevent the destruction it entails' (Ransley 2002: 50).

14 For Lacanian- (as opposed to Freudian-) inflected theorising on time-travel loops and paradoxes in science fiction cinema, see Zizek 1999: 299–305 and Rascaroli 2001. One of the focuses of Rascaroli's discussion is Bigelow's 1995 film, *Strange Days*.

15 Trivia department: *The Terminator* was directed and co-written by James Cameron, Bigelow's husband from 1989 to 1991. Cameron would serve as executive producer on *Point Break* (1991); he also co-wrote, produced and did some uncredited editing work on

Strange Days. Lance Henriksen, who plays Jesse (leader of the vampire clan) in *Near Dark*, had a role in *The Terminator*, as well as in the Cameron films *Piranha 2: The Spawning* (1981) and *Aliens* (1986). Jenette Goldstein, Diamondback in *Near Dark*, is another Cameron regular, having appeared in *Aliens*, *Terminator 2: Judgment Day* (1991) and *Titanic* (1997). The same goes for Bill Paxton, Severen in *Near Dark*; his Cameron films include *Aliens*, *True Lies* (1994) and *Titanic*.

16 See Coburn interview (1987).

17 For a discussion of the gay subtext in *Near Dark*, see Sara Gwenllian Jones' essay in this volume.

18 Concerning this scene, Bigelow states, 'It's an entire reel. In a way it's a film within a film, with a beginning, middle, and end. It's very lyrical in a way, its rhythm. Its strength is its patience. It's ultimately about turning a bar into an abattoir, but it's turning that process into a state of art. Hard to shoot' (Smith 1995). Although arguably 'gratuitous', it is hardly a 'free-form ... slaughter' – the phrase Sharrett (1996: 261) uses to describe it.

19 My sincerest thanks go to Chris Sharrett and the editors of this volume, whose constructive feedback on an earlier version of this essay was invaluable.

CHAPTER FIVE

Redressing the Law in Kathryn Bigelow's Blue Steel

Robert T. Self

Early in Kathryn Bigelow's film *Blue Steel* (1990), a male detective tells a joke to another detective: a hooker gives a blow job to a man in the back of a cab and bites off his penis when the cab hits a pothole. During the ensuing chaos, in which the screaming victim refuses to go to the hospital because he's 'somebody', the prostitute takes out a needle and thread and sews the penis back on. Punch line: 'She sews it on backwards.'

The joke is a collection of significant images that represent the psychological energies in the film: female subservience, masculine authority, sex as economic exchange and guilty pleasure, woman as threatening and domestic, and castration anxiety. One of the most disturbing images suggested by the joke is that of the penis rejoined at the head to the male body so that the suture puts back the severed member but leaves a gaping wound. The joke thus represents the woman as the subject of a doubled castration. The function of the joke to displace the fear of castration to laughter at male dysfunction is frustrated by the joker's choice of the word 'backwards' instead of 'upsidedown'. This slip undoes the needle's work and restores the fearful image. For the joke to succeed, laughter must arise from the perception of deflated male strength and the recognition of a certain justice in punishing male guilt. The discursive situation in which the joke is told reflects another displacement in which male embarrassment at being overheard by a woman while telling the joke gives way to an attack on the woman for overhearing.

The conflicting anxieties that comprise the joke and its narration reflect key aspects of the disruptive scenarios of sexual identity in the film. They further reflect D. N. Rodowick's argument that 'phantasy is always a form imperfectly realised' in part because 'sexual identity always remains fragile and in flux' (1991: x–xi). In contrast to the 'binary machines' of much psychoanalytic film theory, which construe maleness as an 'imaginary coherence' and femaleness as a 'negativity', Rodowick argues that 'psychoanalysis understands the development of sexual identity as an experience of division and loss' and that

> any attempt to associate subjectivity with criteria of unity, coherence, or mastery, especially as one side of a binary equation, is meaningless. … From the perspective of psychoanalysis' understanding of sexual identity, the goal is to understand the range of scenarios that describe the different experiences of division and loss where sexual positions are constructed (1991: 68).

Narrative discourse is one of these binary machines by which society specifies and attempts to shore up such ideological unities as masculine and feminine identification. Susan Faludi in *Backlash: The Undeclared War against American Women* chronicles the ways these identities became a major battleground during the 1980s as a result of the feminist movement. Hollywood narratives enthusiastically participated in what she describes as a cultural effort to push women back into their 'acceptable roles as Daddy's girl or fluttery romantic, active nester or passive love object' (1991: xxii). Faludi points to 1987 in particular as 'a scarlet-letter year for the backlash against women's independence'. In the top-grossing films of that year, Faludi claims that the 'good women are all subservient and bland housewives (*Fatal Attraction* and *The Untouchables*), babies or voiceless babes (*Three Men and a Baby* and *Beverly Hills Cop II*). The female villains are all women who fail to give up their independence, such as the mannish and child-hating shrew in *Three Men and a Baby,* the hip-booted gunwoman in *Beverly Hills Cop II,* and the homicidal career woman in *Fatal Attraction*' (1991: 116). *Fatal Attraction* particularly warns successful, young, married, professional men with healthy libidos against the homicidal tendencies of single, professional women deprived of domestic bliss. In the repeated representation of tough-guy heroes in such violent action movies as *Predator, Die Hard, Robocop, Lethal Weapon,* and *Days of Thunder,* 'Women have been reduced to mute and incidental characters or banished altogether' (1991: 138).

The same misogynist backlash also appears throughout the 1980s in the 'slasher' film. Active, independent, intelligent, and ultimately helpless young women encounter males with significant Oedipal dysfunctions in films such as *I Spit on Your Grave* (Meir Zarchi, 1978), *Friday the 13th* (Sean S. Cunningham, 1980), *He Knows You're Alone* (Armand Mastroianni, 1980), and *Don't Answer the Phone* (Robert Hammer, 1980). In these films when the woman looks, the killer strikes, and the narrative cinema explicitly reconfirms the potency of male subjectivity in the dismemberment of the female anatomy.

Within this social context, then, the castration joke in *Blue Steel* reflects the kind of crisis in sexual identity described by Kaja Silverman:

> The spectacle of male castration may very well result in a destructive questioning of the dominant fiction. Male subjectivity is a kind of stress point, the juncture at which social crisis and turmoil frequently find most dramatic expression. Major rifts between the dominant fiction and the larger social formation can almost always be detected within a classic narrative film through the breakdown of sexual difference – through the disclosure of male lack or impotence (1983: 114).

Other films contemporary with *Blue Steel* depict women cops in stories that are generally complicit with the binary ideology of masculine and feminine identifications. *Impulse* (Sondra Locke, 1990), *The Silence of the Lambs* (Jonathan Demme, 1991), *V. I. Warshawski* (Jeff Kanew, 1991) and *A Stranger Among Us* (1992) variously develop female private detectives, undercover detectives, or FBI agents in narratives that take a coherent stance toward the politics of gender roles. *Blue Steel*, however, deploys a narrative that neither reaffirms the Oedipal trajectory of stable heterosexuality nor seeks to counter the terms of that social negotiation.

Narrative Drive of Blue Steel

Jamie Lee Curtis is a cop whose bifurcated role of female victim and female hero is never resolved into a narrative coherence. Curtis brings to this contradictory role a divergent star persona from her work in the early 1980s as the 'scream queen' of such slasher films as *Halloween* (John Carpenter, 1978), *Terror Train* (Roger Spottiswoode, 1980) and *The Fog* (John Carpenter, 1980) and in the late 1980s as the teasing and tough object of sexual desire in *Trading Places* (John Landis, 1983) and *A Fish Called Wanda* (Charles Crighton, 1988). Bigelow's film aggressively marks this female as transgressive: she is the subject of the narrative, the figure of the law and the possessor of its power and authority; she is simultaneously the object of masculine investigation, desire, hostility and aggression.

When Megan Turner puts on the uniform of New York 'policeman', holsters her own Smith & Wesson service revolver, and takes the police oath at the beginning of *Blue Steel*, the narrative establishes a complex motivation for its victimisation of the disruptive female. On the one hand, the narrative demonstrates the same energy that Tania Modleski analyses in *The Women Who Knew Too Much* as paradigmatic in the films of Alfred Hitchcock: 'Men's fascination and identification with the feminine continually undermine their efforts to achieve masculine strength and autonomy and is a primary cause of the violence towards women that abounds in Hitchcock's films' (1998: 8). The representation of the woman as the law constitutes a major destabilisation of the symbolic order in which gendered subjectivity is a central project. Thus, the narrative drive of *Blue Steel*, like so much classical cinema, is oedipal and sadistic in its need 'to resolve the female as simultaneously castrated and phallic' (Penley 1989: 41).

It is possible to produce a summary of the events in the film that gives its narrative the illusion of coherence: On her first assignment, a rookie female cop named Megan Turner confronts and kills a man attempting to rob a grocery store. Because one of the witnesses to the shooting, Eugene Hunt, steals the robber's .44 magnum revolver, the rookie cop is suspended for excessive violence in the killing of an apparently unarmed man. The witness Eugene then begins simultaneously to romance the rookie Megan and to embark on a series of random killings, using bullets on which he has etched her name. When Megan discovers Eugene's identity as the killer, he begins to focus his attack on her while masquerading with the police and his lawyer as the innocent victim of her accusations. Since no one but her detective partner, Nicholas Mann, believes her, Megan is forced to search for Eugene on her own, finally killing him in a shoot-out in downtown Manhattan.

The numerous strands of relationships in the film seem hardly so explicitly connected, however; they appear to displace each other, rather than following each other causally. Indeed, when the woman in *Blue Steel* dresses as the law and uses her revolver to defend the law, the film mobilizes a range of divergent and discordant stories with variously gendered subjectivities that fail to cohere finally under the authority of classical narrative closure. Although the image of castration constitutes the unsettling master trope of the film, the terms agent and recipient, subject and object, active and passive, sadism and masochism, and masculine and feminine blur and baffle in their references. Analysing the overlay of scenarios in Freud's 'A Child Is Being Beaten', Rodowick describes how unrestrained sexuality … confronts a social authority demanding that sexual division be represented by only two choices, and thus legislates who gains what rights of sexual identity by deciding what their bodies may signify. The phantasy is therefore the product of an explicitly ideological struggle between desire and the Law that is never resolved. Rather the very architecture of the phantasy is an unconscious evasion of the demands of patriarchal law. (1991: 72)

Narrative Tensions in Blue Steel

A similar competition and instability among sexual identities emerges in *Blue Steel* from the conflicting narrative tensions, which reflect a multiplicity of desires. Megan's desire to put on the power of the masculine occurs most dramatically in the spatially and temporally minor story of her abject mother and abusive father. Her deadly possession of the revolver motivates Detective Mann's investigation and persecution of her. Eugene's witnessing of the shooting and theft of the robber's gun motivates his adulation of Megan and his killing spree. Megan is at once the sign of castration and the object of desire – the female in the male's sadistic fantasy of Oedipal mastery – and a femininity of plenitude.

The shifting registers of sexual identification generate three dominant scenarios of contradictory relationships in the film – between Megan and her father, Megan and Mann, and Megan and Eugene. These sexual identifications also appear paradigmatically in the three short, almost incidental narratives that occur at the beginning of the film: the precredit scene, the credit sequence and the castration joke. The story in the castration joke posits a feminine identification that oscillates between sexual subservience of the prostitute and her accidental act of castration. Detective Mann tells the joke with an energy that oscillates between a masculine delight at the prostitute's domestic wielding of the needle and thread to punish the masculine 'somebody' and the hostility of his attack on Megan's use of lethal force. Thus, the joke, its telling and its central trauma constitute an unresolved anxiety about sexual identity and power, guilt and retribution that dominates the film.

The initial scene of the film reflects this same contradictory pattern of sexual subjectivity. The film opens with a hand-held camera tracking down a long, narrow hall behind a police officer who with drawn gun approaches the closed door of an apartment from which come the protesting screams of a woman. The officer breaks in on a scene of domestic violence and shoots the man; the abused wife then surprisingly shoots the officer. The perceived reality of this scene as the depiction of police combat dissolves perceptually, surprisingly, into the theatricality of a police academy test of cadet Megan Turner, but it also insistently returns later in the film's representation of Megan's intervention in her father's physical abuse of her mother. This traumatic scenario marks her entrance into the space constructed and directed by the law as a violent intervention into gendered difference. Her failure to assume the identity of the liberating officer of the law is marked in the fiction by the 'shooting' of the female cop by the abused 'wife'. Her failure of identity is further marked as the failure of a test: 'Congratulations, Turner', the instructor says with heavy sarcasm, 'You killed the husband, and the wife shot you.' The woman, in resisting the tyranny of the masculine, steps into the contradictory logic of retaliation as self-destruction; the armed feminine confronts itself as the subject and object of a violence previously activated by the male.

The credits then roll over a series of slow-motion images that examine in extreme close-up a police .38 special and then look into its empty cylinders and watch its loading and finally its holstering – an emptiness then a fullness, a presence then a hiding in plain sight. This scrutiny of the gun yields to the spectacle of Megan dressing in her police uniform, still in slow-motion, close-up cinematography accompanied by a droning electronic music that connotes another imaginary reality. The first shot tightly frames a woman's chest; her lacy brassiere disappears as the woman buttons the front of a police uniform blouse. The close-ups reveal different parts of her body disappearing beneath the uniform – blouse, boots, gloves and hat – captured in a rapt, slow-motion, close-up gaze. The camera finally assumes the place of a mirror.

The images culminate in a medium shot of Megan Turner staring directly into the lens of the camera as she straightens her cap, a look of satisfaction on her face as she stares into the mirror of the spectator's eyes, the specular (female) other as the law. The sequence concludes with her graduating from the police academy in another close-up of her androgynous face as she repeats the words of the police oath, 'I promise to uphold…' evoking from the subject position of the sentence the legal code, the name of the father, the Law. Thus, the credit sequence constitutes a slow-motion reverie over the symbols of authority and the female acquisition of them, a dreamy recollection of hiding the breasts with the uniform, of the disappearance of the woman into the law, of her positioning as subject to the law and the subject of its enforcement. These two initial scenes set in motion the film's imaginary scenarios of shifting sexual identities.

Classical narrative cinema characteristically resorts to self-conscious narration and more lyrical modes of discourse during opening sequences, but the metaphoric juxtaposition of images and situations here characterises much of the narrative style of the entire film. Indeed, these initial scenes generate a number of displacements of anxiety about gendered subjectivity – most notably in the police uniform and in the revolver – that reverberate throughout the text. Megan's uniform is a constant marker of the dissonance of desire. Megan's mother visits the police station early in the film and says. 'So this is where you work.' 'Yeah, Mom, this is where I work. See all these other people wearing the same outfit as me.' Megan responds with an irony recognised by the spectator who has just witnessed her suspension and the narrative's need to separate Megan's authority from the uniform she wears. Even in casual ways – 'Well, look at you!' the janitor blurts out when seeing Megan in her uniform for the first time – the film represents the woman and the uniform as a remarkable coincidence. During the celebration after graduation, the transgressive quality of the credit sequence is explicitly marked by Megan's friend Tracy. She says: 'I can't believe it! You're a fuckin' cop! You're on the right side of the law.'

Tracy's exclamation is one of pride and love for Megan, and the scene with which the story begins after the credits is remarkable because it both denotes Megan's isolation from the scenes of family celebration going on around her and celebrates the same-sex bonding between her and Tracy, also a mother who has come to the ceremony with her husband and two children. The scene also introduces a verbal image that ambiguously recurs throughout the narrative. 'Nobody fucks with a cop!' says Megan's black partner when they discuss why they became police officers. The robber asserts to Megan before swinging his gun on her, 'Look, bitch, I didn't come here to fuck with you!' But the text also drives toward the fucking of Megan – as the law and its transgression – by Mann and Eugene, as an act of desire and retribution. 'Nobody' is a subject position in sexual intercourse with a cop whom the film designates as (Lieutenant Nick) Mann. Eugene assumes that position in his romantic quest for the female cop, just as he wields the gun, in fear of the stability of his own heterosexual masculinity. Megan may assume that position only when she becomes the desirable woman, stripped of her uniform, naked, no longer a threat to Mann. From the outset the organising energy in the text links the positive accession of the woman to police authority with aggression, hostility and sexual intercourse.

Each of these narrative vignettes is a self-contained story that flows from one to another without the metonymic clarity of cause-effect logic but with a metaphoric intensity. Each represents the instabilities of sexual identity that the classical trajectory of oedipal narrative would contain. Each displaces a variety of anxieties and desires that overdetermine the representation of Megan. Each reflects the shifting identifications of the desirable female as a figure of power and authority and the Oedipal desire that arises from the 'radical sense of inadequacy and lack' (Silverman 1983: 177).

The central diegetic event in this contradictory representation of the woman as the law is Megan's killing of the robber. Eugene is lying at her feet and witnesses her powerful, deadly use of the gun. Then, during the ensuing disorder, he steals the hold-up weapon and slips away from the scene. Thus, Megan appears guilty for killing an unarmed man. This event triggers three connecting, parallel, yet disturbingly separate sequences of events that occur simultaneously with each other and with another series of confrontations between Megan and her father that situate Megan within the discourse of the patriarchal family. Her interactions with Detective Mann work to reposition her as the object of heterosexual desire. Her interactions with the police department and with Eugene's lawyer diminish her authority and seek her castration. Her romance with Eugene parallels his cold-blooded crimes and his psychotic effort to establish a partnership with her in a shared authority of killing. These three narrative strands focus on the circulation of the robber's very big gun – present at the scene, then absent, stolen, hidden, murderous – the central object in a struggle for masculine identity and power and, ironically, for feminine innocence.

The destabilising of sexual subjectivity by the armed and authoritative woman is everywhere displayed in this text – as is the strategy of interrogating this threat. Megan is asked three times in the film why she wanted to be a cop, the second time by a potential date who runs away from her parody of police authority. He expresses a central fear in the text, 'Do you wear a gun?' and then states its oedipal alternative: 'You're a good-looking woman, beautiful in fact; why would you want to be a cop?' Detective Mann echoes this interrogation of her sexuality when he says, 'You're a pretty girl; maybe you've gone with someone who had a violent streak.' Then, to her negative response, he scornfully queries: 'No boyfriend? Is that a personal problem?' Both situations presuppose Megan's guilt in the betrayal of heterosexual conduct. The same anxieties surface in the love relationship between Megan and Tracy and ultimately mark Tracy as a victim of Eugene's psychosis. Too masculine. Megan endangers the hierarchical status quo of gender roles; too feminine, she threatens the heterosexual requirement for social reproduction.

But the anxiety that marks the woman-uniform image more aggressively underlies the desire to take away Megan's gun, badge and uniform. The absence of the robbery weapon and Megan's apparent overreaction in emptying her revolver into the robber – an aggressive and explicit representation of male lack and female plenitude – become the cause of a series of tellingly hostile interrogations in the departmental investigation of Megan's actions. In the first interrogation, Megan is taken off the streets by the chief, who in a revealing *mise-en-scène* sits in a half-lit room under a large gold replica of the police shield that hangs behind him on the wall. Obviously hostile, Mann questions her with only one object in mind: to demonstrate her inappropriate, hysterical willingness to use her revolver. The second interrogation is shown only in its result – the announcement of Megan's suspension by a hearing board, followed in close-up by her surrendering her badge and gun to the chief. The suspension also results in the loss of her uniform until she takes her guard's uniform in the final sequence of the film. In the third investigation, she is explicitly set up to be a target for Eugene and is temporarily given a detective's shield, an identity under the law 'in name only'. Mann reminds her, 'You know nothing, less than nothing.'

This pattern of police hostility toward Megan constitutes indifference toward the killer. Eugene is out there in the dark killing people while the police investigate Megan as a threat to be controlled. 'Every aspect of your life is my business. I own you!' Mann says. Mary Anne Doane observes that in films in which the woman is an agent of the gaze, 'the woman's exercise of an active investigating gaze can only be simultaneous with her own victimisation. The place of her specularisation is transformed into the locus of a process of seeing designed to unveil an aggression against itself' (1987: 72). 'People like you get people hurt', Mann asserts, but only the audience hears Megan's response: 'Yeah, but it's me who should worry.'

A central logic in the narrative establishes the armed woman as guilty of Eugene's criminal excesses, establishes her sexuality as the object of investigation, and then sets her up as both the romantic and homicidal object of the very masculine violence she is arraigned for causing. 'Fucking entrapment!' yells Eugene's lawyer after Megan has correctly arrested his client for murder, but Megan is the target of the textual trap, the trap of the social formation, of the dominant fiction, the Oedipal trap. When she is queried for the last time, now by Mann, 'Why did you become a cop?' her simple answer is, 'Him' – the singular male pronoun, third-person, objective case, and the antecedent is every male in the text, from the robber, to the chief, to Mann, to Eugene.

At this point, late in the film, Megan is referring to Eugene. But 'him' also refers to her father. Another narrative sequence interwoven among the others begins in the scene at the Turner family dinner table after Megan's graduation from the police academy. Shot in close-up one-shots of the father, mother and daughter, this very short scene aggressively represents the abject mother, the defiant daughter and the father's angry gaze of rejection and words of denunciation: 'I've got a goddamn cop for a daughter!' Megan's threat to the masculine is explicitly evoked in this scene, but the motivation for that threat – the father's abuse of the mother – is repressed.

In the subsequent scene, in which the mother visits the police station to apologise for the behaviour of the father, Megan asks the telling question: 'Does he still hit you, Mama?' This is a complex moment in the representation of sexual identities, because Megan has just been suspended from the police force; the image of mother and daughter drinking coffee together within the walls of law enforcement signifies the abjection of the feminine by which the masculine purchases its defense against lack. E. Ann Kaplan argues that 'the mother becomes for the child the realm of the abject that must constantly be struggled against through identification with the Father in the Symbolic' (1992: 133). The impotent father takes his anger out in violence against the woman, and the daughter seeks redress for his crimes from the Law.

One of the most uncanny movements of the film occurs after Eugene kills Megan's best friend, Tracy, and Megan arrests him a second time. Again Eugene is released from police custody. Again Megan is the target of hostility from the police, and again Eugene's attorney threatens Megan's position on the force: 'I'm going to have your job!' Returning to her parents' home, she finds bruises on her mother's arm. The mother attacks and accuses the father, whereupon the daughter arrests him, handcuffs him, reads him his rights and transports him to jail. In one of the most seminal scenes of the film, abjection becomes power. After he breaks down and tearfully confesses his crimes against the mother, Megan relents and takes her father home – only to find Eugene waiting for her in her father's chair. The cutting then produces a series of close-up one-shots of solicitous Mother, frightened Megan, duplicitous Eugene, and no shot of the father.

The *mise-en-scène* of the family runs as a central subtext in minimal, fleeting ways throughout the film and comes to a dramatic climax here. Unable to arrest and keep the killer in jail, Megan arrests the father but succumbs to his suffering admission of guilt and releases him only to find the killer has taken his place in the family living room. Cinematography and editing remove the impotent and abusive father from the scene and replace him with the homicidal and manic 'lover'. Megan became a cop because of 'him' – the father, the lover, the killer.

The Oedipal economy requires a masculine accommodation to the authority of the law and a disavowal of impotence through an objectivisation of the woman's threat. *Blue Steel* inaugurates a range of sexual instabilities within this dynamic by dressing the female body in the uniform of the law. Megan configures the identification with the abject mother within the history of the family and the concomitant desire to have the phallus. Representing an assumption of masculine power, she constitutes threat by usurping authority rather than by signifying its lack. This intolerable assumption of power is contained by the investigatory and debilitating gaze of Mann, but when Eugene seeks to locate his identity in the image of the law, the text represents masculine subjectivity under stress as an oscillation between a regressive desire for the punishing plenitude of the feminine and a sadistic drive to control her threat to masculine subjectivity.

Eugene's Crisis of Sexual Identification

The extent to which *Blue Steel* represents what Rodowick calls the 'entropic character of desire' (1991: xi) emerges in Eugene's crisis of sexual identification. He is psychotic in his efforts to submit before the power he discerns in Megan and in his murderous attempts to appropriate that power. Eugene is a successful gold trader on the floor of the New York Stock Exchange, a middle man in the economic exchange of the most desired symbol in the material treasury. But his witnessing of Megan's shooting the robber is a moment of submission combined with a recognition of lack. Lying on the floor of the grocery at Megan's feet, he steals the gun of the man she has just punished in the extreme for his transgression of the law. A key moment occurs later when Eugene leaves the empty floor of the Stock Exchange, goes to a rest room, pulls the stolen revolver from the front of his pants, and points it at himself: the male perpetrator facing himself in the mirror with the stolen weapon from another male perpetrator shot to death by the female cop. He imagines the position of authority he witnessed in the shooting at the grocery store, her position, the killer of men, and subsequently signifies the authorisations for his murders by etching her name on the bullets in his gun.

As he then simultaneously romances Megan and attacks her, Eugene reflects a sadomasochistic instability similar to what Modleski discovers at the base of the Hitchcockian crisis in masculine subjectivity. She sees *Vertigo* (Alfred Hitchcock, 1958) for instance, 'soliciting a masculine bisexual identification because of the way the male character oscillates between a passive mode and an active mode, between a hypnotic and masochistic fascination with the woman's desire and a sadistic attempt to gain control over her, to possess her' (1988: 99). Eugene assumes Megan's desire in her wielding the pistol, and he kills in order to replicate her powerful use of it. But masculine subjectivity is driven by two 'inspirations': one supine at the feet of the powerful feminine and the other driven by divine voices of command. When he kills, Eugene acts under the impetus of a voice inside his head that tells him, 'You are God, Eugene. You are unique, Eugene. … You are not alone, Eugene.' Indeed, in this regard he is yet another avatar of the other sadistic figures in the text, Father and Mann.

Here is also a paradoxical renunciation of the very phallic power that permits Eugene to violate the law. The stolen gun enables Eugene's crimes, but those crimes position him for retaliation by Megan, for professional but largely for personal reasons. Eugene's crimes are both a means of attacking Megan and of submitting to her authority, reflecting a passive adulation of her strength. At the very same time that Eugene stalks the street as a serial killer, he pursues Megan romantically in another masquerade motivated by a longing for the impossible reunion with the woman. Telling word play between the two of them during one dinner date echoes the narrative play of names in the text: 'Why me?' 'Why you?' Mann is the threat to come between *Me*(gan) and *Eu*(gene). In one scene, Detective Mann forcefully asserts his controlling surveillance over Megan; in the next scene, Eugene takes her for a helicopter ride over Manhattan, where other people 'don't matter very much' and 'we're the only people in the world'.

Figure 3 Worshipping the phallus in *Blue Steel*.

These multiple desires emerge quite explicitly in the scene when Megan discovers that Eugene is not only the lover she had supposed but the killer she has sought. At the moment of sexual engagement, Eugene reveals his murderous persona. As they kiss, Eugene feels her gun and asks her to take it in her hand and point it at him. When she does, he kneels before her and places the muzzle against his forehead. 'I have found my brightness', he says. 'I have seen that brightness in you ... You shot him without blinking an eye ... You're the only one capable of understanding ... The two of us, we could share ... I know you better than you know yourself ... We're two halves of one person.'

Once it reveals this guilt and ends part of the masquerade, the text can no longer maintain the masochistic energy of masculine submission to the powerful woman; masculine subjectivity can no longer adhere to passive, romantic identification. As he continues to kill, Eugene begins a new masquerade of innocence before the law that works another form of control over Megan: his lawyer begins to attack her integrity. The psychic strategy here initially involves the establishment of Eugene as Megan's 'kindred spirit', through his guilt, his abjectness, his disavowal, his masquerade first as lover and then as innocent. These masquerades serve two contradictory goals of the textual project: they prolong the extent of Megan's quest to arrest Eugene, and they continue the legal hostility against Megan by 'officially' warning her to leave Eugene alone. The last quarter of the film then constitutes a play of attack, sex and death.

Positioning of Megan as Distressed Female

The 'him' who motivated Megan's fear and desire for the law includes all the major masculine figures of the diegesis in a metonymic chain of displacement, from the father to the robber, to the police chief and Detective Mann, to Eugene – all of whom ironically echo the robber's words of denial as they swing their weapon on the police woman: 'Get outa my face, bitch ... I didn't come here to fuck with you!' The narrative logic finally is a perverse structure of substitutions for these male figures, in which Megan is the object of phallic competition, hostility and disavowal. The narrative refuses an unambiguous cause-effect logic of guilt but constantly posits Megan's authority and at the same time targets her strength in order to thrust her into positions of vulnerability. This energy culminates in the penultimate sequence, when Megan handcuffs Mann to the steering wheel of their squad car and goes off on her own – emotionally and ineffectively – leaving Mann inadvertently at the mercy of the killer. She wounds Eugene just as he is about to kill Mann. The effect again is to prolong Megan's punishment of Eugene as well as Mann's punishment of Megan. Mann's narrow escape from this situation coerces the woman into a position of apology, to recognise and confess her guilt: 'I almost got you killed. I never should have put you in that position.' So positioned by the textual economy, Megan now becomes the distressed female, ready to be rescued from her fears by the solace of sex with Mann.

The divergent psychic energies that distinguish and link Mann and Father and Eugene figure significantly in the final sequence. The romantic scene of sexual intercourse between Megan and Mann – full of erotic music, soft shadows and slow-motion close-ups – finally repositions the woman as an appropriately passive object of sexual desire. But the wounded Eugene is uncannily everywhere in his competition with Mann to control Megan. Insistent masculine violence against the armed woman means first coitus and then death. Eugene shoots Mann, effectively removing him from the remainder of the text, and takes Mann's place on the postcoital bed. The lovemaking between Megan and Mann gives way to Eugene's attempted rape of Megan, which is staged by the editing and cinematography as actually a violent parody of rape and which can only be stopped again by Megan's power – her shooting Eugene a second time. With a stolen gun, from the usurped seat of the father, as a substitute for Mann in Megan's bed. Eugene provokes the final violent confrontation with Megan. 'Being with Megan is the ultimate kick', he says, echoing the words he utters in submission to her arresting gaze: 'Death is the ultimate kick.'

With both Mann and Megan wounded in the hospital, and Eugene wounded and having escaped into the New York night, the film's narrative energy seems apparently spent. But the crisis engendered by Megan's dressing as the law continues inexorably toward death. Megan leaves her hospital bed, knocks her police guard unconscious, and dresses once again in a police uniform. In a slow-motion haze, she stalks the streets until finally, inexorably, Eugene reappears and they engage in the extended shoot-out of the last scene. At the end Eugene is dead in the street, and the police woman is led away from the scene, like Melanie in *The Birds* (Alfred Hitchcock, 1963) in a catatonic state.

The homicidal personality of *Blue Steel* swings between a desirable image of feminine power and the masculine need to assert its own power. This oscillation mirrors a textual fabric woven of multiple desires, multiple narrative structures, multiple identifications. Megan Turner crosses sexual boundaries at the outset of the film in the theatrical moment of her intervention into the scene of male violence against women, her test for accession to the law. The female cop becomes the unstable centre of desire (to be protected, to be romanced) and of hostility (to be accused, to be investigated) and of nurture (to be revered and feared). Sexual identities in *Blue Steel* are articulated across the same fissures of difference that constitute its divergent diegetic relationships. Subjectivity is variously situated by identification with the active and tough police woman and by identification with the desirable and passive female. Megan is the focus of narrative lines that oscillate among emotions of sadistic aggression (Megan as hero, the pleasurable subject of narrative action) and of masochistic pain (Megan as victim, the passive object of fear and delay). The conflicting desire of the text is to see the phallic power of Mann asserted against the dysfunctional Eugene and to restore the passive objectivity of the vulnerable and beautiful female.

Rodowick describes the Oedipus complex as a social process that organises the divergent possibilities of sexual identity into an acceptable duality:

> In sum, the Oedipus complex is a cultural agency and an ideological machine whose product is women and men, each failing and searching out compromises, in their particular ways, with the idealized norm of Woman/Man. Little wonder, then, that phantasy life, so closely tied to the Oedipal situation, organizes scenarios of crisis, renunciation and the problem of identity. (1991: 73)

Conclusion

The number of films at the beginning of the 1990s that thrust women into figures of the law reflect many problems of identity surrounding the changing status of women in the culture. Most of these films develop a traditional narrativity of the police/detective film that works around conflict and its resolution, guilt and punishment, and that ultimately recuperates feminine subjectivity to Oedipal subject positions.

Blue Steel, however, activates instabilities of sexual difference without containing them. The narrative seeks to motivate the generic trajectory from the police action film of transgression/guilt, investigation, capture/punishment, but its organisation deconstructs those connections, turning Megan's act of law enforcement into a motive for her investigation by that law, laying the blame for Eugene's crimes on Megan, and using those crimes to engage Megan's punishing investigation of Eugene while simultaneously desiring her punishment and punishing her desire.

The complexity of plot construction in the film draws us into an awareness of the contradictions of gendered identification. The film's metacritical pattern, like that Modleski finds in Hitchcock, 'actually allows for a critique of the structure it exploits and for a sympathetic view of the heroine trapped within that structure' (1988: 25). The text reflects the displacement of guilt from its appropriate locus, on the killer, to the woman who has usurped the law by putting on its uniform. The deeper understanding of female victimisation yielded by the film holds that to be aggressive is to be transgressive, is to unleash a force of repression and hostility of which the transgression is both cause and target; it further yields as a prior and final knowledge that to be either an active or passive woman is to be a victim. What finally is central to sexual identity in *Blue Steel* is the constant veneration, contestation and instability of authority.

CHAPTER SIX

All That is Male Melts into Air:
Bigelow on the Edge of Point Break

Sean Redmond

> Bigelow makes 'high impact films that get in your face': gut-wrenchingly
> kinetic, explosively visceral, poetically violent; like a female Walter Hill crossed
> with Sam Peckinpah. While fellow directors Penny Marshall and Martha
> Coolidge are content to scour the emotional battlefields, Bigelow goes for a
> rush response: all fast edits, upfront camerawork and almost fetish-like respect
> for weaponry. (Salisbury 1991: 27)

Point Break (1991) is Kathryn Bigelow's most profitable 'studio' film to date, taking
approximately $100 million at the American box-office during the year of its release,
and yet it remains one of her least well-received films, both in terms of commercial
reviews and academic analysis. Critical attention of her work has tended to focus on
what have become, in part, canonised films like *Blue Steel* (1990) and *Strange Days*
(1995) – analysed and re-discovered for their complexity and contestation over gender
and genre. An indicator of what is most valued in the Bigelow oeuvre came when
the call for papers for this collection of 'new' essays on Bigelow found the editors
inundated with abstracts for *Strange Days*, but absolutely nothing on *Point Break*.

However, When *Point Break* has been written about it has generally been from a negative perspective. *Point Break* is often perceived to be one of Kathryn Bigelow's least politically radical, generically transgressive or feminist films: the more critical readings of the film point to its Oedipal trajectory; to the way it valorises an excessive, testosterone fuelled, individualist masculinity; and to the adherence to the visual and narrative formula of the dumb, adolescent action film, from which *Point Break* takes its generic form. Hannah Ransley's brief assessment of the film shows how the film has been read as a superficial, lightweight high-concept movie:

> The 1991 film *Point Break* is Bigelow's biggest commercial success to date, perhaps because it most successfully conforms to its action genre ... Its examination of masculine relations and the lines between right and wrong is complimented by adrenaline-pumping action sequences. Bigelow's familiar group of outsiders living by different rules are presented here as whole-heartedly cool. (2000: 47)

Nonetheless, there have been some important supportive interjections around the ideological meaning(s) embedded in the film. Two of the more positive (although still rather skeletal) readings of *Point Break* have come from Needeya Islam (1995) and Yvonne Tasker (1999). Islam and Tasker have commented on the way the film plays around with gender and sexual identity, and film form, and how counter-hegemonic values are principally promoted or given real narrative determination through the positive representation of 'outsider' groups and individuals. They both read the film as if it has depth, contestation, and as if the author, Bigelow, has been able to sign the film (in spite of or perhaps because of, studio and generic pressures) with her own transgressive obsessions, themes and interests.

In a similar vein to both Islam and Tasker, what I would like to do in this essay is to re-visit and re-discover *Point* Break through this positive ideological framework. I want to both explore what I consider to be the stylistic and political depth(s) of this supposedly sugar coated action spectacle, and to find Bigelow's voice, her knowing and troubling cinematic gaze in the film's obsessions, themes and interests. The overarching premise of this essay, then, is that *Point Break* is a (perhaps *the*) seminal Kathryn Bigelow text. Through a close textual and contextual reading of the film I hope to show that there are a set of recognisable, intertextual Bigelovian traits, traits that circulate or coalesce around the following three areas: a political, counter-hegemonic radicalism; a gendered and sexualised identity crisis; and finally, a supra-cinematic subversion of generic form (and indirectly of the mechanics of the Hollywood cinema machine). Bigelow, I will contend, is an outsider on the inside, subverting the machine from within.

First, *Point Break* can be read as a politically radical text, at least in the context of Hollywood where a conservative ideology is argued to generally inform both the structure and the content of the films produced there (Kellner 1995: 56). *Point Break* is politically radical in the Hollywood context because its cause and effect narrative seeks to undermine, satirise, and by the end of the film, abandon the dominant political order for, at least implicitly, counter-culture values and lifestyle. In short, *Point Break* is engaged in a sort of Gramscian hegemonic battle but here the battle over ideas and values are to be 'won' by the subordinate culture.

At the closure of *Point Break*, long haired, unshaven, *surfer-cop* Johnny Utah (Keanu Reeves) lets bank robbing surfer Bodhi (Patrick Swayze) go 'free', free to surf that final, existential, 'once in a lifetime' wave thrown up by the fifty-year storm. Seconds later, in a symbolically related act, he throws his cop badge into the ocean, and now, as *surfer* Johnny Utah, exits right, out of the frame and out of the film. In so doing, he has finally rejected surveillance culture and the dominant system of law and order that had, in part, fashioned him as a narrative agent, and driven him to this moment in the film in the first place. When long-haired, unshaven, surfer Johnny Utah exits right, out of the frame, at the end of the film, he does so for a life (style) of moments out of time, *outside* of the dominant order.

Second, *Point Break* offers up an arguably transgressive, textured and contradictory representation of its male/female characters and masculinity/femininity in turn. While strong, athletic male 'star' bodies populate the screen, and engage in heroic, mythical encounters, the homoerotic (homosexual) relationship that develops between Johnny Utah and Bodhi, and the centrality of androgynous, yet eroticised male (and female) bodies in the film, undermine traditional notions of gendered bodies and heterosexual, patriarchal encounters. In short, *Point Break* articulates an identity-in-crisis, and frames its representations through a queer aesthetic.

Contextually, the film appears at a particular juncture in American cinema where 'new man' images had begun to replace the 'hard bodies' found in so much of the 1980 action movies (Jeffords 1993: 197). Bigelow, who I would argue is clearly conscious of such hyper-masculine representations emanating from the Reagan-Republican 1980s, is one of the first directors to deliberately re-shape and re-imagine masculine identity in the early Hollywood filmwork of the 1990s (although, as I will argue shortly, the political films of the 1970s are also a key reference point for Bigelow).

Third, *Point Break* re-imagines and transcodes the visual and narrative conventions of the action film. The film is a breathless text of attractions, one that is so full of emotional intensity and physical ingenuity that I think it can be appropriated as a film that fits within Linda Williams' concept of what constitutes a 'body genre', or a film that revels in the showing of 'bodily excess' (Williams 2000: 219). Further, the film is a knowing, playful, and at times subversive staging of the action film. Bigelow is playing with film form, invigorating the process of spectatorship, and self-consciously referring us to her own authorship and the constructed nature of film representation. *Point Break* is a giddy work of art.

Cultures of Subversion

> The unique thing about surfing is that it kind of exists outside the system, the people that embody it are of their own mind set, they have their own language, dress code, conduct, behaviour and it's very primal, very tribal. I tried to use the surfing as a landscape that could offer a subversive mentality. (Bigelow in Salisbury 1991: 27)

Kathryn Bigelow (in an interview with Andrew Hultkrans (1995)) has defined her involvement with film-making as a desire/need to work with an art form that was accessible, and which could have a social consciousness. If we were to examine Bigelow's oeuvre so far we would see this commitment to both the popular and the political being played out across the body of her work. Bigelow takes mainstream popular film genres and invests them with a radical political ideology, or to use her words, 'subversive mentality' (see Steven Schnieder's essay on *Near Dark* in this reader for an example of how Bigelow can been read as a radical film-maker). Nowhere is this accessibility and consciousness more apparent than in *Point Break*.

The film constructs, in different ways, two opposing cultures, lifestyles or life systems. On one side of the political spectrum there is the life system of the dominant order, crystallised through the organisational culture of the FBI – surveillance and technology-based, individualist, regulation bound, trapped by a relentless bureaucratic time piece – a life system dead from the neck down. On the other, there is the life system of a subordinate order, crystallised through the resistant, bohemian counter-culture of the surfing tribe – 'naturally' formed, community based, free to roam with room to roam, outside of manufactured time – dead, perhaps, from the neck up.

Bigelow satirises and parodies and undermines the systems of law and order, and while (masculine and individualist) elements of the counter culture are critiqued, its counter-hegemonic centre is finally valorised. *Point Break* is a film then in which the legitimation crisis of modern America are played out but to a final, liberating curtain call. In this sense Bigelow's *Point Break* is also a return to or a conscious re-working of the type of political film made in Hollywood in the 1970s, when, according to Robin Wood (1986) 'the dominant ideology almost disintegrated'. In fact, as I shall shortly argue, *Point Break* seems to directly invert the fascistic ideology of *Dirty Harry* (Don Siegel, 1971).

Figure 4 *Point Break* 'establishes Utah's and Bodhi's relationship as a love affair through a series of looks.'

How does Bigelow parody and subvert the dominant order in *Point Break*? She does it through the construction of an apparent black and white binary opposition between the two life systems represented; through the character of Johnny Utah and his differing relationships with Bodhi, Pappas, Tyler and Hick; through the foregrounding of scientific, rationalist investigative and surveillance techniques; and through the different representations of time and space in the film. The opening title sequence incorporates many of these parodic and subversive elements, setting up mirrors and 'foreshadows' for the rest of the film. It is worth, then, spending some time examining this opening sequence.

The opening shots of the film are of the ocean, the surf, bathed in a duskish orange glow, a warm, tranquil, expansive set of images. The 'transparently' rendered title of the film *Point Break* and the two star names emerge from both sides of the frame to cross over one another, and to merge. A series of shots of an idealised, balletic surfer (Bodhi) gliding on the waves follows, as white water literally pours over the camera. At this moment in time the cinematography, choreography and iconography could place the viewer in a surfing documentary, *Crystal Voyager* (David Elfick, 1972) perhaps, or as knowing witnesses to a self-referential homage to *The Big Wednesday* (John Milius, 1978) (Bigelow's own echo of an intertextual relay here?). From the beginning of *Point Break* there is constant movement of the camera, of what is in front of the camera, and merging or transition; the titles flow into one another, the two star names dissolve into one another, and the water flows over the camera. But, also, here on the surf, in slo-mo, the action seems to be happening outside of time, or regardless of time. Absolute spatial and existential freedom is being connoted here.

The sequence continues with what we imagine is parallel action: the camera cuts to a rain soaked Keanu Reeves/Johnny Utah chewing gum, flexing muscle, loading rifle. The blue light, gray drizzle, and the low key lighting of the land-based *mise-en-scène* stands in stark contrast to the limitless feel of the warm ocean and Bodhi's oceanic ballet that has just gone before. A whistle blows: a stop watch is clicked, and Utah, up against time, all tight black vest and honed muscle, has to kill all the baddies and save all the goodies on a simulated target practice range. There are strong echoes here then to other Rookie Cop Movies: to the opening of *Blue Steel*, where Meg (Jamie Lee Curtis) has to respond to an armed domestic dispute, and to *Silence of the Lambs* (Jonathan Demme, 1991), where Clarice (Jodie Foster) is up against the physical and psychological demands of the assault course. However, while a certain degree of failure marks the opening to these *women-centred* cop movies, Utah is here, at least on the surface level, supremely successful, and supremely masculine.

Utah, at this introductory point in the film, does seem to be very like the muscle-bound, silent, retro males of 1980s 'boy's own' action films, or even of (a modernised) Harry Callaghan. Utah's jaw line and body mass is übermensch in appearance. He is seemingly an unambiguous lethal male killing machine taking out the assassins with absolute, deadly accuracy ('100 per cent Utah', the trainer shouts out at the end of the practice). Nothing, it would seem, will get in the way of his already encoded masculine, manifest destiny.

As the title sequence continues, Utah hurls himself, in real time, between barrels and barriers, and lets off his automatic weapon with sure-fire accuracy. Through a series of cross cuts a ('non') relationship is set up between the mysterious surfer Bodhi (shot in slo-mo), the cardboard cut-outs of assassins and children that Utah is supposedly accurately unloading his gun into, and with Utah himself, who because of the way the sequence is edited together appears to be also intermittently shooting at Bodhi (the sound of gunfire actually bleeds into the shots of Bodhi surfing). The implications of this linking together of two parallel actions are significant.

In terms of the surfer/cop opposition, Bodhi surfs 'out of time', and out of place, in a shimmering and romantic endless ocean. The slow motion shooting accentuates the sensation that time is being slowed, unwound, set free. Similarly the blue hum of the synth score romanticises the action. By contrast, Utah is caught chasing 'real' time (he has to beat the clock, to be the best, to prove his skill as an FBI agent). He is regulated and primed by the law and order system. His 'action' movements (diving behind fences, aiming straight, firing rapidly) are lethal and programmed or machine-like. The sound of the heavy rain and the gunshots are aural, staccato punctuations that shatter the romance of the music that carries across the two planes of action. Movement and space mark both protagonists out as different, as 'other', but it is Bodhi's surfing dance, on an endless ocean, that is positioned positively – natural beauty to Utah's machine beast.

Bodhi, then, is immediately being imagined as a free agent, an outsider, a part of a romanticised counter-culture diaspora. Utah, by contrast, is an FBI agent, a servant of the state, programmed to violently oppose the freedoms being imagined on the surf. When he metaphorically shoots Bodhi in this scene, through the trickery of the editing, the repressive state apparatus (Althusser 1971) that he works for comes into ominous play, and the contest that eventually emerges between them in the film (a contest that is actually between dominant and subordinate culture), is portentously foreshadowed. However, there is another way to read Utah's performance, and the juxtapositions formed with Bodhi, in this opening sequence.

First, Utah's representation, characterisation and performance can be read as a clearly signalled, knowing, excessive parody of the hyper-masculine male. It is the constructed nature of his masculinity that is actually being foregrounded in this scene. Not only does Reeve's boyish star image undercut the representation but also his performance (and the way Bigelow shoots him) clearly establishes the performance as a simulacrum, as cardboard as the people he shoots on the range. This is a (highly camp) masculine performance, and one that Utah/Reeves will throw off or reject by the closure of the film (the performance then actually foregrounds and problematises gender in much the same way as *Blue Steel* and *The Silence of the Lambs*).

Second, the juxtapositions are actually tied to the transitional nature of the whole opening title sequence. Just as Keanu Reeves and Patrick Swayze's names pass through one another; and just as water and movement mark out much of the *mise-en-scène* and cinematography, Utah (whose masculine performance has been set up as 'performance') is being mirrored against Bodhi as if they are indeed fluid figures, or doppelgangers, destined to meet, destined to change, destined (as I will argue presently) to love one another. The representational meaning of these two characters, to appropriate Stuart Hall (1997: 23) is deliberately *never finally fixed* in this opening sequence.

The beginning of *Point Break* is the beginning of a classical narrative, with Proppian characteristics, but nonetheless one that is saturated in radical, politicised representations. What is really being foreshadowed in this opening sequence is that masculinity is a constructed identity (a masquerade), that the dominant culture is relentlessly time-bound, regulated, conformist and brutal, and that the subordinate culture will (through the heralded transformation of Utah) win out. This subversion of the dominant order continues through the film: time, technology and the body are the markers for what is a dystopian critique (on a par with *Strange Days*) of the conformist, repressive culture of modern America, transposed onto the FBI.

The first time that Special Agent Johnny Utah enters the L.A. headquarters of the FBI, a continuous hand-held, Steadicam shot follows him around and through the building for 1 minute 53 seconds of screen time. The movement and kinetic energy of the single shot is meant to capture the hive-like activity of these headquarters, and provides a continuum with the opening scene, or at least Utah's sequence (it is also a visual trademark for Bigelow). Computer terminals, faxes, video surveillance banks, security devices, telephones and headsets, a maze of corridors, and drones of agents rushing past Utah (and the camera) give the impression of supreme efficiency, and of an army of technologically advanced (white) people dedicated to the law and order ethic, and the relentless imperatives of time. The FBI chief Hick personifies this zeal as he grills Utah about his eating habits, diet and fitness regimes. The FBI is a lean, efficient, conformist/functionalist organisation dedicated to snuffing out crime, negating deviancy. But it is also clearly a place, therefore, without individual identity, without human embodiment, all technology and no soul. (Pappas is, of course, by contrast, all gut intuition, a rebel maverick who serves as both Hick's binary opposite, and Utah's mentor. There are traces of Harry Callaghan in his anti-authority rhetoric, but this is precisely why he, and Utah, finally, do not fit in.)

The white corridors and white reflecting surfaces – and faces, there is a white hegemony in place in these corridors of power – that permeate the colour, the feel of this entire 113-second shot bleach out difference (everything is the same) and help suggest the impersonal nature of the institution itself. Similarly, the cinematic headrush of the shot here suggests not real freedom of movement but the over-determination of time in the FBI (and in the modern world – time is money, time is measured in milliseconds, everything has to be done in a hurry). Time is commodified not just for efficiency purposes but because time, so Hick's/the FBI's paranoia runs, is itself under threat from counter-culture and subversive forces which, if given the chance, would let time run free and blow the time pieces of capitalism asunder.

One of the main reasons why the FBI/Pappas have so far been unable to catch the 'Ex-Presidents' bank-robbing surfers is because they measure time in terms of the seasons passing, and so they exist outside of the routinised conception of time held by the FBI. As Pappas says later on in the film 'they go with the money', or in effect they go in and out of time. One of the clear dislocations that Utah experiences throughout the film is the rigid time restraints of the FBI and the out-of-time surfing lifestyle (after making love to Tyler for the first time, on the beach, where time seems to have stood still, he is late for his own bust). In this hysterical attempt, then, to regulate and control time, it is as if one second of time is lost then the battle for ideas, values and attitudes will be lost. (In the 'real' world one only has to think about American foreign policy in the 1980s for an indicator of how crucial it was to act decisively, quickly, 'yesterday', against the imagined 'red threat' of Russian expansion.)

If time is a priority here then so is also the regulation and control of the human body. In this regulatory discourse the human body mirrors the body of the FBI institution: it has to be lean, efficient, healthy, primed and programmed. As Utah mocks near the end of this scene, 'Sir, I even take the skin off my chicken.' The problem here, of course, is this training of the body limits its freedoms and possibilities, it produces an effective but docile body. As Michel Foucault observes:

> The human body was entering a machinery of power that explores it, breaks it down and rearranges it. A 'political anatomy', which was also a 'mechanics of power' was being born; it defined how one may have a hold over others' bodies, not only so that they do what one wishes, but so that they may operate as one wishes, with the techniques, the speed and the efficiency that one determines. Thus, discipline produces subjected and practiced bodies, 'docile' bodies. (1979: 138)

For Utah this lack of real embodiment is a living death. Even in this early encounter we get a sense that Utah wants to be more than a working drone, that he will want to do more with his body. Utah, on one level, is the classic narrative agent maverick, the individualist in a bureaucratic, white-collar, rule bound institution that will do everything to curb his initiatives (again, clear echoes of Harry Callaghan). However, what is different, or progressive, about *Point Break* is the subversive type of embodiment that is offered up as a positive alternative to this institutional body politic.

The surfing lifestyle that is imagined in the film is, especially early on, heavily romanticised. Catching waves is articulated as a transcendental, life-changing activity (as one of the unnamed characters in the film prophetically says to Utah, 'surfing is a source, it will change your life, I swear to God'). When the Ex-Presidents surf, and when Bodhi catches his first real tube, the ecstasy, the pleasure is over-determining. The sounds, the frenzy, and the way Bigelow captures this type of carnival, suggest bodies beside themselves with pleasure. In these particular surfing sequences Utah's body is opened up and moves into liminal spaces. Blood rushes through his veins, muscle and bone are tested, his inner spirit comes into existential being, on the wild, free and expansive surf. As Bigelow herself has said:

> Thrill-seeking adrenaline addicts have always fascinated me. The idea seems to be that its not until you risk your humanness that you feel most human. Not

until you risk all awareness do you gain awareness. It's about peak experience. (in Hultkrans 1995: 84)

Once Utah has experienced his body in this way (once he has tasted bohemia) then his return to the dominant order is severely threatened. The narrative trajectory of *Point Break* charts his transformation from a 'young, dumb, and full of come' All-American, to a counter-culture slacker. So, while in one clear sense he is like Harry Callaghan in that he despises the system he works for, on another he inverts the representation. Harry Callaghan despises the diaspora scum who roam the streets of a disintegrating America. He throws his badge away at the end of the film both because 'bureaucracy' and the political institutions have feminised law and order, but also because, in fact as a direct consequence, it had failed to keep this scum under control (i.e. within routinised time).

By contrast, at the end of *Point Break*, when Utah lets Bodhi go 'free' (freedom to surf, to die, to transcend) and he throws his badge into the ocean, it is because he has rejected law and order, or the dominant order, because it has no place, no space, no time for the ideas, values and attitudes of the subordinate culture. Utah has become a man out of time, and he has to walk free. But Utah is also different to Callaghan in another sense: while Callaghan is all heterosexual man and rages against queens, faggots, pimps, drug pushers and pros, Utah is a new man, simultaneously hard and soft bodied, and consequently liminally androgynous.

One final key motif in the film, in terms of its political radicalism, is the attention to investigative technology and surveillance. Scientists, labs, police checks, security cameras, stake outs, undercover cops populate the narrative. The FBI are wired and equipped and investigate crime through these technological devices. So, not only is time relentlessly regulated here, not only are bodies subject to and objects of regulation and training here, but the social world in its entirety is kept under close scrutiny *from here* – an all-encompassing modern version of the fascistic panopticon.

However, the critique of technology and surveillance is more specific. At the beginning of the film Utah is as 'wired' as the next agent, and initially investigates through these surveillance techniques. While these devices are in part successful in searching out who and where criminals are they also ultimately fail to correctly locate and arrest these 'criminals'. It is only when Utah and Pappas go with their gut feelings and intuition, finally, that they can close in on the 'Ex-Presidents'. The message here is similar to that of *Strange Days*. Where technology over determines human action, and where mechanical surveillance replaces human interaction, humanity and social difference are threatened. In *Point Break*, technology is set against nature; machine against man; regulation against freedom; bureaucracy against individuality; and docility against blood, tissue and bone.

> In order to have self-realisation, its weaning, but it's also searching for androgyny. Man and woman become fused. (Bigelow in Hultkrans 1995: 84)

Susan Jeffords (1993) has argued that 1991 was a pivotal year for locating a fundamental change in the way masculinity was to be subsequently represented and understood in American popular film. For Jeffords, the hyper-masculine men who had populated so much of the 1980s Hollywood output were either being transformed into 'new men' (she cites Schwarzenegger's appearance in *Kindergarten Cop* (Ivan Reitman, 1990) the year before as leading this evolution), or were being replaced by 'new men' (new stars) who were 'sensitive, generous, caring, and, perhaps, most importantly, capable of change' (1993: 197). Body size was slimmed down and hyper-masculinity itself critiqued (articulated as part of the problem) within the diegesis of a range of key films. Jeffords suggests that the diegetic (and cultural) rationale for this transformation was the 'new man's' need to return to the family that he had been ostracised from or had neglected or never really had in the disenfranchising 1980s.

According to Jeffords the representation of the body in the revisionist action film is encoded to fail in some way, 'through wounds, disease or programming' (1993: 201), and this failing masculine body is an attempt to show how constructed, manufactured, the hyper-masculine body had actually been – an exterior shell hiding, denying the real caring man underneath (*RoboCop* (Paul Verhoeven, 1987) is cited as an example). While Jeffords recognises that this change is in some way positive, she argues the actual meta-representation always leaves the new man, generally a white man, in a continued state of privilege and power. Although Jeffords does not mention *Point Break*, it seems to me to be a key film for locating this revisionist 'moment' in the transcoding of the action body and gender identity formation. The trajectory of *Point Break* seems to follow a number of Jefford's key conceptions for this type of revisionist film.

First, Reeves seems a perfect choice for the role of one of the 'new man' found in *Point Break*. His threshold boy/man persona, his not being quite there, produces a fractured, polysemic masculine/feminine quality perfect for allowing him to reject his 'lone ranger' marriage to the job for his heterosexual love affair with Tyler – an apparent particularised return to family values.

Second, Utah's body in the film repeatedly fails him at crucial moments. His weakened knee (an injury sustained from playing top level American football) gives way during his pursuit of Bodhi, and, again with Bodhi, when he crashes to the ground during the head-to-head, 'just in time' parachute jump. During his first attempt to surf he nearly drowns (his body unable to balance on the board, or master the wave), and in the doomed drug bust the criminal is seconds away from pressing his head into the whirring blades of a lawnmower (only to be blown away by Utah's mentor-partner, Pappas). Similarly, when up against four surfers in a fistfight he is losing badly until Bodhi arrives to rescue him.

Rescue is in fact another characteristic related to Utah's failing masculinity. When he nearly drowns on the surf, it is Tyler who pulls him to safety; when he is arrested for aiding and abetting the Ex-Presidents, Pappas removes the handcuffs; and in the two 'action' sequences mentioned above, it is Pappas and Bodhi who come to his rescue. When Reeves first uses his gun and kills someone for real he is queasy with the thought of it, with the sight of blood (just like a woman?). Reeves is a new man, flawed like every man, vulnerable to attack, reliant on others (male and female) to keep him from harm, and keenly aware of the meaning and sanctity of human life.

Finally, the film seems to be partly driven by a new man-inspired, heterosexual love affair between Utah and Tyler. In classical narrative style, they meet dramatically, fall in and out of love, he needs metaphorical rescuing: she needs literal rescuing, and it is their love for each other, finally, which acts as the dynamo behind the film's closure. By the end of the film she is his central reason for being and he will do anything to rescue her from the clutches of the Ex-Presidents, and in particular his anti-hero nemesis, Bodhi.

However, there is also a much more transgressive articulation of gender in the film. Not only is *Point Break* particularly knowing and self-conscious about the power relations of gender identity but the film sets out to undermine and blur 'classical' masculine/feminine oppositions, and heterosexual, defined 'man-to-man' relationships. It is clearly, then, a Bigelow picture, concerned with androgyny, the body, and gender dislocation. As I have previously argued, almost from the very first moments of *Point Break*, masculinity and male-to-male relationships are foregrounded and problematised.

Keanu Reeve's beefed-up Utah is a knowing parody of the hyper-masculine ace cop, and the parallel edits that connect him with/to Bodhi foreshadows the intense relationship that the two men will have in the film. The beginning of *Point Break* is the beginning of a love story, between two (androgynous) men, without a woman in sight. However, I think the subversion of the masculine male originates with the casting of its two male stars, Reeves and Swayze (and in terms of feminine identity this is also the case with the casting of Lori Petty whose androgynous, dark looks allow her to mirror Reeves in several key moments in the film).

Textually, Reeves brings with him the 'youth culture' baggage and the in-between masculinity/manhood of *Bill and Ted's Excellent Adventure* (Stephen Herek, 1989). This star-signified intertextual relay allows him to shift more easily from cop to surfer dude in the film but also, conversely, undermines the ace cop persona from the off (it is difficult to take Utah/Reeves seriously with the echoes of *Bill and Ted's Excellent Adventure* in the air). But the nature of Reeves' star image is also transitional or fluid in form: he has the same sort of textual and extra-textual vulnerability as Tom Cruise: and their boyish, beautiful good looks, and Reeve's wide eyes suggest a softness, a femininity to their star sign. (Reeves, like Cruise, is a pin-up star for legions of gay men.) Rose Dublin (Reeves' Community Theater Director) describes Reeves as, 'Goofy and sort of macho and sort of uncertain. On the threshold of growing up but not quite there' (Anon. 1995: 52).

As indicated earlier, there is something far more transgressive about Utah, about 'masculinity' and his relationship with Tyler and Bodhi. It is my argument that he is actually as much woman as man, his sexual identity is blurred, because he is a mixture of lots of competing impulses and identities, never quite there. Similarly, the same can/must be said for both Tyler's femininity and Bodhi's masculinity/sexuality. It is in the love triangle that exists between the three of these central figures where the drama of the transgression is played out.

Utah and Tyler's first meeting is the rescue scene in which she plucks him out of the ocean and saves him from near certain death. Not only does this place her in the role of an active narrative agent (a woman doing a man's job) but the way this is shot, and the star casting of Petty and Reeves together, actually blur their gender differences. One cannot initially tell who is doing the rescuing (man or woman) from the underwater shots (in fact it almost looks like there are two Utahs under water). When the two do emerge from the water their similar size, hair length, hair colour, and even their facial bone structures conjures up a doubling, a shared androgyny between them.

This sense of sameness and simultaneity is reproduced elsewhere in the film, most noticeably in a post-coital lovemaking scene. Utah and Tyler are filmed from above. They are stretched out and naked apart from the sheets that cover their lower torsos. Utah is looking up, facing the camera, deep in thought. Tyler is face down, asleep, her arms neatly slotted into the spaces in and around Utah. There is great stillness to the shot: it has the feeling of a photograph, or of a painting (Klimt comes to mind in the way the two figures are entwined or interconnected in the most intimate way). But what is most striking about the shot is their likeness to each other, a likeness encoded through their masculine and feminine traits – they are both muscular, short-haired, but they are both pretty, 'soft', fragile, echoes then also of the two stars' biographies.

If this is a post-coital, lovemaking image then there also has to be confusion around the heterosexuality of the act, an ambiguity around the genders involved in the lovemaking (love making that we never get to see in the film – a homosexual taboo too far?). Tyler and Utah lie side by side in this shot but it is Tyler who is face down, arms and legs resting beside but also on top of Utah, in what, therefore, seems to be the more active post-coital position. If we were able to fill in the ellipses here, and add in the lovemaking scene, Tyler's active position here would indicate that she would be on top during the sex and fucking Utah – like a man – from the patriarchal inscripted missionary position (when Utah prints out a police profile for Tyler she has a record sheet as long as your arm, for speed violations and indecency – phallically charged deviant acts usually assigned to male anti-heroes or antagonists). If I return to Jefford's idea of 'failing' masculinity, Utah's failing masculinity in this context is not simply to do with a liberal but still distinctly patriarchal 'new man' revisionism but with a more progressive and culturally transgressive gender confusion and gender blurring.

It is worth noting that in this shot and in fact throughout the film there is a corresponding passive but ambiguous 'to-be-looked-at-ness' (Mulvey 2000: 487) that frames both Tyler and Utah (and also, as I will presently argue, Bodhi). During the film we get a number of Utah point-of-view shots looking at Tyler, at one point in the film while she is undressing, and master shots of the camera gazing at Bodhi (his face, eyes, body). If there is ambiguity or blurring around both Utah's and Tyler's gender then there is ambiguity at the way he looks at her in the film – a man-woman looking at a woman-man.

In short I think in *Point Break* Bigelow deliberately interrupts the 'normal' looking codes for men and women that are generally found in popular film. Islam in fact locates the to 'be-looked-at-ness' of Utah as one of the reasons the film can be defended from feminist objections, 'the film is not simply recoupable as a 'boys' own adventure', since the status of the active agents as the locus of identification is tempered by their position as the locus of desire' (1995: 116). However, the androgyny, the to-be-looked-at-ness serves another more transgressive service – it allows for a more daring reading of what I think of as the real love affair in the movie, that between Utah and Bodhi.

Bodhi (the name taken from the Buddhist Bodhi tree, to mean 'enlightenment') is another androgynous figure. Patrick Swayze brings to the role the same star-gender ambiguity as Reeves and Petty. In *Dirty Dancing*, for example, he is both a masculine love machine and balletic dancer, both hard (bodied) and soft (tissued, curvy). This ambiguity is embedded in Bodhi's character – a surfer in tune with nature, with water (where water symbolises the feminine side) yet also hard-bodied, sculpted, individualist, ruthless, and into masculine encoded 'extreme sports'. However, it is his physical appearance that roots this or his particular man-woman fusion. Muscle-bound Bodhi has long, flowing, 'bouncy' hair, embroidered clothes, and a softness to his voice. While the beard he dons displaces some of this feminine form because neither Utah nor Tyler can offer a more physically feminine opposition, he looks the most 'glamorous' in the film. These three 'versions' of androgyny lay the film open to a queer reading. At the centre of *Point Break* is a love triangle of sorts.

Tyler's 'first love' we are told was Bodhi. Utah's first love is (supposedly) Tyler. But the real love affair in the movie is between Utah and Bodhi, on a number of direct and implied levels.

First, if we were to transpose the same sort of active/passive reading we gave for Tyler's and Utah's love affair and lovemaking onto Tyler's largely extra-diegetic relationship with Bodhi, the active/passive dichotomy remains (in fact it might be argued that Bodhi takes the part of the loose, flirtatious woman, and Tyler the part of the no-nonsense male). Second, if we continue the analogy that Tyler and Utah are similarly androgynous figures, then Bodhi's relationship with, and his desire for, Utah springs from this (it becomes a mirror for, or an inverted replay of his relationship with Tyler). If Utah is very like Tyler then his desire for Bodhi comes from this: he sees Bodhi through her/his eyes. There is a key scene early on in the film where the three of them meet for the first time. Initially, Bodhi is surfing beautifully and Tyler catches Utah standing, gazing admiringly. A two-shot then catches both of them standing, staring-gazing admiringly. Tyler says enigmatically, simply, 'That's Bodhi.' *That* is love at first sight – his, theirs, hers.

Third, Utah uses and deceives Tyler very much in the classical style of the duplicitous woman (his androgyny calling up the echoes of a femme fatale?) to get to Bodhi. All throughout *Point Break* Utah seems to be undercover, in disguise, with his true identity masked in some way. The film starts with Reeves-Utah's parody of the beefcake cop; Utah literally goes undercover and delivers the 'I have lost my parents, too' routine to Tyler, to secure her trust; and Utah pretends that his love interest is Tyler when it really is Bodhi.

Fourth, the film directly establishes Utah's and Bodhi's relationship as a love affair through a series of looks (including the first 'look of love' mentioned above) and through a series of heightened moments, where their bodies are entwined together or are in close proximity in sequences of body frenzies. There are numerous occasions in the film when the two exchange glances, and while these are sometimes framed in the man-to-man 'sizing you up' trope there is one key scene when the exchange of glances is literally *penetrating*.

At the end of the (Steadicam-filmed) bank robbing chase sequence between Utah and Bodhi, Utah falls to the floor clutching his injury-prone knee (failing masculinity, again). As Bodhi continues his escape, Utah directly points a gun at him but cannot shoot (queasy with the thought of all that blood being spilt?) or will not shoot – adrift, as he clearly is, in an exchange of glances. Utah stares at the masked Bodhi – all that is visible of his face is his eyes. Bodhi returns the stare, and in a close up shot that lasts for four or five seconds, he literally seems to be looking into Utah, beneath his series of disguises. Through a series of shot-reverse-shots the intensity and drama that is going on between the eyes is established. They are outing one another. Utah cannot shoot

Bodhi and Bodhi knows this: they are in love with each other, and all that was once encoded as male melts into air.

Genre Frenzy

> Playing with genre is both conscious and unconscious, because I don't think you're ever immune to genre ... But I have a desire to subvert and redefine. Genre exists for that purpose. (Bigelow in Salisbury 1991: 27)

Point Break subverts and redefines the action film in two clear ways. First, its kinetic, pulsating and thrill-a-minute set of encounters is very like the type of 'body genre' that Williams (2000: 208) has reserved for the horror, melodrama and pornography genres. It is my contention that spectators are meant to ride (feel) *Point Break* (and in fact, much of the action genre) in much the same way as the protagonists in the film. Second, this over-determination of excess and spectacle, and the textures of irony and parody that ripple through the film, point to the subversion of the genre and to a self-referential critique of the Hollywood machine that produces it. Bigelow's knowing, telling radical signature is all over the film. (It is also my contention that *Point Break* has to be read at the level of self-reflexivity.)

Williams (2000) defines the body genre film as that which catches the human body at its most heightened and aroused state. Visually, the body is either crippled with fear (horror), sexually aroused (porn), or racked with grief (melodrama). Aurally, body genre films are filled with the sounds of screams, sobs or the moans and groans of sexual pleasure. In terms of the type of body that is caught and heard in this way, Williams argues that it is the female body that is generally subject to the torture, fear, pleasure, pain, and mourning – for example, she argues that it is women that spectators see writhe and moan with pleasure (and pain) in porn movies. In terms of spectatorship, Williams argues that there is 'an almost involuntary mimicry of the emotion or sensation of the body on the screen' (2000: 210). Or, in other words, there is a close correlation between the aroused or frightened or grief stricken bodies on screen with the bodies of the spectators in the cinema.

Point Break is a film that is full of bodies beside themselves, caught 'in the grip of intense sensation or emotion' (Williams 2000: 210). In the five or six action and 'extreme sports' sequences that run throughout the film we see bodies shudder with excitement and roar out with sheer, almost orgiastic pleasure. In fact, the extreme sports sequences could be argued to be a displaced type of sex or masturbation – this is how (we see) the 'men' in the film reach the height of sexual excitement and fulfilment. The bodies in *Point Break* are caught twisting and turning on a wave, or free-falling from an aeroplane, or running, diving, chasing one another in bank-robbing scenes. Visually, because of the constant camera movement, these moving, often ecstatic bodies are shot in constantly moving cinematic spaces (through fast edits, Steadicam shots and so on). The energy and drive and 'rush' that is generated from such spatial and body simultaneity, coupled with the sounds of these bodies enjoying themselves, place the film, at least textually, in the body genre category.

However, extra-textually, in terms of spectatorship, *Point Break* works as being part of the body genre. The spatial and body simultaneity is the most kinetic, charged type of cinema (outside of 3-D) that you can watch. Rather than sitting back and putting your feet up, as Richard Dyer (1994) has suggested the normal male viewing mode is for the action film, *Point Break* compels you to sit forward and put your feet down, in mock escape mode. And, to use a slightly reductive audience profile, just as some men get erections while watching porn films; and just as some men and women sob along to melodrama; and just as some teenagers hide their faces and scream along to horror films, some spectators will break out in sweat to the daredevil sequences and feats of courage found in the rollercoaster ride of a movie that is *Point Break*.

The body (hands, palms) may not only sweat but register other physiological changes: the heart may beat quicker – may almost jump in the mouth – in an almost exact copy of the protagonists' own transformation in the film, or in direct response to the breathtaking action sequences and stunts that take place; the stomach may knot or go queasy; and in the skydiving sequences a fear of height or vertigo may take place. In short, there is – to appropriate a Williams term – a body frenzy at the core of *Point Break*, and potentially in the viewing position offered and taken up by spectators to the film.

However, a key difference does emerge between Williams' conception of the body genre and *Point Break*. The rapturous bodies found in *Point Break* are not female bodies, but hybrid male-female (to-be-looked-at) bodies – particularly the bodies of Utah and Bodhi (which, in the sky diving scenes, for example, are entwined). I have already established the reasons for this: gender is blurred and sexuality re-imagined in the film and it is, finally, through the ecstatic bodies of the two principal protagonists where this is most firmly rooted. Utah and Bodhi share numerous intimate body moments that are framed by both a desiring point of view and an impassioned and glorious intimacy – *Point Break* then is not that far from a (gay) porn movie after all.

In terms of spectatorship there are further, clear consequences for reading the film in this way. If these are male-female bodies engaged in this body frenzy and if the film does produce bodily reactions in its spectators, then the identification and cinematic immersion is one that is itself hybrid, fluid, potentially queer, and in terms of normal viewing positions, possibly liberating.

The conventions of the action movie are subverted from the off in *Point Break*, in ways that I have already examined at length in this essay: *Point Break*'s radical political message, its gender blurring and 'outing' scenario clearly re-work the ideological underpinnings of the genre, and the set of (heterosexual, patriarchal) expectations associated with the genre. But there is much more to the way the genre is played with here.

Narratively, the film seems to be awash with self-reflexive irony and parody, so much so that *Point Break* seems to be also engaged in a critical dialogue about the action film, and, less directly, the cinema machine. For example, the knowing casting of Reeves, Swayze and Petty sets up the androgyny, bohemia, and counter-culture aesthetics that does so much to foster this sense of an inverted intertextual relay – this extends to the casting of Gary Busey, a nod to his role in the surfers' surf movie, *The Big Wednesday*, to the 'dude' language taken from *Bill and Ted's* and inserted into the early surf encounters involving Reeves, and to the appropriation of *Dirty Harry*. Similarly, throughout *Point Break* there are a set of clichéd authority figures, who deliver a range of clichéd lines but because of the manner of the performances and the style of the delivery of these lines the cliché is deliberate or conscious. *Point Break*, then, is both knowing and critical of the action film, and through this offers another way into the film for spectators.

These sets of intertextual references allow or call for the film to be read as a mediation on film itself. So not only is *Point Break* a body genre film, producing bodily responses from its spectators, but it works in terms of its own 'cultural capital', asking spectators to make the references and decode the critical dialogue embedded. This is also what makes *Point Break* such a radical text: it appeals to the both the critical mind and the liberated body – spectators are asked to think and feel their way through the movie.

However, the real self-reflexivity in the film comes from the action and spectacle sequences, or at least, in terms of a defining moment, from the skydiving sequences onwards. *Point Break* seems to have the makings of a natural, 'classical' ending after Tyler has been kidnapped and Utah goes in pursuit. Bigelow could have staged this final contest on the beach, or in Bodhi's house, with guns and explosions, possibly. What we get, however, is a shoot-out, two extended skydiving sequences and, finally, a fist fight on an Australian beach (with Tyler nowhere to be seen, the ending a mirror of the opening sequence but with Utah and Bodhi now literally side-by-side). These sequences take up another forty minutes of screen time.

While these scenes are dramatic in their own right, and allow the Utah/Bodhi relationship to develop, they also feel like a deliberate form of cinematic excess – an extra turn on the rollercoaster that you weren't expecting, or hadn't paid for. There is delay in the ending, to the resolution, but not really because of any sophisticated plot deviation but because of the decision to show a number of each more stunning action (body) sequences. Given the knowing and self-reflexive nature of the film, this cinema of excess seems in one sense to be a direct reference to the cinema machine that demands these high-concept production trends and the blockbuster aesthetics. Bigelow gives us the extra forty minutes at the expense of the studio system and its (sometimes) reductive template for the action film.

In another sense, though, the self-reflexivity refers us back to the hands, eyes of the director – a knowing presence throughout the film – layering the film with its irony, relays and radical political agenda, filling the screen with this visual and aural excess. These are there to be experienced (rode) but they are also there to be read, like Bigelow herself. Bigelow is constantly on the edge of *Point Break*, of all the films she makes, and of the cinema machine itself. An outsider on the inside, subverting film form, offering up a radical political agenda, and blurring, destabilising gender.

CHAPTER SEVEN

Cherchez la femme: The Weight of Water and the Search for Bigelow in 'a Bigelow film'

Deborah Jermyn

> Artistically speaking, *The Weight of Water*, Kathryn Bigelow's first
> film in five years, is her richest, most ambitious and personal work to
> date: commercially, however, it may be her most problematic. (Levy
> 2000: 32)

In these opening comments following the film's Toronto Film Festival screening,
Emanuel Levy's *Variety* review quickly got to the crux of the matter regarding the
difficult reception met by *The Weight of Water* (2000). While numerous reviews
acknowledged the film's impressive cinematography and the complexity and intricacy
of the film, revolving around a dual narrative structure of two stories removed from
one another by over a century, they were also rather baffled by what to make of
it. Though it clearly was not the kind of action-packed adventure audiences have
come to expect from Bigelow, was it quite art-house? In fact, the dilemma that Levy
points to above could be said to be true of most of Bigelow's work which, with the
exception perhaps of *Point Break* (1991), has never sat comfortably in the presumed
division between mainstream ('*commercial*') and art-house ('*personal*') cinema. In

this essay I want to explore the sentiments behind the disappointment expressed by fans and reviewers to date about the film, and to examine *The Weight of Water* in terms of it being 'a Bigelow film'. More broadly, I want to pursue why the very notion of a Bigelow film has become an increasingly troubling one. In my analysis, the search for 'a Bigelow film' suggests the fraught place of authorship in post-classical cinema while *The Weight of Water*, I argue, can itself can be understood as a film which is very much about writing, creativity and storytelling in various guises, exploring the tenuous and multivalent nature of authorship. What follows then is not so much an attempt to 'rescue' a maligned film as it is an attempt to suggest ways of reading it that would add to our understanding and conceptualisation of Bigelow's work. To do this I make textual analyses of both *The Weight of Water* and of reviews and profiles of Bigelow, exploring the dialogue around Bigelow as a form of cultural 'evidence' that is bound up in the reception of her films. What I unravel is a kind of parallel between the tensions that have permeated the popular and critical construction of Bigelow's persona and authorship, and the tensions that have permeated the reception of *The Weight of Water*. Both of them, it would seem, are an uncomfortable mix of apparently conflicting impulses that defy easy definition.

Bigelow's refusal to be easily compartmentalised, to be labelled a 'female director' or to work within the confines of a given genre, has often made the concept of a Bigelow film a slippery one and thus a frustrating entity for film critics and academics to deal with. As a director in a post-classical cinema, whose work has eclectically moved between genres and has pivoted around a collaborative approach to art and film, Bigelow does not always fit neatly into an auteurist concept of film-making. Though film studies debates over some four decades have amply demonstrated the shortcomings of auteur theory, one should not underestimate its enduring resonance in film culture, nor its significance for feminist film analysis and women film-makers, as a peculiarly phallocentric account of, and approach to, film history. A cursory look at Bigelow's reviews recurrently reveals the frustration of critics trying to place each new release within the pedigree of what came before it, indicating the auteurist interest in her. For example, Yvonne Tasker has noted 'the critical bemusement' that met *Point Break*, received as 'not *noir*ish enough, ironic or feminist enough, not a worthy successor to the cult status of *Near Dark* or what was widely felt to be the latent feminism of *Blue Steel*' (Tasker 1999: 15). It was evaluated then, as problematic in terms of its refusal to 'fit in' with the concerns and style of its predecessors. However cine-structuralist accounts of authorship (though not unproblematic) suggest that it is 'not a coherent message or world-view' that is at stake in auteur analysis. Authorship in this light is not about re-making the same film throughout one's career, but rather about 'preoccupations' which can be identified even through the 'disparate elements' which figure (Wollen 1972: 146).

Despite some of the apparent contradictions in Bigelow's work then, and though mindful of the provisos about the difficulties of her claim to auteur status, an expedition through her oeuvre undeniably returns to a series of qualities that lend themselves to identification as her 'signature'. One recurrently notes, for example, a pronounced and self-conscious fascination with the cinematic gaze and genre distinctions; a curiosity with sub or counter-cultures; and a complex engagement with the dynamics of gender, putting the essences of 'masculinity' and 'femininity' under the spotlight while exploring an intriguing vision of 'androgyny' in which such essences begin to blur. The term 'auteur' has in fact been sprinkled fairly liberally in accounts of Bigelow's work, suggesting a status that in many ways seems self-evident. As early as 1994 Anna Powell was ready to declare unequivocally that Bigelow has 'produced a sufficiently substantial body of work to have now reached auteur status' (1994: 136). For a director moving into Hollywood in particular she has been able to 'maintain impressive control over her movies' (Svitil 1997: 88) for example, ensuring that, in her own words, 'Everything I've done I've had input into the writing' (Bigelow in Smith 1995: 42, reprinted in this collection). Nevertheless her auteur status still seems under negotiation, partly due to the perplexity of her oeuvre, partly due to her collaborative relationships and partly due to the Hollywood mythologising that has arisen around her, a mythologising which has conferred 'star' status upon her.

As one of the few high-profile female directors in contemporary Hollywood cinema, and one who has distinguished herself in the action genre at that, she has become a curiosity, an oddity and object of fascination, whom critics and academics struggle to place. Even leaving her 'decidedly un-ladylike' (Svitil 1997: 88) penchant for stylised violence aside for a moment, Bigelow is a journalist's dream, that most beguiling of creatures in the writing of Hollywood mythos; a woman who can claim both brains and beauty. *Film Review* is one of many commentators to have observed in some shape or form that 'Tall, dark and beautiful, Kathryn Bigelow looks more like a Hollywood actress than a film director' (Rynning 1996: 22). (Indeed, while not endorsing the larger presumptions behind this comment, the physical resemblance between Bigelow and Liz Hurley/Catherine McCormack in *The Weight of Water* is striking on occasion; one wonders at times to what extent Bigelow is conscious of this and may in fact be playing with her own iconography through her portrayal of them). This conjunction, this meeting of femininity with authority – terms which are still apparently held to be mutually exclusive – is constructed as entirely surprising, novel and incongruous. One is reminded in fact of the scene from *Blue Steel* where the camera pans up Megan's body while she does up the buttons of her starched, blue police shirt to unexpectedly reveal a lacy bra beneath. This construction of Bigelow, as almost some kind of femme fatale behind the camera, is ubiquitous in interviews and borders on hyperbole in some instances. For example Ian Nathan from *Empire*, tongue in cheek or not, seemed quite overwhelmed when he met her in the flesh to discuss *Strange Days* (1995). He sets the scene thus:

> Tall, svelte, sculptured like a Greek statue (with arms), the 43-year-old Kathryn Bigelow is a remarkable mix of beauty and drive, the ice-maiden intellectual who makes a habit of casting Hollywood convention asunder. (Nathan 1996: 78)

One wonders if John Ford was ever greeted in such a fashion by *Cahiers*.

Such airy musings on a director's mien do however very much echo the discourses which circulated around another female 'pioneer' in (Classical) Hollywood, Dorothy Arzner, who was similarly dogged by press and magazine commentators 'who felt compelled to comment on her appearance' (Mayne 1994: 152). Judith Mayne has provided a fascinating account of the promotion and publicity which sought to place and define Arzner in relation to popular standards of femininity during the three decades of her career, a struggle made all the more perplexing by Arzner's overtly 'butch' persona. Though Bigelow adheres far more readily to conventional standards of female beauty – where Bigelow 'looks like a Hollywood actress' Arzner very much 'contradicted established notions of what a woman should look like' (Mayne, 1994: 152) – in both cases one finds the discourses surrounding them marked by a quest to grasp and harness how 'feminine' qualities co-exist with their apparently 'masculine' traits, thereby rendering the latter qualities less threatening. This is one of numerous parallels one might draw between the construction of 'Arzner' and 'Bigelow' as women directors in Hollywood, one which would seem to indicate that the novelty and challenges wrought by such a conjunction (woman + director) are still negotiated and diffused in remarkably similar ways, some seven decades later.

In the critical and popular struggle around Bigelow and the 'conventions' she undoes, there are three particular inter-related discourses writ large in the battleground that seeks to define her. Firstly, interviews and reviews routinely try to find the woman in the text, scanning her films for evidence of a quintessentially female point-of-view and probing her feminist or non-feminist credentials, a process she has resisted. Secondly, the reception of her films recurrently ponders whether or not she amounts to an auteur, a status excitedly debated but often inherently presented as potentially compromised by the eclectic diversity of her oeuvre and her (often repeated) collaboration with key (and, crucially, male) colleagues, most notably James Cameron.

Finally, and linked to both of these issues, is the popularisation of Bigelow's misnomer as an 'action director'. While this label is obviously appropriate to a number of her films, such is its appealing novelty value when applied to a female director that it has stuck at the cost of all else. When a Bigelow film doesn't 'do' action then, it becomes not an example of a broader repertoire, but an uneasy departure that refuses to fit. In what follows then, I want to look at how each of the three themes outlined above has contributed to the elusiveness of a 'Bigelow film'. To do this I examine how each of these themes might particularly contribute to an understanding of *The Weight of Water*, both the film itself and its reception. References to its reception here draw largely on reviews garnered from festival and fan sites on the web since, for reasons that this essay begins to open up, at the time of writing the film had yet to receive a general release in the UK or US.

Firstly, some contextualisation. *The Weight of Water* is based on Anita Shreve's 1997 novel of the same name, based itself on a real life murder mystery. As Shreve's Author's Note explains, 'During the night of March 5, 1873, two women, Norwegian immigrants, were murdered on the Isles of Shoals, a group of islands ten miles off the New Hampshire coast. A third woman survived, hiding in a sea cave until dawn' (Shreve 1997: i). Shreve's story merges historical fact, including verbatim passages from the court transcript of The State of Maine v. Louis H. F. Wagner, with fictitious narrative. She explores the events leading up to the murders of Anethe and Karen Christensen and the testimonies of those involved, in an investigative thriller that is pursued in the present day by Jean, a photojournalist. Jean travels to the scene of the crime on Smuttynose Island with her husband Thomas, a celebrated poet, and their daughter Billie, on a magazine assignment about the murders. Sailing there on her brother-in law Rich's boat, who also brings his new girlfriend Adaline, what starts off as a pleasant enough adventure rapidly turns sour. As Jean becomes increasingly wrapped up in the testimony of Maren Hontvedt the cracks in her marriage, precipitated by the flirtation between Thomas and Adaline, begin to show. In the novel, the trip ends in tragedy when, distracted during a storm by their own crises, they fail to notice Billie falling overboard and the little girl drowns.

Shreve's book was inevitably going to be seen as an intriguing project and/or 'departure' for Bigelow for a number of reasons. Firstly, it is an adaptation of a novel and as such a first for Bigelow, who is a director with a history of co-scripting a number of her films (*The Loveless* (1982) with Monty Montgomery; *Near Dark* (1987) with Eric Red; *Blue Steel* (1990) also with Eric Red and taking an active role in the script for *Strange Days*). Secondly, its dual narrative, which travels between a contemporary and nineteenth-century setting, would entail Bigelow entering into the territory of historical drama. Thirdly, this dual narrative pivots around two women, allowing

Bigelow ample opportunity to return again to a contemplative exploration of a female point of view, a sensibility which won her so many plaudits in *Blue Steel*. Finally, other than the depiction of the murders and the storm, the story was never going to lend itself to 'action movie' territory. Rather, with its brooding, uneasy build-up of tensions and jealousies on the boat, its painful account of the breakdown of a modern marriage; its reconstruction of the daily chores, hardships and isolation of life for an immigrant fisherman's wife on the Isles of Shoals, this would be a character study. In other words it wouldn't sit easily with the expectations which follow a Hollywood 'action director par excellence' (Keane 1997: 23).

It was perhaps no real surprise, then, when reviews started to appear before any general release which at best floundered over what to make of the film, and at worst dismissed it. Though it may be rather premature in the film's circulation to write it off as critically maligned, its early reception indicated just that. When the film premiered at the Toronto International Film Festival, Scott Feschuk's (2000) review in the *National Post* bemoaned its 'protracted build-up'; meanwhile Vassar Girl's (2000) review was contradictory, on the one hand calling it 'a fast-paced story' but on the other noting 'a lack of action'. Other reviews situated it as constituting another shift in Bigelow's work. At upcomingmovies.com Greg Schmidt (2000) noted that 'Bigelow appears to be making a drastic (as drastic as the first film in 5 years can be) change in mood' while on the IMDb user comments board 'pipsorcille' (2001) wrote: 'Well, this is a very different film for her in part because it's made completely differently than any of her other previous films.' For *Variety*, the film marked a tangible and welcome turning point in Bigelow's career, suggesting, rather patronisingly it might be argued, that 'the good news' from herein is 'Bigelow has given up on her attempt to belong to Hollywood's boys' club by making viscerally exciting, ultra-violent actioneers' (Levy 2000: 32). Elsewhere Kirk Honeycutt's review of 'this weighty drama' following the Toronto premiere nicely summarised the problems that *The Weight of Water* could expect to meet. While noting that it 'might be the tonic adult movie goers seek' following a year bereft of 'intellectually and visually stimulating movies' he observed nevertheless that, '*Weight*, which is seeking distribution, will be no easy sell. Even in art house terms it's hard to label the film; it's a psychological drama with a murder mystery attached, but the murders took place 127 years ago' (Honeycutt 2000).

It is this difficulty in ascribing 'labels' to her work that is, paradoxically, characteristic of 'a Bigelow film'. Like *The Loveless* in particular, *The Weight of Water* is a film which clearly demonstrates Bigelow's art background, her first film since then to so obviously undermine some of the expectations of the Hollywood mainstream. While on the one hand it boasts stars like Sean Penn and Elizabeth Hurley and ultimately delivers two predominantly resolved narratives, the dual narrative sometimes disrupts the conventions of filmic time and space. For example, in one sequence we cut between Maren hiding on the rocks and Jean, mirroring her movements, clambering over them with her camera. Later, as the film reaches its climax, Jean sinks in the sea during the storm only to encounter Anethe and Maren floating eerily beneath the surface. Indeed it was precisely Bigelow's rendering of the dual narrative that often came in for criticism; Manohla Dargis' review of the film at the London Film Festival bemoans Bigelow's 'inability to connect the stories persuasively' (Dargis 2000: 20) while Levy noted that 'cineastes will praise this boldly innovative structure, but mainstream viewers may feel distanced by the excessively fractured story' (2000: 32). In these ways the film occupies an uneasy space on the border between art cinema and Hollywood, a quality which is characteristic of Bigelow but which the reviews above reveal perplexes those expecting the latter. In Lizzie Francke's words Bigelow is 'a disquieting presence … difficult to accommodate' (1995: 6) and as such her work provides a mass of apparent contradictions that resist easy mapping. So how might one better understand the responses to *The Weight of Water* in terms of the expectations that circulate around Bigelow; as 'action director', as 'woman director', as 'auteur'?

Cherchez l'action

As Yvonne Tasker has noted, 'Bigelow's status as *the* female action director in Hollywood brings her a strange visibility' (1999: 13). In effect though, the 'action director' moniker has been as big a hindrance as a help. While her action credentials have made her one of just a handful of contemporary Hollywood women film-makers who can command any sizeable degree of recognition, they have also been responsible for a delimiting and restrictive sense of what her film-making amounts to. Thus when she does not deliver action it seems, as the reviews of *The Weight of Water* above suggest, she is somehow perceived to have got it wrong, to have misled the audience about what to expect from her films or even to have let them down.

The expectation attached to *The Weight of Water* was particularly pronounced given Bigelow's five-year absence from film-making since *Strange Days*. It seems all the more pertinent, then, that she returned not with a blockbuster but with a quietly observed drama. Responses on the IMDb user comments board for the film reflect this sense of unfulfilled anticipation. Fabio Pirovano (2001) writes, 'I waited with a particular attention for a next Bigelow's project after the Great *Strange Days* … but I Thought Better!' [sic] whereas Palermo-3 (2001) notes with disappointment: 'My hope was that *The Weight of Water* would finally bring Kathryn Bigelow the recognition she deserves … And so it's with a certain dismay to find myself reporting that *Weight of Water* is a mess … It's hard to know what Bigelow was going for here.'

There seem to be two different but inter-linked discourses operating in the various responses indicated above, with commentators sometimes talking about *The Weight of Water* and sometimes talking about Bigelow more broadly; in fact, commentaries are not always expressing disappointment in *The Weight of Water* as a flawed film in and of itself but in its failure to be a 'Bigelow' (read 'action') film. Arguably this latter sensibility has often led to commentators neglecting the more understated accomplishments that one might find in the film; its intriguing interweaving of the two female protagonists from each narrative, the intricate and painful exchange of looks that accompany the narrative's crumbling relationships, its meditative play with point-of-view and voiceover. While the film does perhaps suffer from some clumsy plotting around Jean's uncovering of the murder mystery and an unrelenting air of gravity, there is still much here which makes it an intelligent and thoughtful piece.

What these reviews also arguably overlook is that despite its lack of 'action', *The Weight of Water* consolidates continuity across Bigelow's oeuvre for other reasons. If we recognise Bigelow as a director whose 'mastery' of *melodrama* is just as prevalent in and characteristic of her work as her mastery of *action*, the film sits rather more comfortably within her oeuvre. Indeed despite melodrama and action being genres which are oppositionally 'gendered', their mutual preoccupation with 'excess', in performance, aesthetics and narrative, suggests they nevertheless share much common ground. In this light, the generic space of melodrama is just as pertinent and germane a way into understanding Bigelow's films as action. Similarly, in his account of masculinity in John Woo's 'extremely violent' Hong Kong films, Julian Stringer (1997) suggests that a fuller understanding of them will be gained from seeing them as a fusion of two genres, where the gangster film meets with melodrama. In the rush to champion the novelty of a woman succeeding in a 'male' genre however, and no doubt not wishing to banish her to the predictable realms of the one genre where women have prevailed as writers, stars and audiences if not directors, the melodramatic concerns of her work have been rather more neglected. While Bigelow can indeed 'do' action, she has also demonstrated a penchant for contemplative and explosive explorations of the textures, tensions and turbulence of families, relationships and domestic spaces, themes which form the mainstay of melodrama. As a director who has attracted interest for the ways in which she straddles both mainstream and independent cinematic forms, the critical debates around melodrama form a fitting parallel to, and intriguing entry into, her work. While melodrama was once largely seen as a conservative form, seeming to lend support to the institutions of patriarchy and capitalism through narratives which could be read as underlining their sanctity, the critical re-appropriation of melodrama since the 1970s has amply demonstrated the complexity and contradictory nature of the form and its potential for politically charged debate. While melodrama might in some ways be said to celebrate the institution of the family, then, its depictions of tortured relationships within families simultaneously suggest its institution is deeply flawed. In Geoffrey Nowell Smith's words, melodrama 'cannot accommodate its problems, either in a real present or an ideal future, but lays them open in their shameless contradictoriness' (1987: 74).

These concerns have always been at the core of Bigelow's work, not so much an alternative to her action films as a component of them all, bringing with them melodrama's critical angle on capitalist and patriarchal institutions. We can find melodramatic traditions in the rotten, incestuous and repressive father-daughter relationship which haunts *The Loveless*, leading Telena into a destructive Sirkian mission which sometimes echoes the familial corruption of the Hadleys in *Written on the Wind* (Douglas Sirk, 1956); the 'perverse' nomadic family at the centre of *Near Dark* transposes the radical but enticing lifestyle of vampires onto the less than engaging nuclear family unit; the domestic violence endured by Megan Turner's mother in *Blue Steel* lies at the core of Megan's decision to become a cop and finally to use her own legitimised power to overturn her father's; the loaded looks and passionate exchanges between Johnny Utah and Bodhi in *Point Break*'s homoerotically charged central relationship speak pure melodramatic excess; while Lenny's obsessive refusal to relinquish his failed love affair in *Strange Days* is as integral to his character and the film's drama as his SQUID dealing.

When Bigelow's work is looked at in this light, *The Weight of Water* isn't such a surprise or aberration at all. Rather its sibling rivalries, its exploration of a marriage in crisis and the unspoken jealousies and resentments that haunt Jean and Thomas, like the intense, incestuous and ultimately destructive bond between Evan and Maren, all sit firmly within the melodramatic interests that have underlined Bigelow's films and what Powell has called her predilection for 'family horror discourses' (1994: 138). Families, then, recurrently hold secrets and tragedies in Bigelow's films, with women often bearing the brunt of their destructiveness; beyond the domestic violence suffered by Megan Turner's mother in *Blue Steel*, Telena's mother in *The Loveless* took her own life rather than endure her brutish husband any longer and Telena ultimately chooses the same fate rather than withstand further sexual abuse from him; the Colton family's oddly absent mother in *Near Dark* is never spoken of and instead the family appear to co-opt (and thereby constrain) Mae into her role; while Mace in *Strange Days* is a struggling but determined single mother. Despite the prevalence of these melodramatic themes in Bigelow's work and their concurrent exploration of familial and social convention, reviews of her films have tended to neglect them for the more frenetic and spectacular pleasures of her action. This is not to suggest we discard the concept of Bigelow as an action director; rather that a more expansive account of her work will result when we temper it with recognition of the melodrama that pervades it.

Cherchez la feministe

Next to 'action director', the moniker of 'woman director' looms large. Few critics have been able to resist probing whether having a female director at the helm makes Bigelow's films 'different' to those of her male peers. On the one hand this has involved repeated entreaties for her to give an account of her position on feminism and her experiences of being a woman director in Hollywood. On the other it has meant that her films are recurrently examined in terms of a search for the tell-tale signs of female 'difference'. Indeed some of the earliest and most influential work in feminist film studies sought to do exactly this, reclaiming the work of film-makers like Dorothy Arzner by highlighting how their female authorship lent aspects of their work a different sensibility, even a subversive impulse, when compared to the larger mass of Hollywood films made by men (Johnston 1975). But the search for feminism in Bigelow's films has been hampered somewhat by her reluctance to engage with this line of enquiry. Again this seems much like Arzner's apparent resistance 'to explicit feminist interpretations of her work', something that Mayne attributes to Arzner being understandably 'a bit suspicious about the sudden attention' in her that, in Arzner's words, the growth of 'women's lib stuff' had given rise to (Mayne 1994: 191). For example, when asked in interview if there is a feminine way of expressing violence Bigelow replied that:

> I don't think there's a feminine eye or a feminine voice. You have two eyes, and you can look in three dimensions and in a full range of colour. So can everybody. What about a woman's background would make that vision different? (Bigelow in Bahiana 1992: 34)

This resistance to being 'feminised' and her penchant for violence and action have made Bigelow a tricky subject for feminist analysis, not always easily recouped by feminist readings. It suggests she does not want to limit her appeal or be 'ghettoised', yet ironically this is to some extent what the characterisation of her as an 'action director' has achieved. Unlike other women directors of her generation such as Susan Seidelman and Sondra Locke who have spoken openly about their experiences of, and the challenges of being, women working in Hollywood, Bigelow has recurrently thwarted this line of questioning (Hillier 1992). She has steadfastly resisted being drawn on whether she herself, as a woman, consciously seeks to take on 'traditionally masculine subject matter', implicitly refusing the feminist mantle such a quest would entail and instead playing down gender difference, asking:

> What is a masculine subject, what is a feminine subject? Those notions tend to ghettoise men and women, and ghettoisation is unproductive. I don't mean to gloss over it, but there's nothing more counterproductive than the notion of gender-specific film-making. (Bigelow in Fuller 1995: 44)

While *Blue Steel*, then, was celebrated for its articulation of a resilient and active heroine who takes on the 'masculine' position of cop on the New York streets, *Point Break* became its kind of negative inverse. Though Needeya Islam has persuasively argued that the 'exaggerated to-be-looked at-ness' surrounding its male leads means *Point Break* is not merely regressive (1995: 116), a theme developed by Sean Redmond's essay in this collection, it was nevertheless difficult not to conclude that Bigelow had virtually ignored the development of any female characters and left them firmly on the sidelines to revel in the male angst and taut bodies of a surfer movie. It was *Strange Days* that proved particularly perplexing for feminist analysis however, becoming the bête noire of Bigelow's oeuvre. While containing the infinitely independent and resourceful Mace (Angela Bassett) it was lambasted by critics for its depiction of the rape and murder of a prostitute. The controversy over this notorious sequence focused on its particularly vicarious enactment of the rape, which through the futuristic device of SQUID technology (virtual-reality-like head gear which records individual's experiences on discs which others can later 'jack' in to), meant that other characters, and by extension the audience, get to re-play and experience the attack as both victim and attacker.

Unsurprisingly this sequence was widely accused of a perverse and exploitative voyeurism, 'a terrifying, first-person participation which has upset sensibilities enough to cause walkouts in many screenings' (Nathan 1996: 78) and which was met in some instances by 'boos and much talk of a need for censorship' (Rynning 1996: 22). The fact that it was directed by a woman added an interesting subtext into the mix. Was this sequence somehow worse, was it all the more objectionable, *because* it was directed by a woman? As Todd McCarthy wrote in *Variety*, 'Ironically for a film directed by a woman, more than a few women will have problems with these scenes' (McCarthy in Francke 1995: 8). As she stood apparently accused of being 'anti-women' (Rynning 1996: 22), was this Bigelow's betrayal of all those commentators who had claimed her as one of the precious few female voices in Hollywood? Of course to condemn this sequence on the grounds of its voyeurism neglects the other kinds of readings it lends itself to. Is it precisely in its perplexing excess, its deliberated manipulation of the spectator, forcing them into an uncomfortable position whereby they experience a rape from the dual-gendered position of both male rapist and female victim, which makes it a daring, confrontational and politically charged representation of male sexual violence? Or is this kind of 'progressive' reading merely a wilful justification of the fact that a woman directed it and therefore it must surely amount to 'more' than mere exploitation and voyeurism?

The Weight of Water provides some similarly challenging material in the search for a female perspective in Bigelow's work. On the one hand it is arguably the most female-centred film she has made. Firstly, of course, it is an adaptation of a novel by a woman, with Shreve being an author who enjoys a large and loyal female readership. The lead protagonist in each of its two narratives is female and a female point of view is inscribed through a number of devices; two sets of female voiceovers, the use of Jean's camera to give her point of view (freeze-framing the action and rendering it black and white, though this device dwindles as the film progresses) and the curious mirroring and intermingling of the two women's stories across time and space. In each of their stories we find an empathetic insight into the tensions and struggles of their daily lives. The drudgery and isolation of Maren's life as a fisherman's wife is a vivid depiction of the harsh existence that would have met many immigrant women in this period, her days an endless repetition of cooking, cleaning and passionless sex with a husband she barely speaks with. When her siblings come to live with them, repressive social and familial etiquette means she must endure the exacting company of her sister and stifle her affection for her brother, the barren landscape of Smuttynose Island all the while forming a perfect setting on which to play out the bleakness of her life. Over a hundred years later, Jean is married to a Pulitzer Prize-winning poet but is a successful photographer in her own right. Though able to enjoy a comfortable lifestyle, her relationships are similarly fraught with anxiety and repressed emotion, as she witnesses the growing flirtation between her husband and Adaline. Through Jean, Bigelow taps into the preoccupations thought to characterise women at the start of the twenty-first century, enjoying the independence of their own careers but still carrying the traditional responsibilities of wives and mothers and still often in careers which enjoy less recognition or rewards than their partner's. And all the while of course, they must struggle to live up to the ubiquitous and exacting standards of female beauty and sexuality which pervade popular culture, amply demonstrated by Hurley as Adaline, who does so much, whether consciously or otherwise, to knock Jean's self-esteem.

But though this may indeed be 'a contemporary women's picture' it is also as Dargis notes 'one with a toxic heart' (2000: 20). While our female protagonists are compelling they are unrelentingly dour and introspective, not women who warrant sympathy easily, if at all. Furthermore, both women are tainted by their complicity in the suffering of other women, even before the revelation that Maren was responsible for the hideous deaths of Karen and Anethe. The women are linked then not simply through Jean's reading of Maren's story but through their shared culpability in vengeance on a rival and the brooding resentment that each bears the women around them. When Anethe wants to help Maren with her chores in the house, Maren coolly allows her to go to read to their lodger Lewis Wagner in his room, fully conscious both of Anethe's naïveté and vulnerability and Wagner's predatory desires. The attack on Anethe that follows, then, can be seen at best as one that Maren might have averted, at worst as one that she manipulated into taking place. Jean's parallel moment to this, though perhaps more ambiguous, comes during the storm, when she sees Adaline sea-sick and confused on the deck of the boat without a life-jacket. As she calls out to her to put on a vest, she appears to pause when she notices that the sail is going to swing out and hit Adaline. She grips the railing herself but fails to shout out a warning to Adaline who is knocked overboard, perhaps not prompting the accident then, but certainly choosing in that split second not to try to avert it. The fact that this scene is intercut with Maren's attack on her sisters – one woman literally a killer but both 'guilty' – seems motivated by more than attention to frenetic editing, underlining the murderous impulse they share.

In these ways the film explores the terrifying possibilities of female rage and the horror of the female murderer, in narratives which would frustrate audiences hoping to find more obviously sympathetic female characters from a female director. Once again, Bigelow refuses characterisation which would sit happily within the 'feminist'/'female' director mantle recurrently thrust upon her. Maren in particular is a potent example of an 'unnatural' woman; barren, incestuous, 'bisexual' and finally murderous, she typifies archaic and ultimately reactionary fears of woman as duplicitous and monstrous. Both women, who have hitherto been conspicuous for their self-restraint in the face of trying circumstances, now speak of being overcome by a frenzy or momentary madness that is so encompassing, it physically overwhelms them. On the boat, Jean says in voiceover, 'The anger is so swift and so piercing. An attack of all the senses. Like a sudden bite on the hand', while Maren observes that no-one can predict 'how he will react when rage overtakes the body and the mind'. Perhaps what is most terrifying here, then, is the implicit suggestion that anyone (any woman?) in their position might snap and do the same. These are complex, thought-provoking, perplexing women, testimony to Bigelow's characterisation skills and rich pickings for feminist analysis, but as likely to appal as to please.

Arguably though the sequence, and indeed performance, which will prove most troublesome to a feminist analysis centres on the glorious Hurley. The scene where she lies prostrate on the deck of the boat, topless, sucking on and rubbing an ice-cube over her overheating body, while Thomas and Jean watch both her and each other watching, is as sensational in its way as the *Strange Days* rape scene. It certainly warranted more attention than any other scene in reviews. Feschuk's (2000) *National Post* review (titled 'Hurley's naked ambition') for example, opens by drawing immediate attention to it: 'Let it be stated plainly that there is much to celebrate in any film in which a topless Liz Hurley delicately runs across her exposed rack an ice cube'. Like the *Strange Days* rape scene, it is a scene that proves to be similarly awkward and problematic in terms of locating the signs of 'difference' that a female director might bring to the text. But equally the same kind of polysemy applies again. Is this another moment of outrageous objectification all too typical of Hollywood – or is its lingering excess and laboured exchange of looks a kind of self-conscious and critical commentary on cinematic voyeurism from Bigelow?

The character of Adaline arguably loses the nuances and ambiguity she holds in the novel where one is never entirely certain just how much of her interest in Thomas' work is mere flirtation, just how aware she is of the tensions she produces in those around her and indeed, just how reliable a narrator Jean is in interpreting Adaline's affecting presence for us. Instead, in the film she becomes rather more unequivocally a teasing siren, and though her knowledge of poetry remains a characteristic which implies greater depth, this is still a notable shift (with implications which I return to below in terms of reading the film's authorship). Hurley in the role is a brave, provocative and ultimately winning casting decision, however. Given the baggage that goes with her 'actress-cum-model-cum-famous girlfriend' persona, some reviews jumped predictably at the opportunity to berate her performance, a performance that is arguably entirely capable in fact. But beyond this Hurley carries intriguing cultural connotations that endow the role with another level of meaning. She is a woman whose face and figure have become almost iconic, known to millions worldwide as the (former) face of Estée Lauder's advertising, gracing film premieres and *Hello* magazine a thousand times over as the impeccably styled companion to Hugh Grant and sundry millionaires. Despite her early acting credentials as a Dennis Potter protégée, Hurley's stardom was borne of the paparazzi and the still image. There is something fascinating then in watching her perform on film; not captured, frozen, inanimate in a photograph as she is best known to us, but moving and speaking. That Bigelow uses Hurley, then, to play Adaline – the focal point in the exchange of looks which bespeak the tensions on the boat – adds another element of reflexivity to the role and underlines the sense that Bigelow may be using it to explore the objectifying power of the cinematic gaze again.

Ultimately, tempting as it may be to look for 'the woman in the text' in Bigelow's films the evidence remains in many ways equivocal. This is partly due to the seemingly contradictory sympathies in Bigelow's oeuvre, partly due to her unwillingness to engage with such readings, but also partly because the quest to locate a 'female/ feminine' specificity per se is doomed until it is able to contend with the diversity encompassed by these terms. Certainly to expect some kind of simple correlation between women directors and 'positive' female characterisation or politics is in itself arguably a reductive process which risks underestimating the vast array of individual and institutional influences brought to bear in the film-making process, and in Hollywood in particular. Furthermore any desire for 'positive' female characterisation, be it in women film-makers' work or elsewhere, must first engage with the subjective and mutable notion of a 'positive image' as an indistinct concept 'which has plagued the feminist movement from its inception' (Waldman 1990: 16). Rather than pursuing the search for something in her films we can label a female sensibility (which arguably itself risks being reductive and essentialist, a perspective which may account for Bigelow's reluctance to discuss her work as a 'woman film-maker'), we should perhaps welcome the fact that, here at least, Bigelow is endowing female characters with the kind of complexity and contradictions that we take for granted in their male counterparts.

Cherchez l'auteur

It is partly Bigelow's recurrent play with gender and genre distinctions, then, that has enabled an auteurist claim on her. The dialogue this has produced about her is worth looking at more closely since the rise to auteur status inevitably involves attention to more than the auteur's films. If authorship is about more than an oeuvre, if it also in some ways about popularising a 'personality' with a particular extra-filmic history and persona, Bigelow still fits the bill. Beyond her place in post-classical Hollywood history as arguably the first prominent female director of action movies, she is also known as an intellectual, an artist trained at the Whitney Museum and Columbia film school, endowing interest in her action films with a level of gravity not always evident in the genre but fundamental to auteur status. While maintaining her independent bent, she is also firmly enmeshed in Hollywood A-list society (or at least the hearsay surrounding it) by virtue of the fact that she was formerly married to Hollywood giant, *Titanic* (1997) director James Cameron. This is a fact which bridges personal/ professional interest in her, still emerging with predictable regularity in interviews and profiles despite their divorce in 1991. It also brings with it a visibility which seems to sit uncomfortably with her somewhat reserved demeanour in interviews and her personal reluctance to engage with questions about her status as a 'woman director', since it is an observation which very often carries the sneaking implication that her position in Hollywood has been enhanced by her association with Cameron.

Similarly again, Dorothy Arzner had to counter claims that she won her first directing contract when her early mentor James Cruze asked Paramount officials to give her a chance – both women then have had to contend with speculation about their careers being aided and 'shaped by male authority figures' (Mayne 1994: 34). The Bigelow-Cameron relationship, in addition to the commentary on her 'Hollywood actress' looks and controversy about her 'un-ladylike' film-making, has meant that Bigelow has come to be constructed as a kind of 'star' in her own right (see also Lane 2000: 103), a fascinating combination of personal and professional intrigues which warrant public speculation and make her a far more visible entity than many of her peers.

In fact the association with Cameron has proved tricky for Bigelow's auteur status. On the one hand it raises the issue of film's status as a 'collaborative' art, which has of course always been a thorny one for auteur theory. But beyond 'collaboration' their relationship brings a further and even more highly charged inflection to bear on Bigelow's claim to authorship through the gender dynamics it implies. Since their marriage in 1989 Cameron has gone on to become one of the most powerful men in Hollywood and it is all too easy to assume that Bigelow has stood to gain from this, since at the very least he was executive producer on *Point Break* and producer, screenplay writer and an (uncredited) editor on *Strange Days*. Indeed Will Brooker's essay in this collection shows the ease with which on-line commentators in the pages on the Internet Movie Database recurrently refer to *Strange Days* as 'a Cameron film' while Christina Lane's essay refers to it as a 'doubly authored text'. Elsewhere, Lane has written frankly about Bigelow's response to a manuscript she had written about Bigelow, which commented on her relationship to Cameron. Lane admits her manuscript had 'inherently granted Cameron more authority in their collaboration' by virtue of the fact that it contained the observation, 'Married to Cameron at one time, Bigelow's ability to push her projects through certainly relied somewhat on him.' Bigelow gave this suggestion short shrift, replying that she had suggested Largo Entertainment bring Cameron in as executive producer on *Point Break*, and commenting:

> For some reason, it would appear that whenever analysts (whether they be journalist or academics) study the career of men and women in the entertainment business, they assume that any collaborative effort between a man and a woman, somehow is more beneficial to the woman than the man. (Bigelow in Lane 2000: 102)

Furthermore, the implication that Cameron aided Bigelow's career neglects the fact that the film he was most prominently involved in, *Strange Days*, was the film that won her the most critical disapproval. It would be intriguing by comparison to examine how often accounts of Cameron's career credit elements of his success to *his* relationships with female collaborators, numbering among them not just Bigelow but also producer Gale Ann Hurd. Lane notes that any discussion of a single author in regard to Bigelow and Cameron is particularly complicated by their relationship, 'because they share similar visual and narrative styles, with an emphasis on special effects and physical violence' (Lane 2000: 103). In the same vein, Tasker has noted that for Bigelow 'as with Cameron, concept and image come first' (1999: 14). But this entanglement of authorship is surely then a reciprocal one, problematising the auteur status of *both* directors with Bigelow feeding into Cameron's style just as he is believed to have contributed to hers.

In fact Bigelow has recurrently collaborated with a number of men in her films, co-writing and co-directing *The Loveless* with Monty Montgomery, co-writing *Near Dark* and *Blue Steel* with Eric Red, while Jay Cocks worked on the script for both *Strange Days* and the thwarted *Company of Angels* project, and Howard E. Smith edited/co-edited *Near Dark*, *Point Break*, *Strange Days* and *The Weight of Water*. Interestingly, in these collaborations where the men are of course much less celebrated and powerful than Cameron and where Bigelow, if anyone, has prominence, her working relationships with these figures have not invited interest. Bigelow's male mentors and inspirations are undoubtedly numerous. For example it was Oliver Stone who 'helped get *Blue Steel* made. Without his involvement it would never have been made' while at film school it was Peter Wollen who 'was great. He's illuminating. Until I met him I was just looking at light reflected on a screen' (Bigelow in Hamburg 1989: 168). Meanwhile she lists her favoured directors as 'George Miller, Sam Peckinpah, Martin Scorsese, (James) Cameron, Walter Hill' (Bigelow in Bahiana 1992: 34). With an acknowledged pedigree like this, Bigelow's reluctance to engage in a discussion of gender and Hollywood seems to turn a wilful blind eye to a state of affairs she is inextricably bound up in. What all these relationships surely point to more than anything however, is the extent to which Hollywood is still a male dominated industry. Rather than indulge in speculation about the nature of particular male-female collaborative relationships in Hollywood, we should perhaps note that these will inevitably predominate among female careers as long as women in Hollywood, and powerful women in particular, are still such a relative rarity.

The Weight of Water throws up more intriguing questions about Bigelow's auteur status and indeed seems to consciously play at many levels with the notion of authorship, and female authorship in particular. As noted above, the film makes a number of changes to Shreve's novel and it is tempting to attribute these to Bigelow's authorial vision. Without production knowledge however this is speculative and, furthermore, Shreve herself is credited as co-writer of the screenplay. Crucial changes though result from the decision to cut the role of Thomas and Jean's daughter,

Billie, the impact of which is felt in various ways. Much of Jean's warmth is lost in the absence of her very loving relationship with her child and so too is some of the ambiguity and intrigue around Adaline and her intentions, since in the novel she also enjoys an affectionate relationship with Billie and is revealed to be a mother herself, who has relinquished her child to her former partner.

Finally, the absence of Billie means that the film has a very different conclusion to the novel, when it is not Billie who drowns but Thomas, in the act of saving Adaline. Rather like Bodhi riding his final wave at the end of *Point Break*, this elevates Thomas to the status of tragic hero, finally fulfilling a death-wish mission to leave behind a world where he will never quite 'fit'. In this way the film version of Thomas ultimately amounts to more than the rather woeful image of a 'used-up' poet who was once great but now drinks too much; his noble death recasts this image into a Byronic romantic portrait of the self-destructive poet as auteur. This vision of flawed but ultimately redeemed masculinity seems familiar from Bigelow not just in terms of Bodhi but in terms of *Strange Days*' Lenny, whose misery after all is nobly drawn from unrequited love. Yet the film also casts doubts on the concept of the auteur; Thomas admits he took one of his best lines ('I stole "poignant flesh"') from Rich who can't remember saying it, his recurrent reciting of other poets points to the interactive or reciprocal nature of all arts, while his half-hearted claim to be William Burroughs when recognised by a young fan almost suggests that the canon of great male writers is interchangeable. As an actor who was once known for his 'bad-boy' persona but who has more recently been recognised for moving into directing, gaining a reputation for producing intriguing rather than commercially successful work, the casting of Sean Penn in this role also adds a certain degree of reflexivity to the notion of Thomas as auteur. Finally it is Jean, along with the deceased Linda, who provided the muse which led to his most productive period of creativity. Still, both Thomas and Jean are situated as 'auteurs'; the novel and film make concrete the link between Thomas' poetry and Jean's photography in the anecdote about their first meeting where Thomas told her, 'We're both trying to stop time'. This is a metaphor that one might equally extend both to Shreve as novelist and Bigelow as director, but also one that Thomas later laughingly dismisses as a chat-up line and 'pretentious shit'.

There are in fact multiple and self-conscious levels of authorship imbuing the text(s), a layering which demonstrates authorship's tenuous nature. One might list these variously as including Shreve's novel, Maren's hand-written testimony, the translation of that testimony, Jean's reading of that transcript, Jean's photographic rendering of that story, Jean's own narration, the adaptation of Shreve's novel to screenplay, Bigelow's rendering of that screenplay to film and our own reading of the novel/film. Roland Barthes of course would have it that 'the death of the author' comes with 'the birth of the reader' (Barthes 1968: 213). Indeed Maren's authorship of her own story is actually rejected; her murder confession, undermined further by the 'false' flashback which shows Wagner committing the murders, is suppressed in the film by the authorities who file it away on the grounds that women are 'not always to be believed', while in the novel it is simply mislaid and forgotten till Jean rediscovers it in the archives a century later. In the novel particularly, the possibility of a single 'author' or perspective is further undermined by our doubts about Jean's reliability as a narrator, as one wonders if she is reading too much into the tensions around her and whether Thomas or Adaline's telling of events would amount to two other very different stories. These questions about the viability of self-contained authorship also extend beyond the text(s) to the extra-diegetic world in a sense; while Shreve is undoubtedly 'the author' of the novel her story is drawn in part from real-life events and incorporates verbatim court testimonies. Finally, then, though the film can certainly be seen as 'a Bigelow film' in some respects, particularly pertaining to its use of melodrama and cinematography, and though Bigelow herself has described it as 'a very personal piece for me' (her message read at the 2000 London Film Festival screening), it simultaneously points again at numerous levels to the fraught nature of authorship.

Waiting for Bigelow

In the brief account here of some of the themes and controversies that have characterised Bigelow's career, I have argued that *The Weight of Water* is not so much a radical departure as another idiosyncratic choice in a career which has been marked by such choices. Directing *The Weight of Water* seems a move that was characteristically motivated by Bigelow's own interests rather than the expectations of those around her. While its problematic reception suggests on the one hand there are genuine 'flaws' in the film which will continue to disappoint audiences, on the other, its reception seems also at least partly to be testament to the audience frustrations that Bigelow's career is destined to inspire. The interest in Bigelow as an action-director/woman-director/auteur both points to and has contributed to her significance in contemporary Hollywood. More broadly it points to some of the difficulties thrown up by these classifications and by attempts to make genre/gender/authorial distinctions in post-classical cinema. If, for a moment, we look at Bigelow's career itself as a 'story', *The Weight of Water* seems not so much a symbolic finalé of some sort, then, as another episode in a particularly beguiling and accomplished serial, one that promises 'to be continued' in characteristically original and perplexing fashion.

PART TWO: THE STRANGE GAZE OF KATHRYN BIGELOW

CHAPTER EIGHT

Strange Days: A Case History of Production and Distribution Practices in Hollywood

Romi Stepovich

Judging from its individual constituent parts alone, Kathryn Bigelow's *Strange Days* should have been a success. With a headlining actor in Ralph Fiennes, a block-buster writer/producer (James Cameron), a large budget from a major Hollywood studio, and with Bigelow being a known action director herself, 20th Century Fox should have had a success on its hands. Instead of a smash hit, however, this formula wound up a recipe for disaster.

In fact, many things were done correctly during the planning of the film; however, many more went wrong – even more so than the usual pitfalls that habitually occur in pre-production (and even pre-pre-production) of a movie. In many respects, pre-production is all about what can possibly go wrong – figuring out all feasible shooting scenarios, solving casting problems, location logistics and so on – while all the time attempting to save money. However, before any of this planning and attempted money-saving could take place, the financing of *Strange Days* was in jeopardy – the first in a series of events that would lead to ultimate financial box-office failure of the film.

From pre-production to distribution, I intend to analyse key elements in all phases of the history of financing and producing *Strange Days* to uncover what went wrong with Kathryn Bigelow's sixth film. Was Bigelow's vision usurped by the studio's desire for a certain type of genre film? Who was the intended target when the film was made, and subsequently, did the studio's marketing strategy result in decreased interest with the potential target audience? Additionally, in analysing the production and distribution practices pertaining to *Strange Days*, I call into question institutional practices within the studio system in the mid-1990s and ask whether, in these conditions, Bigelow's film could ever have been anything other than a box-office failure. To answer these questions, it is prudent to go back to the film's inception, which begins with writer/producer James Cameron.

Making The Deal

In early 1992, James Cameron, Larry Kasanoff – then head of Lightstorm – and Jeff Berg, Cameron's super-agent and former chairman of ICM, negotiated one of the largest film production deals in Hollywood history. This deal began with a plan developed by Cameron and Kasanoff that had the potential to develop Lightstorm into a global distribution firm. At the time, Cameron and Kasanoff are quoted as stating, '[T]he deal immediately achieves our objectives of turning Lightstorm into a self-contained motion picture/entertainment company' (Fox 1992: 1). The deal's principle was simple: to maintain control over a project, a producer needs to have the least possible interference from the studios. That said, to secure the financial backing for any production which hopes to have a decent release in the US and Canada, a producer must obtain, at the very least, domestic distribution for the project; the best way to accomplish this is through one of the major studios. Securing a strong domestic distribution deal was therefore critical for Lightstorm to succeed. A strong distributor with deep pockets always means one of the major Hollywood studios.

Although 20th Century Fox – the eventual winner – was the studio with which Cameron had the best relationship at the time, Fox was not the only studio in the running for the deal: Cameron's own Lightstorm Entertainment, Sony Pictures Entertainment and Warner Bros. were also in heated talks (Busch 1992: 1–6). One of the greatest incentives for Fox to be successful in securing the deal was Joe Roth's decision to add high-quality action pictures to their production slate. Roth, the head of 20th Century Fox at the time, called the deal a 'coup' for the studio and that he hoped for 'high-octane' films from Cameron: 'It's clear that he will make the kinds of films that we were familiar with in the past' (Fox 1992: 1). Roth went on to describe the deal as a 'partnership', which in his view distinguished it from the kinds of pacts that Fox and other studios have with other producers. Importantly and, as it became clear, ironically, the deal's structure was supposed to protect Fox from risks involved in science-fiction action pictures, where budgets can mushroom out of control (Lippman 1992: 1). The deal that Lightstorm stuck with Fox would ultimately set both up for two films, *True Lies* (1994) and *Strange Days*. The costs of both films would draw critical comment during production – particularly *True Lies*, whose budget acquired the adjective 'runaway' on more than one occasion. However, neither film would have been possible without the unique structuring of Lightstorm's deal with Fox.

James Cameron's precedent setting, exclusive five-year, twelve-picture financing and domestic distribution deal with 20th Century Fox was reportedly worth in excess of $500 million (Busch 1992: 1–6). Originally, Fox was supposed to put up a fixed percentage of the negative cost of each film up to a certain cap, estimated at around $15 million per film (Brennan & Aysough 1993: 1). During the early 1990s many independent production companies and producers had distribution deals with studios: Castle Rock with Columbia Pictures, Imagine Films with Universal Pictures and Morgan Creek and producer Arnon Milchan with Warner Bros. Even Steven Spielberg's Amblin Entertainment, located on the Universal Pictures lot, does not have an exclusive distribution deal with the studio (*Hook* (1991) was distributed by Tri-Star) (Fox 1992: 1). For a number of reasons Cameron's deal was special. First, the arrangement was unusual because typically, studios acquire worldwide distribution rights, cover the entire production bill and consequently own the pictures outright. Producers usually make their films for a lucrative fee and a possible profit participation (Lippman 1992: 1). At this point in film production history, there were two traditional ways of financing films: the first way described above, and a much more lucrative but risk-laden alternative, which saw the producer finding foreign distribution through presales – usually at film markets such as Cannes and the American Film Market better known as the AFM.

Financing any film through foreign presales is always risky, and James Cameron's decision to do this with rather large budget action films set a precedent, as previously mostly only small budget sexual thrillers and art house films were financed through presales; in fact, such presales were the main source of revenue for those two genres in the early 1990s. Ironically, Kasanoff is quoted as stating, 'We certainly will not be in the quirky, art-film business' (Fox 1992: 1). At this time it was not unheard of for an action film to be financed through foreign presales. However, an action film financed in this manner usually meant questionable production values and B actors, two areas not synonymous with the Cameron name. Questionable too are the foreign distribution deals that were struck with the medium-size foreign distribution firms. This could mean that Lightstorm most likely would be unlikely to get 'top dollar' for their product, and, in the event that they did manage to secure a lucrative deal, it would probably stretch the ability of the foreign distributors to pay up front. Yet despite these risks, Lightstorm sewed up foreign distribution deals with four medium-sized foreign distributors; UIP in Britain, Jugendfilm in Germany, Nippon Herald in Japan and Artisti Associati in Italy.

An Unlikely Pair: True Lies and Strange Days

To piece together the production history of a film, and to understand the factors that contributed to that film's problems, it is often not sufficient merely to go back to the beginning of production. In the case of *Strange Days*, one must go back to the film before the film, and look at what happened to the financing deal of *True Lies* to see what went wrong with *Strange Days*. Indeed, it is impossible to discuss the production history of *Strange Day*s in any meaningful way without also addressing the history of *True Lies*, as the Lightstorm financing deal tied them together.

As pre-production activities progressed on *True Lies*, financial troubles started brewing for Cameron and his project. The largest problem was the completion bond issue. Completion bonds are a standard part of a film's production budget. A completion bond is exactly what its name suggests: a bond, secured from an outside company, insuring a film's financiers so that if the film goes over-budget or over-schedule, the bond company will provide the funds to complete the film. This guarantee comes at a rather high price. In the early 1990s the fee for the completion bond ran anywhere from 7 to 10 per cent of a film's budget. However, if the film was full of stunts or other such risky procedures, the bond could run as high as 20 per cent. The true high cost, however, was not the money paid to secure the bond; rather it was the creative price to be paid in the event the production should start to run over-budget and over-schedule. In that case the bond company would bring their people in, take over the decision making process on the production and work in tandem with the studio or financiers to make sure as little money as possible is spent on what remained of the film to be shot and edited.

At this same time in the early 1990s, fluctuating film budgets and increases in salaries across the board had led to the completion bond companies feeling the financial squeeze. Since many films were going over budget, times were becoming harder and harder in the bond business. The slightest hint at trouble on a production would cause the bond companies to send in representatives. This was the climate in which *True Lies* was produced.

Due to the worries of all that can go wrong on a big-budget action picture, and, the uncertainty of the foreign distribution contributions, Cameron felt it prudent to go back to 20th Century Fox and try to re-negotiate his financing deal for two of his biggest budgeted films that were being readied in various stages of pre-production: *True Lies* and *Strange Days*. One of the first hints of any financing trouble for *Strange Days* came in the form of a *Hollywood Reporter* article dated 9 July 1993, about the re-structuring of Lightstorm's distribution deal with 20th Century Fox. The article opens with the lines: 'James Cameron, the creative force behind the two "Terminator" blockbusters, has been forced to alter the scope and structure of his highly publicised, 12-picture, $500 million distribution deal with 20th Century Fox and a consortium of foreign distributors, sources said' (Ulmer & Marich 1993: 1). The terms of the re-structured deal entailed complete financing of *True Lies*, then budgeted at $70 million and *Strange Days* budgeted near $30 million. The article credits the primary reason for the deal shift as 'the nearly $70 million budget of *True Lies*, which is set to go before the cameras in August, as well as the crisis in the independent finance and completion bond market' (Ulmer & Marich 1993: 1). Furthermore, if there was a hope that *Strange Days* would be better off fully financed by Fox, that was dashed when it the same articled reveals:

> While the new deal structure incorporates the initial two pictures, it is currently refashioned to accommodate the production of only one, 'True Lies'. As one source close to the deal put it, 'The bowl containing the deal is still there, but the soup in that bowl is a lot different consistency now – a lot thinner.' (Ulmer & Marich 1993: 1)

The industry trade magazine, *Variety*, reported much the same information that same 9 July, implying *Strange Days* might be in trouble:

> Cameron countered rumours still circulating in Hollywood this week that his $500 million multi-pic deal with several foreign partners, 20th Century Fox and United International Pictures, had been reduced to one costly pic. 'Everything is fully funded and absolutely perfect and the deal is exactly the way it was originally set up.' (Brennan & Aysough 1993: 1)

It was not just Cameron's production financing deals that were at stake. In a move that drew comment, Cameron chose Larry Kasanoff, the former key Carolco executive, to become the new president of Lightstorm. Carolco was going through a possible bankruptcy at the time of Cameron's decision and had been mentioned and linked with Lightstorm's troubled times just one month earlier in a *Los Angeles Times* article which implied both production companies were in serious danger of running dry of their funding resources. The ominous tone for both companies' situations is set at the beginning of the article:

> Parents wanting to steer their children clear of professions might want to add independent film executive to a list that typically includes policeman, lion tamer and soldier of fortune. Sure the perks and pay are good. But consider the downside: near-insurmountable odds against success, nervous banks, forced alliances with foreign partners who can be fickle, pesky bonding companies or no bonding companies at all. And the list goes on. Carolco Pictures and Lightstorm Entertainment, two of the most prominent players in a field already littered with casualties, know the problems well. Cameron's idea was to own his own films and control his own destiny. But destiny may have other ideas. Sources close to the company say Lightstorm is struggling to hold together its patchwork alliance of foreign partners ... There are widespread reports of short-term cash-flow problems. (Citron 1993: 4)

Cameron was indeed struggling with 'destiny' and he managed to secure a $10 million loan to help keep the company operating. This loan came at a price: it was reported that the amount of the loan gave Fox territorial distribution rights to France, as well as reduced licensing fees for the US and Canada (Brennan & Aysough 1993: 1). It was under this new financing situation that Kathryn Bigelow would be directing *Strange Days*.

Strange Days – The Production History

It is a popular Hollywood practice to stay in pre-production for as long as possible before going into production. This is hardly surprising: it costs only a fraction of a film's budget to pay for pre-production, whereas, once a film goes into production a full crew is hired, all rentals either are in use or being wasted, and actors are paid enormous sums of money for their presence for a specific amount of time. If things go wrong in this period of film-making, they can affect the outcome of not only the rest of the shoot, but also how the studio handles the picture from post-production to distribution.

The script

Strange Days was in a precarious position even before it started in pre-production. Cameron was the original writer and had been working on a treatment of *Strange Days* for ten years, describing the feature in multi-generic terms: 'It's an erotic suspense thriller set in the very near future' (Bahina 1994: 4). In a discussion regarding literary influences on the story, Cameron notes: 'I wanted to do a David Mamet science fiction film … I wanted to do a film that was so character-based and realistic that the rhythm of the words, the way the people talked, was a critical part of the overall design and style of the film' (Anon. 1995a: 6). However, Cameron never intended to write more than a treatment of the story; nonetheless, the more involved he became in developing ideas with Bigelow, the larger the treatment grew. Cameron explains his expanding treatment, and defines it as a 'scriptment' – a hybrid between a script and a treatment. He notes, 'I always tell myself 'I'm not writing a script, I'm just writing a treatment' (Anon. 1995a: 5), an attitude that stems from Cameron's practice of typically juggling writing three scripts simultaneously. With *Strange Days* he allowed himself to expand since 'he just wrote the scenes because the characters [became] so real to me.' (Anon. 1995a: 5). He describes his 'finished' scriptment as a sort of novelistic template for a movie, will all the scenes in it (Anon. 1995a: 5). Despite his increased involvement, Cameron's work on the scriptment never culminated in a finished screenplay: instead, in a joint decision made with Kathryn Bigelow, screenwriter Jay Cocks (*The Age of Innocence* (Martin Scorsese, 1993)) was hired to finish the screenplay. Cameron's involvement with *True Lies* and that production's timetable made further work on the *Strange Days* script impossible.

Although Bigelow had been excited by the idea of *Strange Days* while it was still a treatment, her approach differed from Cameron's on a number of standpoints. In an interview with *Box-office* magazine's Ray Greene, Cameron explains that although he felt his story is a classic science fiction film, Bigelow had always rejected the generic term. Cameron explains, 'She treated it as a very straightforward relationship thriller with political overtones, and let the technology weave itself into the fabric' (Greene 1995: 10). In the same interview, Cameron revealed he wrote *Strange Days* with Bigelow in mind to direct it. When asked by Greene if Cameron believed gender influenced Bigelow's vision, Cameron explained that he was the one always pushing to make the film more romantic and Bigelow was always pushing to make it harder-edged (Greene 1995: 10). Obviously, Bigelow's vision won out.

Casting

After a finished script is financed, the most crucial job in pre-production is casting. The casting director is one of the first below-the-line individuals hired during pre-production. This is usually because the director, producer and studio rarely get their first choice concerning the actors, including the leads. If the project is a studio feature,

A-list talent is always sought first. Casting is a precarious job not only because of actor's availability (and the more the actor is worth, the less available he or she is) but also because of fees and studio approval. *Strange Days* proved to be no exception to the gruelling casting process.

Although the script for *Strange Days* was completed by 1993 and the production was set to start shooting in the early spring of 1994, the two leads had not been cast by early January. Lacking the lead actors can affect the film's scheduling process due to such considerations as other actors' commitments, availability of locations, etc. All these factors ultimately cost more money in the budget which increases pressure on everybody – especially the director and producer.

On 10 January 1994 there was a small excerpt in the Buzz section of *Weekly Variety* regarding the casting of *Strange Days*:

> At Fox, they're putting pictures together at a frenzied pace. They're close to getting Andy Garcia to star in the Jim Cameron scripted *Strange Days* which Kathryn Bigelow will direct. Angela Basset, who played Tina Turner in *What's Love Got to Do With It*, is in talks to co-star. (Anon. 1994: 4)

Bono was rumoured to join the *Strange Days* cast in his acting debut as a sleazy concert promoter who is Juliette Lewis' love interest. In the 3 March 1994 'Just for Variety' column in *Daily Variety*, Army Arched notes: 'Bono is up for a role in *Strange Days* for Jim Cameron, starring Oscar nominees Angela Bassett and Ralph Fiennes. It deals with the underbelly of the music biz in LA.' However, by May, those rumours proved to be partially inaccurate.

Ultimately, three Oscar-nominated actors secured the leads: Ralph Fiennes as Lenny Nero, Angela Bassett as Mace, and Juliette Lewis as Faith. It was Fiennes' role in *Schindler's List* that impressed Bigelow enough to want to cast him as Lenny. Bigelow felt that 'the role of Lenny Nero required somebody who had a tremendous amount of intelligence, complexity, depth, a series of qualities that I really felt only Ralph could supply'. In contrast, Cameron did not see Fiennes in the role. He felt somebody 'glibber and slicker' would work better, though he felt Fiennes made Lenny a much sexier character – a guy you can care about very much (Anon. 1995a: 6).

This triple powerhouse of A-list actors headlining should have served to draw a wide audience. Juliette Lewis is known for her diverse roles across genres from *Natural Born Killers* (Oliver Stone, 1994) to *What's Eating Gilbert Grape?* (Lasse Hallstrom, 1993). However, she has never been known as a show opener. Angela Bassett garners great respect and should have been able to pull in the African-American audience, but this audience would probably have been the same group that went to see her as Tina

Turner – women. Ralph Fiennes' appeal runs across gender boundaries, although with a genre film such as science fiction, which traditionally is thought to appeal to more males than females, his ability to draw both sexes risks being less pronounced.

The power of the Oscar – or at least the Oscar nomination – can usually be relied on to count for something but in this genre it must be largely discounted because the 'typical' science fiction fan does not really care about Oscar-calibre acting; they do care about good action stars, hot women and great special effects. These observations may sound cut-throat and sexist, but it must always be remembered when discussing Hollywood that such factors are still the key dynamics at work, which may in part go to explain why this all-star cast could not open a science-fiction, film noir, action-thriller.

The shooting

According to the *Films in Preparation* section of *The Hollywood Reporter*, there were a number of start dates for *Strange Days*. In the 22 March 1994 issue of *The Hollywood Reporter*, the start date (which had been previously mentioned as an early spring shoot) was slated as 12 May 1994. This was also mentioned in a 3 March 1994 L.A. *Daily News* celebrities column. However, according to a report in *The Hollywood Reporter* on 17 May, the start date had been pushed back in the listings to 6 June 1994. By 22 March, Ralph Fiennes and Angela Bassett were included in the cast list. It was not until 17 May that Juliette Lewis had been added to a somewhat more sizeable cast list. Although not without precedent, this was cutting it rather close for a film slated to begin filming in just a little more than two weeks time.

The film was shot entirely in the Greater Los Angeles area. In terms of locations, the scope of the production was extensive. There were two scenes that were important enough to be noted in the Los Angeles press due to the unusual scope of the scenes. The first scene entailed filming on Sunset Boulevard – a massive undertaking at any time, day or night. According to *The Hollywood Reporter* on 22 June, over a two-day period in June 1994, the production received permission from the West Hollywood film commission to film on Sunset Boulevard. The crew erected elaborate holiday decorations along the boulevard and shut down several lanes of traffic. The Hollywood Chamber of Commerce furnished the decorations. At this point in time, it was rather unusual to receive permission and get more than one city agency to co-operate with a production on any front. This probably meant that a very substantial location fee was paid to the City of West Hollywood, and perhaps a donation to the Hollywood Chamber of Commerce.

The second scene of great scope, the rave scene – actually a giant 1999 New Year's Eve bash – at the end of the film was more ambitious. *The Hollywood Reporter* on

Figure 5 The strange gaze of Kathryn Bigelow.

28 September reported that shooting the scene necessitated shutting down several blocks in downtown Los Angeles for the day. Approximately five tons of confetti were dropped from the Bonaventure hotel, large parts of which had been rented for the night, more than fifty off-duty police officers and a dozen on-duty police helped with crowd control, which included transporting five people with Ecstasy overdoses to hospital. For final footage of other New Years Eve celebrations, Bigelow went to New York, the New Year before, to shoot footage, while producer Steven Charles Jaffe went to Spain. Several other camera crews were dispatched around the world to get footage for this event. It took several months of planning by city and production officials to pull off the project on 17 September. *Strange Days* benefited from the Los Angeles Film Commission's new campaign to keep production in Los Angeles. The city was especially helpful at this time because many productions had been leaving the area due to inflated location fees and difficulties in obtaining shooting permits for densely populated areas in the city.

In order to gather a large enough crowd, and to avoid paying thousands of extras, the film-makers hired concert promoters Moss Jacobs and Philip Blaine, who planned a huge rave which featured performers Dee-Lite and Aphex Twin, plus all the cyber-techno bands they could garner. The event was set to start at 9pm on a Saturday night and run until dawn in a four-block roped-off area. The tickets were only available in advance for a $10 price tag, including secured parking downtown; in essence the film-makers were charging the extras for their participation. Nevertheless, both the party-goers and the film-makers gained – the film-makers got their huge party scene at a controlled cost and the party-goers 'got to be in a film' (Parisi 1995: S64).

Cinematography is, of course, always one of the key elements to the *mise-en-scène* in a film, but in the case of *Strange Days*, it was essential to have multi-faceted cameras. One of the aspects of the story James Cameron wanted to emphasise was the number of POV shots because of the SQUID technology (the head sets) used throughout the film to view other peoples' experiences. These POV scenes are some of the most ambitious in film history. To help accomplish their goals, Cameron and Bigelow hired Director of Photography Matthew Leonetti, whose credits include *Jagged Edge* (Richard Marquand, 1985) and *Dead Again* (Kenneth Branagh, 1991). It took a year (D'Silva 1996: 10) to build the highly specialised camera which would be able to reproduce the key effect of looking through someone else's eyes – this effect, 'playback', enables a character to relive a slice of someone else's life, be it murder, car chase or steamy sex session. The scenes had to be choreographed weeks in advance and walked through with a video camera to see if they would work. The actors had to wear a special head-mounted 'Helmetcam' which could capture the feeling of looking through someone else's eyes. The camera had to *be* somebody's head.

With all the care and extra work that went into the planning and production of *Strange Days*, it is no wonder the principal photography did not wrap until the week of 14 October 1994. The stunt sequences alone required an enormous time commitment. It took two years to co-ordinate the opening sequence, a sixteen-foot jump between seven-storey buildings by a stuntman without a safety harness. With the care and artistic consideration put into the production, it is amazing the shooting only took four months.

The soundtrack

One of the many problems with *Strange Days* and its marketing was that it was nearly impossible to tell who the target audience was supposed to be. While the trailers promoted sexy slogans ('You Know You Want It' – want what?), the music was aimed at a definite alternative youth market. This was apparent, first, with the staged rave in the film and second with the music choices throughout the soundtrack.

The importance of the music in the film was not lost on Bigelow. In a case study done of the film's soundtrack, Bigelow and music supervisor Randy Gerston (*True Lies*) discuss the strategies employed to successfully integrate the right music into the soundtrack. Bigelow asserts, 'The music is integral in two ways: creatively, and also from a narrative standpoint with respect to Juliette's character' (Parisi 1995: S64).

Bigelow goes as far to call the music 'a character in the piece' (Parisi 1995: S64). Steven Charles Jaffe, a producer on the film, explains:

> Instead of making the tragic mistake of throwing money at the screen, building absurd cars and designing bizarre costumes that will never work their way into real life, we realised that one of the things that would help define the future in a subtle way was the music. (Parisi 1995: S9)

International music was selected for its varied sounds and uses of instruments. Randy Gerston felt that an international sound best captured the essence of futuristic music because 'the world is shrinking and people are getting acclimated to strange languages being part of the pop vernacular' (Parisi, 1995: S9). The British band Skunk Anansie headlined at the New Year's Eve rave and their song was included on the closing credits. Other international bands on the track include French industrial alternative rockers Deep Forest and trip-hop artist Tricky.

Both Gerston and Bigelow were excited about Juliette Lewis because she was able to sing. There was a push in the casting to find actors who could also sing since there was so much music in the soundtrack. Gerston notes: 'We didn't want actors lip-synching … This was a great source of anxiety when we were casting: hoping they could act and hoping they could sing' (Parisi 1995: S64).

Live bands are used through the film, but the rave is notably the most important scene for the appearance of live sound. Skunk Anansie were encouraged to jam between takes so Bigelow and Gerston could record live music and give the rave as much authenticity as possible. Bigelow explains that though the band would ultimately be lip-synching, they would have live sound. Gerston explains how they went about capturing the sound:

> We did it for real. Everything from the speaker placement to the lighting to the stage construction to the live P.A.s and live amplifiers so between takes they could jam. It's important in dealing with musicians that you present to them an atmosphere that's concert-like or club-like if that's what you're asking them to do. Because bands are bands, they're not actors. (Parisi 1995: S64)

With so much effort put into the music track, Lewis' singing certainly didn't change her career to a pop singer, nor did the soundtrack make a huge commercial splash in the US. This was despite the fact that the soundtrack were released a few weeks before the film's opening, and 60,000 promotional *Strange Days* CD-ROMs were available only through purchasing the 'College Special' issue of *Rolling Stone* magazine at record

Figure 6 Kathryn Bigelow collaborates with James Cameron on the set of *Strange Days*.

stores. These CD-ROMs were described by a *Rolling Stone* spokesperson as a 'press kit on disc' (Jordan 1995: 37). The CD-ROM contained audio, video and text material from the film including a movie trailer, production stills and short music clips from the soundtrack. The article notes that the target audience is young, educated and affluent (Ibid.). Once again, the Fox distribution arm, this time the music department, sold its effort short and perhaps narrowed the target audience too much.

The final product

Considering the many genres that *Strange Days* has been described as, it is no wonder the marketing of the film was such a disaster. The *Business Wire*, 14 October, described the story as anything from simply an 'upcoming thriller and techno-thriller' to a 'futuristic erotic thriller' in the same article. Whether the genres of science fiction, action or film noir are mentioned in articles or reviews, the term thriller is not far behind. This hybrid genre caused a great marketing dilemma for the distributors at Fox.

For lack of any other clear direction, the marketing team decided to sell sex. When too many genres are blended, studio marketing departments get confused. Sex seemed the easiest way out with the slogan, 'You Know You Want It' on the trailer and in print ads. Another prevalent advert included a banner describing the film as a 'sexy, kinetic thriller'. These marketing tactics worked so poorly in the US that in Europe the film was going to be marketed as an 'action thriller murder mystery' instead of the US 'cyberspace virtual reality film' slant. This confusing marketing campaign is blamed for the disastrous opening weekend *Strange Days* experienced (Puig & Natale 1995: F1).

Strange Days was set to debut on 7 October 1995 as the New York Film Festival's centrepiece. Despite this it was quickly boycotted by US audiences. *Strange Days* did not break $9 million in the US theatrical market. It was reportedly budgeted anywhere from $35 million to $45 million, and that does not include Prints and Advertising, which typically cost up to 50 per cent of a film's budget.

Critically, the movie opened to mixed reviews, the most positive one coming from the *New York Times*. A reviewer from *Fantasy and Science Fiction* hated the film (Maio 1996: 1), and the *Village Voice* essentially concluded it boiled down to a failure (Hoberman 1995: 1). Most reviews tended to say a few kind words about the look of the film, then dismiss it as a weak story – too long and too confusing.

Outside Controversies

Strange Days had two incidents surrounding the release of the film that added to the overall negative aura of its poor reception in Los Angeles. The first problem involved race relations, the second was the death of a Fox executive the night of the premiere.

During the early to mid-1990s, Los Angeles was a hotbed of racial tension. With the Rodney King beating, the acquittal of the officers on trial for the King beating, the race riots as a result of the acquittal and the Nicole Simpson/Ron Goldman double-murder and the arrest of O. J. Simpson, things could not have been tenser in Los Angeles. This was the climate in which *Strange Days* was released. At the centre of all these was the question of the Los Angeles Police Department and its treatment of minority groups.

The depiction of the brutal execution of a rap singer by the LAPD in *Strange Days* could only exacerbate the situation. A *Los Angeles Times* article, addressing the timely depictions of the LAPD in *Strange Days* noted how the film 'presents members of the Los Angeles Police Department engaging in a range of illegal activities, many aimed squarely at African-Americans' (Richard 1995: F1). Screenwriter Jay Cocks states: 'If incidents like Rodney King reverberate in the movie, it's only metaphorically' (Richard 1995: F1-F8). This may be true, but more images of violence in Los Angeles is not necessarily what North America wanted to see at the time. Saturated with the images of race riots, a beating of truck driver Reginald Denny, the infamous O.J. Simpson freeway chase and eventual trial coverage, arguably the last thing Americans wanted to be reminded of at the time was the violence occurring in reality.

On the night of the Los Angeles premiere, a Fox executive, Dylan Sellars, was driving home another Fox executive, Lewis Cherot, a director of development.

Driving along Sunset Boulevard Sellars hit a tree, killing Cherot instantly. There was some question as to whether or not Sellars was intoxicated by any substance, legal or illegal. Cherot worked on *Strange Days* extensively and attended the premiere to enjoy the fruits of his labour. It is ironic that he should die the night before the box-office disaster that would befall the film. Sellars was charged with manslaughter, but was subsequently cleared. He left his post as an executive and got a deal with Fox as a producer.

Strange Days, then, was a film plagued by many problems. The manner in which Cameron attempted to finance the film made its production almost impossible. Preparation for the film was a nightmare: a special camera had to be built for major sequences; deadly stunts had to be choreographed; years of preparation passed without the film going into production. Three top-named actors headlined the film and it was still a financial disaster. One of the most prominent director/writer/producers in Hollywood supervised the production of the film, in a genre he made his name in and the film still did not break even. A talented director put her energies into a 'thriller' and got a piece critics struggled to define. Even if all the elements go in with the best intentions, in Hollywood, that doesn't guarantee a $100 million return at the box office. It can mean anything, and, in this case, it still resulted in 'failure'.

CHAPTER NINE

'Straight from the Cerebral Cortex': Vision and Affect in Strange Days

Steven Shaviro

Kathryn Bigelow's *Strange Days* (1995) was not a box-office success when it was released in 1995. Perhaps viewers found the film difficult, because of the way it crosses the boundary between mass and elite culture. On the one hand, *Strange Days* is a spectacular, mass-market film, with story and screenplay by none other than James Cameron, the director of *Titanic* (1998), *Aliens* (1986), and the *Terminator* series of films (1984, 1991). *Strange Days* is meant to work in a manner similar to Cameron's techno-thrillers. It has characters that the viewer is supposed to identify with, and a plot full of thrills, exciting action sequences and unexpected twists. But at the same time, *Strange Days* is very much an experimental film, one that questions and inverts the traditional Hollywood structures of identification and involvement, in ways that are consonant with the ideas that have been put forward by feminist film criticism over the last thirty years. Also, *Strange Days* is crucially involved in dialogue with many earlier films. It is self-consciously a 'postmodern' film, by which I mean that it assumes the priority of commodified media over any sort of 'nature'. And as a film by a woman director, previously known for her subversive, revisionary takes on stereotypically 'masculine' action films, *Strange Days* is deeply concerned with gender issues.

Strange Days is a science fiction thriller, with an almost-contemporary setting. It takes place in Los Angeles, on 30–31 December 1999, the eve of the new millennium. 'Millennium' is meant both literally and figuratively. The film's climax occurs during 'the biggest party of all time', an outdoor New Year's Eve celebration during the countdown to the year 2000. But the film's bleak, post-*film noir* urban vision is millennial, as well, in a metaphorical sense; end-of-the-world fears and fantasies are much in evidence. The film directly alludes to the Los Angeles riots of 1992, which erupted after the acquittal of the four white cops who had been caught on videotape, beating a black man, Rodney King. The film's nightmare vision of a Los Angeles riven by racial and class warfare, and under what amounts to martial law, hasn't literally come true as I write these lines in 2001. But the tensions that are dramatised in this vision continue to haunt American society, even if they were temporarily driven underground during the Internet-fuelled economic boom of the late 1990s.

The world of *Strange Days* is thus in most ways still identifiably our own. But there is one aspect of the film's scenario that turns it from a present-day adventure drama into science fiction. The science fictional ploy of *Strange Days* is a technology called SQUID, short for 'superconducting quantum interference device'. SQUID is a kind of virtual reality machine. It is like a tape player that is plugged directly into the brain. It records and plays back actual lived experience, in full multi-sensory detail. The process is called being wired. As the film's protagonist, Lenny Nero (Ralph Fiennes), explains it to a prospective client: 'This is not like TV, only better. This is life. It's a piece of somebody's life. It's pure and uncut, straight from the cerebral cortex.' Being wired is like being literally inside someone else's mind and body. You see exactly what they see, feel exactly what they feel. You can have hot sex, without the risk of AIDS. You can find out what it is like to be another gender. You can experience the thrill of pulling an armed robbery – as happens in the film's opening sequence – without so much as leaving your chair.

In the world of *Strange Days*, SQUID technology is illegal, but it has a thriving presence on the black market. It's mostly used as a kind of sleazy entertainment, filling the market niche that is actually inhabited today by porno films, perhaps crossed with computer games and online virtual environments. That makes it just the sort of thing for Lenny, a cynical wheeler-dealer who used to be a cop, until he was kicked off the force for corruption. Now Lenny makes his living as a peddler of illicit, and mostly pornographic, SQUID tapes. We learn quickly that Lenny has his limits – the one thing that he refuses to deal in is snuff tapes, ones that end with the actual death of the person whose experience provides the material for the tape. But he doesn't seem to have many qualms beyond this. The conventional plot of the film, such as it is, will be concerned with Lenny's ultimate redemption. But as I hope to show, there is a lot more at work here, that doesn't function just on the level of the viewer's identification with the male protagonist.

The power of SQUID is demonstrated at the very start of the film. The opening shot, aside from the titles and a brief computer print-out, indicating the date and time, is a close-up of a blinking eye, accompanied by a brief off-screen dialogue ('Ready?' – 'Yeah, boot it'). Then, we get a single long sequence shot. It's a robbery, seen and heard from the point of view of one of the robbers. They enter a restaurant, wave guns around to frighten the workers and patrons, and grab money from the cash register. But just as they are about to leave, the cops arrive, breaking in on the robbery. The robbers flee up the stairs, and onto the roof. The man who's POV we are sharing is trapped. He tries to escape by jumping from the rooftop to that of the next building over. But he doesn't quite make it. Instead, he plummets into the void, down to the ground. The shot ends suddenly, violently, devolving into static at the moment of his death.

This bravura sequence is, I think, one of the most extraordinary in the history of film. It's all speed, violence and nervous tension. The sequence is a single long take: a 'sequence shot', like the famous opening shot of Orson Welles' *Touch of Evil* (1958). (Actually, Bigelow shot the action in several different takes, and only spliced them together during editing; but the sequence as we see it seems entirely seamless.) In contrast to the sublime detachment of Welles' crane shot, however, Bigelow uses a handheld camera that is in the thick of the action. (Actually, the camera was not held in the hands of the camera operator, but attached to a helmet on his head.) There is much fast, elaborate camera movement. Anything that moves so rapidly on screen has an intensifying effect – just think of the rapid-fire montage of a good music video, or the fluid action sequences in Bigelow's previous film, *Point Break* (1991). Indeed, Bigelow addresses this point specifically in an interview:

> I really only started to work compatibly with the Steadicam and trust it in *Point Break*. You can create an edit-free situation, yet it has the pace and sense of a quickly cut sequence. People move in and out of their coverage, and the actor and camera can move counter to one another. I love the purity of an unbroken shot, and I love that juxtaposed with a sequence that has tremendous editorial intrusion. (Bigelow in Smith 1995: 50)

This contrast between edited sequences and unbroken shots is taken even further in *Strange Days*. It becomes a central structural principle of the film, because of the way it is built into the conception of the SQUID technology. The fact that the opening sequence of *Strange Days* is a seamless single long take makes it relentless as well as intense, in a way that goes far beyond most music videos and action sequences. Here, the absence of cuts means that there is no space for us to breathe. This is all the more the case, in that the sequence ends with the death of its anonymous protagonist.

Its worth noting how innovative Bigelow's sequence-shot is, in contrast to the delirious cutting techniques that so many recent action films have borrowed from music videos. In James Cameron's action sequences, to take an important contemporary example, the rapid cuts are cleverly designed to mimic the wrenching violence of the diegetic action. The fragmentation and chaos of what's happening onscreen is driven home by the sense of disorientation that comes from the fact that the shots are not matched into typical shot/reverse shot patterns, as well as that no single shot lasts long enough for us to get a clear sense of what is going on. In *Aliens* and the *Terminator* films, Cameron divides time into ever-more-minuscule intervals, and valorises shock and confusion over spatial coherence. This is strikingly different from the way that more 'classical' action directors (like Anthony Mann and Samuel Fuller in the 1950s, or in a somewhat different way John Woo today) carefully maintain our sense of geographical orientation and temporal sequence, even in the midst of the violence and chaos of shoot-outs and other action sequences. Bigelow herself seems to prefer the classical approach; as she says:

> Geography is so important in action sequences. I see a lot of films in which geography is sacrificed, it's just a lot of fast cutting, a lot of noise, a lot of impacts – and I have no idea where I am, or who's coming from the left or right. (Bigelow in Smith 1995: 50)

In *Strange Days* (for which Cameron did some uncredited editing work), Bigelow manages to combine the best of both approaches. By eschewing cutting altogether in the SQUID sequences, but moving the camera rapidly and jarringly, in a way that reproduces the psychological shock effect of quick montage, Bigelow is able to combine the spatial groundedness of classical action, with the non-linear, continual disorientation of Cameronesque action.

But I still haven't mentioned the most important thing about the opening sequence of *Strange Days*. This is the fact that, like all the other SQUID sequences, it is also a first-person point-of-view shot. This leads to a strange paradox. On one hand, the first-person perspective of the POV shot evidently binds us tightly into the action. But at the same time, this perspective is oddly impersonal. For as we watch the sequence at the start of the film, we do not know who the protagonist is; we have no idea whose point of view it is that we are sharing. The action is so immediate and so visceral, that there it abolishes the distance that traditionally separates the film spectator from the scene that is being displayed in front of him/her. But this lack of distance is also a lack of knowledge and of identity. It thrusts us into the action so viscerally, that it affords us no security whatsoever.

As film theorists have often pointed out, photographic technology bears a strong affinity to the one-point perspective of the *camera obscura* and Renaissance painting. The lens of the camera, and therefore the eye of the spectator, remains at an imaginary viewing point, forever outside of the scene being viewed. The position of the spectator is a transcendent one; for this position is not part of the visual field, and therefore the spectator cannot him/herself be seen. In principle, the mobility and duration of cinematic images ought to work against such dualism and idealism of vision. But most of the time editing conventions, like the rules of continuity, make sure that film does not transgress the structure of distanced, fixedly perspectival viewing. In classical film, it is only at certain extraordinary moments – like the one in Hitchcock's *Rear Window* (1954) when Lars Thorwald (Raymond Burr) looks back, and suddenly realises that L.B. Jeffries (James Stewart) – and therefore, by proxy, the movie audience as well – have been watching him, that the invulnerable remove of the spectator is breached. Something similar happens, albeit for quite different reasons, during the SQUID sequences of *Strange Days*.

Another way to put all this is to note that immediacy is not the same as presence. The SQUID sequences in *Strange Days* are quite immediate, but they are also explicitly set in the past, rather than the present. The fact that we know the sequence to be a recording, or a virtual re-creation, ensures that its immediacy is strangely divorced from presence. That's why we hear 'boot it' at the very beginning. And the sequence starts with an out-of-focus smear, further letting us know that it is a recording. The robbers also wear masks, in order to insure that they cannot be recognised, by the subsequent tape-watchers as well as by their victims. All in all, the anonymity of the person through whose eyes we are looking makes the sequence oddly devoid of that weight and density that are necessary to an experience of full subjective presence.

This anonymity is also that of the person who is watching the tape, within the diegesis of the film. We've seen his eye in extreme close-up, and heard his voice; but until the sequence ends, that is all. In a real sense, neither the doer nor the observer is a fixed, identifiable self. It is only with the interruption of the tape, at the death of the person whose POV we have been sharing, that we find out who the diegetic spectator is. This is done through a shock cut from the vertiginous fall of the end of the tape to a close-up of Lenny's face. He is violently shaken by this unexpected conclusion, and he complains angrily to the purveyor of the tape. It is Lenny who said 'boot it' at the start; and it is he who has been directly experiencing the POV shot that we have just seen.

What happens in this opening sequence recurs every time SQUID comes up in the course of the film. Bigelow presents the SQUID recordings as continuous first-person shots. Events unfold in real time, in a single take, from a single point of view. The unedited POV is how Bigelow simulates, for the film spectator, the sense of full sensorial immersion that is a given of the diegetic world of the film. Indeed, these SQUID sequences are tactile, or haptic, more than they are merely visual. The subjective camera doesn't just look at a scene. It moves actively through space. It gets jostled, it stops and starts, it pans and tilts, it lurches forward and back. It follows the rhythms of the whole body, and not just that of the eyes. In this way, Bigelow establishes what I would like to call a presubjective regime of vision: a kind of looking that is affective rather than cognitive, and that is not associated with a fully formed phenomenological self or psychoanalytic ego.

A few words of theoretical explanation may be in order here. I am trying to think about affect without a subject: affect that comes, instead, before or after the subject. Such a formulation appears paradoxical. We usually think of emotions as being properties of the self, or even actions that the self performs. I feel in certain ways, or I have certain feelings. Feelings, therefore, are usually the province of phenomenology. A more radically pragmatic alternative to this is to see feelings as being performative, as when William James suggests that I am afraid (in the sense that I have the conscious feeling of being afraid) because I have the physiological 'fear response' (an adrenaline rush, etc.) – rather than the reverse. As for recent scientific studies of emotion, they generally track how a given emotion works in the brain on a chemical and/or physiological level, by observing what happens in animals (LeDoux 1998). Since animals may or may not be conscious in a human sense, this effectively brackets the phenomenological dimension. (Also, it is not insignificant that fear is the predominant emotion to be studied in this way.) But in any case, these pragmatic and scientific approaches, no less than the more classically phenomenological ones, tend to assume that emotions are attributes of an individual entity (even if not quite of a full-fledged subject).

But there is another, perhaps counter-intuitive, sense, in which I would like to say that affect or feeling is not, strictly speaking, personal. A feeling can take me outside of myself. It can make me lose control of myself, turn me into a different person. A certain feeling may be too much for me to bear. Or it may just be that a feeling does not quite seem to fit. It's a tonality, a quality, something that colours the way I perceive the world. But I'd swear that it isn't just my projection, because it has come to me from somewhere else. It isn't mine, but something alien to me: something from outside, from far away, that has somehow managed to insinuate itself within me. William Burroughs would say that such a feeling is like a virus. It is not a phenomenological attribute of myself; it is not even something that I perform; it is rather something that I passively suffer or endure. It is, in any case, a passion and not an action.

Following Brian Massumi, I use the word affect to designate a feeling that is not personal or subjective (Massumi 2002). I use it in contrast to the word emotion, which continues to designate the more familiar sense of a personal, subjective feeling. Affect is something that comes before the subject has arrived, or that subsists after the subject has departed, or that happens alongside the subject, affecting it but not being integrated within it. Seen in this way, affect is a crucial component of the thought of Deleuze and Guattari and their allies; because it is precisely the sort of concept that is irreducible either to phenomenology on the one hand, or to structural or scientific objectification on the other. As Deleuze puts it, affects are 'impersonal and pre-individual nomadic singularities' (1990: 109). Every affect 'traverses men as well as plants and animals independently of the matter of their individuation and the forms of their personality' (1990: 107).

I want to avoid making a binary opposition between thought and feeling; but I still want to insist that affect is resistant to cognition, or that it happens at a point where thought reaches its limit. To put the point differently: an affect that is re-cognised by thought, or expressed in language, is thereby turned into an emotion. Affect per se is the irreducible ground of emotion, that evades being captured by cognition or by language; or else it is the residue of emotion, the *part maudite* that is not reducible to cognition or to language, even as language endeavours to allude to it.

The SQUID sequences in *Strange Days* are affective in precisely this sense. In these sequences, there are no establishing shots. We are immediately thrust into the action, without any sense of a larger context. Indeed, such a context is inaccessible, for it is the very condition of SQUID recordings that they are played back outside of their initial contexts. Together with denying the spectator any establishing shots, Bigelow also omits the reverse shots that usually anchor cinematic narrative. Except in the mirror, we never get to see the person through whose eyes we are looking. He/she is so close, the intimacy the viewer has with him/her is so extreme, that all sense of a particular self is lost. The vividness of what is happening takes precedence over the question of whom it is happening to. It could be anyone – anyone who chooses to play the SQUID recording back. In this way, subjective experience is commodified: any experience can be exchanged or substituted for any other.

This sort of odd depersonalisation has traditionally been noted as a problem with first-person shots. Films in the past that made extensive use of the first-person camera have generally been regarded as failures. The classical example is MGM's 1946 Raymond Chandler adaptation, *The Lady in the Lake*, both starring and directed by

Robert Montgomery. The entire film, except for a brief prologue, is seen through the eyes of detective Philip Marlowe. The camera looks where he looks, and pans to follow the movement of his gaze: whether he is scanning a large room, following a suspect, or merely glancing at his watch to tell the time. And when he gets punched out, the aggressor's fist hits directly into the camera. At the time, most viewers found this ploy confusing rather than compelling. Contrary to what might have been expected, viewers did not 'identify' with Montgomery's Marlowe as a result of sharing his point of view. It seems – for whatever psychological reasons – that a reverse shot, a view of the person with whom we are looking, is necessary if any identification with the character that does the looking is to take hold.

Today, first-person shots, without reverse shots, are most commonly found in horror films, almost invariably to present the point of view of the monster. Steven Spielberg is probably responsible for initiating this, with his famous shark's-eye POV shots, as the shark glided through the water towards an unsuspecting victim, in *Jaws* (Steven Spielberg, 1975). The monster's-eye POV shot quickly became a cliché in slasher films of the late 1970s and 1980s. It allowed the audience, among other things, to see what the killer was doing, without knowing who the killer was. In these sequences, we are put into the position of the monster; we get the voyeuristic thrills and chills of the kill, but we do not psychologically 'identify' with him/it.

Instead of having reverse shots, the SQUID sequences are generally intercut with reaction shots of whoever is playing back the tape. Usually it's Lenny. He sits with a metal mesh fit tightly over his skull. His eyes are closed. His face is strained in ecstasy or horror. His arms flail about, as he mimes the action in empty air. It's an uncanny sight. The feeling is real, but it has been divorced from any recognisable context. The effect is quite strange, given our customary expectations of film syntax. The reaction shot 'reads' like a reverse shot, which means that it should reinforce our sense of identification with the character that is seeing or experiencing the first shot. But here, the person in the reaction shot isn't even in the same space as the person whose POV defines the initial shot. In the SQUID sequences, therefore, the usual hierarchy between the observer and the scene being observed is inverted. The action is in the main shot, and the observer in the reverse shot. The traditional (masculine) power of the cinematic gaze is thereby shattered. To see is no longer to have a kind of power over what is seen. As a result of all this, the sense of subjectivity is scrambled. Our identification with the camera, or with the scene, is eerily divorced from any identification with the character. We are drawn powerfully into the action, yet not into the mind of the person who is performing the action. The first-person SQUID shots set up a kind of free-floating subjectivity, a constellation or progression of affect that is no longer anchored in any particular self.

Uncannily, this is even the case when someone plays backs tapes from his/her own past. Lenny is stuck on the memory of his former girlfriend Faith (Juliette Lewis), who has long since dumped him. He still wants her back, even though she won't so much as give him the time of day. He obsessively plays back SQUID tapes of their time together. But the gulf between who he was then, and who he is now, as he re-experiences the actions of his former self, is all too painfully, even pathetically, evident. In effect, Lenny relives his past by proxy; he is no closer to the protagonist of these tapes than anyone else, playing them back, would be. Precisely because Lenny's past is so perfectly preserved in and of itself, in a weird sense it no longer belongs to him. It has become an impersonal simulacrum. Is this not the paradox of all nostalgia? As Lenny's friend and bodyguard Mace (Angela Bassett) tells him at one point: 'Memories were meant to fade, Lenny; they're designed that way for a reason.' By not letting his memories fade, but instead reliving them virtually, Lenny makes a futile effort to stop the passage of time. But he cannot succeed; for he himself has already changed, just as much as everyone and everything else.

Bigelow rings many changes on this pattern of the SQUID tapes' impersonality. There's the scene when the villain of the movie breaks into Lenny's apartment, and leaves behind a tape of the experience. Playing it back, Lenny has the odd sensation of seeing himself, asleep and vulnerable, and not even knowing who is looking at him. Then there is the tape of a man running along the beach, enjoying the open air and the sight of the women he passes. Lenny gives this tape to the DJ in the Retinal Fetish nightclub, who has lost his legs and therefore can no longer have such an experience in real life. There's something creepy about the way the DJ thereby uses the SQUID device as his prosthetic limbs (not to mention, in order to enable the most traditional male heterosexual fantasy). Even at its most innocuous, the SQUID-enabled divergence of inner experience from the physical self of the experiencer is troubling. For it means that an experience can be alienated from the person who 'has' it, and turned (like everything else in postmodern society) into a commodity. Moreover, it suggests that our actual selves – as opposed to these enduring tapes of their evanescent, moment-to-moment experiences – are curiously empty.

But there is another, even more troubling, aspect to the problem of the SQUID sequences. The whole opening of *Strange Days* – an extreme close-up of a blinking eye, followed by a long first-person POV sequence, involving the use of replication technology, and culminating in an act of violence – closely recalls the opening, pre-credit sequence of Michael Powell's film *Peeping Tom* (1961). In this film, the image of the blinking eye is followed by a scene that is presented, not through somebody's eyes, but through the viewfinder of a camera, with crosshairs prominently in the centre of the image. The unseen photographer accosts a prostitute, goes with her up to her room, and then kills her. This shocking sequence is followed, as the credits roll, by the same footage being projected on a screen as a silent film (i.e. without synch sound, and overlaid by non-diegetic soundtrack music), and watched by a lone spectator. This viewer turns out to be Mark Lewis (Karl Boehm), the murderous photographer who is the movie's protagonist. Mark fancies himself a film-maker, and his way of making a film is by photographing women as he is killing them by means of a knife that projects out of his camera's tripod.

The most horrific use of the SQUID technology in *Strange Days* – horrific both on the level of the diegesis, and on that of Bigelow's *mise-en-scène* – is a scene that echoes *Peeping Tom* even more directly. In that film, the murderer attaches a mirror to his camera, so that as his victims are being filmed being killed, they see the image of the fear on their faces reflected back to them. Their fear is thereby magnified, in a sort of feedback loop. Powell thus suggests his own complicity, as well as that of the viewer, in the misogynous and objectifying structure of the cinematic apparatus. Bigelow ups the ante on this conception, in a scene at the very centre of *Strange Days*. Max Peltier (Tom Sizemore), the film's major villain, rapes and murders the prostitute Iris (Brigitte Bako), as part of a cynical cover up. Not only does Max record a SQUID tape of his act, but he forces Iris to experience her own victimization through his eyes, at the very moment that she is suffering it, by attaching a real-time SQUID device to her head that is networked with one he is wearing and recording from. This is the sadistic objectification and commodification of the female image, with a vengeance. Lenny is literally nauseated when he subsequently watches this tape, as we see from the reaction shots. But watch the sequence he does, and we do too. There is no escaping our complicity, as an audience, in this technology. For the virtual reality medium projected in the diegesis of *Strange Days*, as well as for the film and video technologies that are its actuality, we can say, quoting Walter Benjamin, that '[mankind]'s self-alienation has reached such a degree that it can experience its own destruction as an aesthetic pleasure of the first order' (Benjamin 1969: 242).

Peeping Tom is all about voyeuristic complicity: film viewing and film-making are equated with objectification, and ultimately with murder. The cinematic apparatus is exposed and denounced for its targeting and destruction of the woman's body. The film-maker himself, and the audience watching the film, are exposed as complicitous in this act of objectification and destruction. It is not surprising that *Peeping Tom* was rejected with horror by reviewers and audience alike when it first came out in 1961. Its release effectively ended Michael Powell's long career as a director. *Peeping Tom* was later rehabilitated, and even gained a cult following, because of the way it seemed to anticipate many of the ideas of feminist film theory of the 1970s and 1980s, starting with Laura Mulvey's influential 1975 article 'Visual Pleasure and Narrative

Cinema' (Mulvey 1999). Mulvey powerfully presented classical Hollywood film as being predicated upon identification with the fantasy position of a male subject, and a corresponding objectification of the body of the woman. The fetishised female body appeared as a fantasy object, but also a threat of castration, for the male protagonist and viewer. The woman, therefore, was stripped of agency, to become either a spectacle for the male gaze, or else an object to be tracked through narrative, and sadistically mastered by the male protagonist with whom that gaze was identified. The task of thus enforcing the patriarchal norm was never entirely successful, in this account, but the project was always being renewed. In such a context, *Peeping Tom* seemed to expose the cinematic mechanism by which the woman was obliterated for the male's sadistic pleasure.

Over the years, *Peeping Tom* has become a persistent reference point for the ways that film theory has evolved. In the 1990s, feminist film theorists tried to move beyond the psychoanalytic models of an all-powerful male gaze or patriarchal vision, and to look instead (or additionally) at the various ways that even classical films rejected, or refused to conform to, the normative model. In particular, *Peeping Tom* was re-examined by critics such as Kaja Silverman (1988) and Carol Clover (1993: 168–91), who discussed how the film's peculiarly masochistic set-up subverted the patriarchal regime of vision that was its ostensible subject. The evident sadism of *Peeping Tom* gets transformed into a masochistic identification, on the part of the viewer, with the woman's victimisation. Mark Lewis, the protagonist of *Peeping Tom* is himself a victim of cinema's objectifying gaze; as a child, his father, a famous psychiatrist, monitored him with a film camera as he was being subjected to experiences of fear. As a result, Mark is unable to occupy the voyeuristic position of male power effectively; his identification with the role of objectified female victim is too strong. This is brought out both in the narrative structure of the film, and in Boehm's sympathetic performance, with its intimations of vulnerability and awkwardness. When Mark kills women, in the act of transforming them into cinematic images, he identifies with his victims far more than he feels a sense of aggrandisement from destroying them. He is actually trying to use film masochistically, to capture and identify with the very moment of death. Mark's secondary identification with the victim, as he watches the films he has made, is his pathetic attempt at redemption from the otherwise intrinsically misogynistic mechanism of cinema. Fittingly, at the end of *Peeping Tom*, Mark films himself in the act of killing himself, achieving the masochistic self-obliteration that he had so long sought, through the detour of victimizing others. In this reading, women's bodies are still being used as a prop for male fantasy, but at least it is an order that tends to undo itself, rather than reinforce its own domination.

Strange Days pushes all this to a more extreme point, as SQUID technology – which is a stand-in here for all of the new digital and virtual technologies that are coming into existence now – replaces that of traditional cinema. The murderer in *Strange Days* inverts the pattern of *Peeping Tom* by forcing his victim to experience viscerally the very sadism that he is in the act of directing against her. Bigelow thus echoes the critique made by *Peeping Tom*. The sadistic and masochistic dimensions of the structure of voyeurism in *Peeping Tom* are conflated in such a way that the latter does not mitigate the former; instead, it actually reinforces the horror. The free-floating, infra-subjective affect of this (and other) SQUID sequences is the point at which power and powerlessness coexist, in an inextricable clench that cannot easily be translated into the conventional terms of confrontation and struggle.

But there is more. The relation between killer and victim in the SQUID sequence at the heart of *Strange Days* is not a movement of identification, but an ever-intensifying feedback loop. This suggests that it cannot be understood psychoanalytically, as the analogous scene in *Peeping Tom* overtly invites us to do. The movement from *Peeping Tom* to *Strange Days* involves a radical paradigm shift. *Peeping Tom* is directly self-referential and self-reflexive, since its subject is the power of cinema itself. But the reference of *Strange Days* is less film as it has existed in the twentieth century, than the new media forms that are emerging on the cusp of the twenty-first. Film is only one element, subsumed within a broader field of video, computer electronics, virtual-immersion technologies, and multimedia entertainment. So Bigelow does not turn film back upon itself, as Powell does, so much as she stages its displacement and absorption. The SQUID technology combines traditional cinema's sense of spectacle with the intimacy of video, the effect of non-present repetition that comes from the possibility of playing back a tape innumerable times, and the promise of full immersion in (as yet nonexistent) virtual reality technologies. The SQUID sequences in *Strange Days* are at best synecdoches for this new, more fully englobing, form of representation. In this posthuman situation, new machines make for new configurations of affect.

SQUID only constitutes one regime of vision in *Strange Days*. The non-SQUID portions of the film have a very different style. Evidently, they are closer to conventional Hollywood film-making. But in fact many of the third-person sequences (if I can call them that) in *Strange Days* also constitute a particular regime of vision, one that is relatively uncommon in mainstream Hollywood film-making. Take the sequence near the beginning of the film, shortly after the opening SQUID sequence, when Lenny is driving through the streets of Los Angeles. The sequence, at first, seems to be anchored in classical shot/reverse-shot form. There is a primary differentiation between Lenny, who is safely inside his car, and the action taking place outside the car, on the streets. But this opposition is not as solid as it could be. The form of the car itself creates a membrane between the inside (Lenny's subjectivity) and outside (the setting for the subject's action); and this distinction is embodied in the editing. But this metaphorical membrane, like the actual ones in our bodies, is highly porous. This is as much a function of the sound as the images. The soundtrack shifts between music Lenny plays on his car's cassette player, non-diegetic soundtrack music, Lenny's voice on the cell phone as he talks to parties unknown, the voices he listens to on talk radio, and ambient sounds seeping in from the street. Meanwhile, in alternation with the close-ups of Lenny at the wheel, the camera weaves horizontally through a crush of traffic and crowds. The camera's movements are fluid, dreamlike, and nearly disembodied. Night time Los Angeles glimmers in subtle gradations of light. The city is a battleground. Cops stand by in riot gear. Tanks sit on street corners. Surveillance helicopters buzz overhead. Fires burn in garbage cans. Teenagers throw rocks at the cops, or smash the windows of cars. Some drag queens mug a Santa Claus, as the camera glides by in a long tracking shot. In the conventional terms of narrative cinema, this is the scene that Lenny is seeing, and the setting or backdrop for his actions as protagonist. But the film's camerawork exceeds this function, and takes on a kind of autonomy. The play of light and shadow, the foldings of space, and the impersonal movements of crowds, all take on a life of their own, rather than just serving as adjuncts to plot and character.

Such fluid camerawork, together with nocturnal blue-black lighting, and a *mise-en-scène* that is alternately overpacked and eerily empty, is something of an authorial signature for Bigelow; one finds it in such earlier films of hers as *Near Dark* (1987) and *Blue Steel* (1990). Later on in *Strange Days*, this sort of camerawork gets even more elaborate. Visual clutter is everywhere. The Retinal Fetish nightclub is a three-dimensional maze of stages, catwalks, multi-level dance floors, alcoves, corridors and pulsating lights. The New Year's Eve celebration that closes the film is filled with crowds, confetti and fireworks. Huge video screens magnify the scenes in front of them. Objects of the most varied sizes and scales co-exist in the widescreen frame. Heads are posed, in close-up, against a swirling background of street life and neon lights. Claustrophobic views from ground level alternate with extreme long shots from above. The camera's movements through space are free-floating and ethereal; the juxtapositions produced through editing divide space rhythmically, in a way that goes beyond ordinary or 'natural' perception.

The second regime of vision in *Strange Days* does not allow the viewer to identify closely with the protagonist. But it also does not give us the third-person objectivity of André Bazin's 'myth of total cinema' (1989: 17). Bazin famously dreamed of the ultimate film as 'a total and complete representation of reality ... a recreation of the world in its own image' (1989: 22). He championed a style of long shots and long the depth and ambiguity of the real world would be 'built into the the image' (1989: 36). Such a dream can only seem ironic today; in since Bazin wrote, instead of the movies having become more like reality has become more like the movies. Bigelow's second regime of vision responds to this condition of hyperreality, in which the world itself may be ironically described as 'a recreation of the world in its own image'. The camera seems to create a new point of view, neither precisely objective nor conventionally subjective, but transpersonal and social. The camera explores the nooks and crannies, the minutest articulations, of social space. Its restless movements and unexpected cuts trace the invisible workings of power. Its images express the rage of crowds, the tensions of class and racial conflict, the dynamics of police control. This is, of course, the way that *Strange Days* endeavours to portray the divisions that have come to define present-day America.

This is the part of the film that most directly alludes to another cinematic precursor, Ridley Scott's canonical postmodern film, *Blade Runner* (1982). *Strange Days* closely follows this earlier film in the way that it uses film noir lighting to portray urban decay and danger: the vision of a dystopian futuristic Los Angeles. Bigelow also takes from *Blade Runner* the sense of a world that has become radically multiculturalised, and that is totally penetrated by media technology. (One wonders if there is a relation between these two developments.) Scott Bukatman (1993) points out how *Blade Runner* is structured around a fractal replication of images along all scales, from the microscopic to the global. *Strange Days* goes even further in the way that it uses contrast of scale, and replication independently of scale, in order to imply the unleashing of film and video technology's capacity to deterritorialise the image.

But there is a significant difference between the ways that these two films thematise vision. In *Blade Runner*, the question of vision has to do with the question of whether the replicants (androids) are human. The film starts with an eye test that is used to make the distinction. The replicant Roy Batty (Rutger Hauer) visits the factory where replicant eyes are manufactured; he pokes out the eyes of his creator, Tyrell (Joe Turkel) when he kills him; and he makes stirring, poetic speeches centred on the motif, 'if only you could see what I've seen with your eyes'. In *Blade Runner*, vision is what makes us human subjects. The pathos of the film has much to do with this humanisation: a residue that somehow, wishfully, is supposed to resist the otherwise totalising power of the media of reproduction. Batty dies reflecting on his memories of the spectacles that he has seen, memories that 'will be lost in time, like tears in rain'. As I have written elsewhere, contrasting Scott with Bigelow, a kind of humanist nostalgia is thus the real source of seduction in *Blade Runner* (Shaviro 1993: 1–9).

Strange Days demystifies this sort of nostalgia. Scott humanises technology, by giving the replicants precious, poetic memories. But Bigelow does something quite different: she materialises memory itself as a technology of electronic replication. The SQUID tapes depersonalise memory, turning it instead into an exchangeable, and infinitely reproducible, commodity. And this also means that memory is preserved in an inorganic physical substrate, which can itself be destroyed. When Mace tells Lenny that memories are meant to fade, she backs up her words by violently stomping on his tapes of his time with Faith. But in this respect, the SQUID technology is no different from earlier prosthetic memory devices, such as ideographic and alphabetic writing, movable print, photography, sound recording, and film and video. All of these media have been condemned, at one time or another, for alienating humanity from its essence or natural state. But all of them can be more profitably seen, in McLuhan's terms, as 'extensions of man [sic]' (McLuhan 1994), that we have projected outside of ourselves, and that have transformed us in turn. Rather than humanising technology – by discovering, for instance that *Blade Runner*'s replicants are actually human after all – we come to realize that the 'human' itself is not a fixed term, but something that undergoes radical mutations, so that the 'human' is always in process of becoming something other than itself.

In the non-SQUID portions of *Strange Days*, in what I am calling the film's second regime of vision, this demystification of nostalgia (and of technology) goes even further. Vision is radically shattered and dehumanised. The camera floats free of any personal viewpoint. It leaves the human eye behind, in a cinematic tradition that goes back to Dziga Vertov in the 1920s (Vertov 1984), and that was extensively explored by Benjamin (1969). This is a very different modernist tradition from the one, involving notions of alienation and authenticity that gets picked up in *Blade Runner*. This is not to say that Bigelow celebrates technology in the utopian, High Modernist way that Vertov did in *Man With A Movie Camera* (1929). Rather, she depicts a world that is so permeated by technology that it would be pointless either to make such a celebration, or to make any sort of symmetrical denunciation. Vertov's camera made itself into the protagonist of *Man With A Movie Camera*, and even took a bow before the audience. Bigelow's camera does not need to do any such thing, because it is already woven into the very texture of social space.

Everything in *Strange Days* is structured around the split between these two transhuman, or posthuman, regimes of vision. It is something like a rupture of the eye. The film's long shots and public scenes extend anonymously beyond the self, even as the SQUID first-person POV sequence shots stop anonymously before it. This split puts conventional structures of subjectivity into suspension. On one side of the split, vision falls short of the subject, while on the other side vision extends beyond the subject.

Strange Days does have a traditionally humanistic plot, but it is necessarily a fragile and tentative one. It exists only in the narrow margin where these two regimes of vision intersect, or interfere with one another. The film is both a love story and a political thriller. But love and political intrigue alike are mediated by SQUID technology; and they are both bathed in the film's atmosphere of nocturnal passion and social strife.

In the film's love story, Lenny is at the centre of a triangle. Throughout the film, he continues to yearn after Faith, even though she unequivocally wants him out of her life. In the SQUID tapes that he watches obsessively, they are totally happy together, and she is all sweetness and light. We see a SQUID sequence in which they are roller-skating together, on the Santa Monica pier, in the bright sunlight. Significantly, this scene is totally out of synch with the urban, nocturnal look of the rest of the film. And Faith herself couldn't be more different from her SQUID image in the present-time sections of the film: she sings early P. J. Harvey songs at the Retinal Fetish nightclub, and tells Lenny plainly to fuck off. Lenny's yearning after Faith is both abject and pathetic; this is only underscored by the way he uses the SQUID tapes in order to fuel his nostalgia.

At the same time, Mace is deeply in love with Lenny, though she tends to be stoic about it; she holds everything in, instead of making a spectacle of her feelings in the way Lenny does of his. For his part, Lenny doesn't scorn Mace in the way that Faith scorns him; rather, he strategically ignores the depth of her feelings, so that he can benefit from her assistance without actually having to commit himself emotionally to her. For Mace is always at Lenny's beck and call; serving as his driver and bodyguard, she comes whenever he needs her, and gets him out of one jam after another. And that's not all. Lenny's love for Faith fits in with the gendered, heterosexual conventions of mainstream Hollywood cinema; the desire is all on his side, and she displays an idealised feminine acquiescence in the SQUID tapes from the past, and a fundamental bitchiness (like a punk updating of the image of the *femme fatale*) in the film's present. But Mace's love for Lenny violates the conventional pattern in several respects. For one thing, she is black and he is white; for another, she is the film's tough guy and action hero.

Bigelow is known for her feminist reconfiguration of action genres; in this respect, *Strange Days* is close to *Blue Steel* and *Near Dark*. All these films feature assertive, active, and even violent female protagonists; while the male characters tend to be either outright psychotic, or else, like Lenny, passive, somewhat effete, and fairly ineffectual. In *Strange Days*, Mace is distinguished from Lenny both by her muscular physique, and by her commitment to action in the present, while he is always dwelling on the past. She frequently expresses her disdain for the SQUID technology, and especially for where it has left Lenny. For his part, Lenny is always getting into dangerous

Figure 7 Caught in the gaze: Lenny (Ralph Fiennes) in *Strange Days*.

situations, from which he is incapable of extricating himself. But Mace kicks ass effectively in a number of bravura fight and action sequences. 'This is what I do', she tells him at the beginning of a nocturnal car chase, which ends with her dousing the flames that are about to make their car explode by driving it off a pier, into deep water. Bigelow and Bassett pull off something difficult here: they create a new kind of female action hero(ine). Mace neither reproduces all the characteristics of male actions heroes with just a nominal change of gender, nor replaces those characteristics with ones that are as stereotypically 'feminine' as Stallone's or Schwarzenegger's are stereotypically 'masculine'. Instead, she evinces a coolness and flexibility that would probably be called androgynous, if one were to try to categorise her in gender terms at all. But I would rather say that, at the same time that Mace is embodied and socially gendered as female, many aspects of her character just are not codable in the binary terms of masculinity versus femininity. In any case, what most distinguishes Mace as an action hero(ine) is that she knows how to negotiate the fluid, continually metamorphosing social spaces that characterize what I am calling the film's second regime of vision. Mace inhabits and operates within this postsubjective realm, just as Lenny does within the presubjective realm of SQUID technology.

It is also significant that Mace is black as well as female, in a world where power is still largely the province of white men. This is not just an example of multicultural tokenism, because the racial divide between Mace and Lenny – and for that matter, between Mace and most of the other characters – is highlighted continually throughout the film, even though it is never mentioned directly in the script. I am inclined to say that *Strange Days* is one of the very few recent films by a white American director that isn't entirely clueless when it comes to matters of race. For instance, the continued racial segregation of ostensibly multicultural Los Angeles is subtly but clearly emphasised, as in the scene when Mace takes Lenny to hide out in the 'hood. More generally, the political narrative of the film turns entirely on race relations. Jeriko-One (Glenn Plummer), a rapper and black political activist, is murdered under mysterious circumstances. Official denials, rumours of racist death squads, and the general public uncertainty over the identity of the killers lead to a tense and dangerous situation. Los Angeles seems ready to explode into a full-fledged race war. This situation is an ever-present background to Lenny's and Mace's interactions. But the political narrative intersects directly with the personal one, when Lenny gets hold of a SQUID tape that reveals the circumstances of Jeriko-One's murder by two racist cops.

Many viewers and critics have found the resolution of the political side of the narrative to be deeply unsatisfying. First, in revealing the identity of Jeriko-One's killers, the SQUID tape also shows that the murder is not the result of any more wide-reaching conspiracy. Then, at the very end of the film, the threat of racial violence is averted when a powerful good guy is brought in to straighten it all out. The incorruptible police commissioner, the very image of traditional white male authority, smoothes things over, arrests the rogue cops – actually they are killed resisting arrest – and thus prevents apocalyptic violence from breaking out. Taken on its own terms, this resolution is clearly a cop-out; it smoothes over the racial tensions that have been dramatised so powerfully earlier in the film, without actually creating any sort of redress. It's almost as if Cameron and Bigelow were frightened by the spectres of turmoil that they had so powerfully dramatised, and therefore pulled back timidly from the brink.

But to my mind, this traditional, genre-bound ending is more than compensated for by the way the film works its conflicts out on the intimate, personal level. When Lenny kisses Mace, at the very end, he finally gives up on Faith, and accepts the love that Mace has offered him all along. He recognises her unrequited desire, instead of wallowing in his own. The poignancy of this kiss comes not just from the way it resolves the characters' dilemmas, and to some extent redeems the deeply flawed Lenny. It also comes from the fact of the unspoken racial divide between them. Such a final kiss between the protagonists is, of course, a traditional genre convention, to give the audience a happier ending. But, unlike the police commissioner's intervention, this kiss reinforces the film's more radical implications – if only because it's the black woman's desire that is being recognised here, something that is all too rare in Hollywood films. Indeed, miscegenation is the only hope the film has to offer.

The personal and the political are inescapably intertwined throughout the film. And they are also surrounded by the two regimes of vision that contain them and go beyond them. This is why we cannot help being aware of how fragile and tenuous the personal, character-driven level of the film is. Lenny's kissing Mace bespeaks a very slender kind of hope, one that cannot be sustained by the film as a whole. That kiss speaks to the resolution of racial conflict, by the elimination of white supremacy. But it also leaves us with the awareness that one person's change of heart, and the union of two people, does not really solve things on a superpersonal, institutional level. The kiss is moving, precisely because it is contextualised and circumscribed by the ways the film has been structured around the split between two impersonal regimes of vision. At the end of the film, the camera lingers, for a long moment, on Lenny and Mace's kiss. The two of them share the screen in close-up. Then there's a cut, to a long shot from above. For a moment we can still make them out amidst the crowd. But the camera inexorably pans up and away, and they are lost in the anonymous distance.

CHAPTER TEN

The Strange Days of Kathryn Bigelow and James Cameron

Christina Lane

The 1995 film *Strange Days* is significant for its engagement of postmodern discourses regarding memory, experience and knowledge as well as for what those discourses say about the film's two authors, director Kathryn Bigelow and writer/producer James Cameron. In *Strange Days*, Lenny Nero lives in the urban street culture of the future year 1999. His dangerous neo-noir world is unravelling with the coming of the new millennium. Racial tensions have heightened to the point where African-Americans and Korean-Americans stand guard outside their storefronts with semi-automatic machine guns, as if the 1992 Los Angeles riots have settled into everyday reality. Almost everyone in this world takes a no-holds-barred, individualistic approach to the surroundings, having been corrupted by greedy capitalism or the lure of male power. Lenny (Ralph Fiennes) is a former vice squad cop who can no longer stay moral in his schizophrenic, out-of-control environment. Instead, he deals out wire trips for a superconducting device (SQUID) worn on the head that allows its occupant to re-live the dangerous or salacious experiences of others through virtual reality. Drawn into an investigation of the rape and murder of a prostitute, he uses a series of these wire trips to solve the mystery, 'trying on' and then discarding other people's memories as he hones in on the perpetrator. These are not just anybody's memories, however. They tend to be those of white female victims, or in one case an African-American male victim, who have died at the hands of white male violence. As a result, the film allows its white male protagonist to experience murder or rape as a second-hand mediary without having to be positioned, for the most part, as a direct victim.

This move suggests that *Strange Days* is working through more than mere anxieties about new technologies or surveillance culture. Although ostensibly Lenny confronts the threat held by the inscrutable confluences of time, space, and fiction, his encounters with technology reveal a more latent vulnerability to the threat of being a racial or female 'other.' It would simplify the film's terms, however, to read these vulnerabilities and threats as just another white male paranoia fantasy. A film as complex as *Strange Days* requires a multi-faceted approach, one that does not dismiss its engagement with postmodernism as ahistorical or apolitical.

In this chapter, I examine four aspects of the film's politics of representation. First, I address its intersection with both postmodernism and historical context. Secondly, I draw out its complicated organisation around gendered structures of looking. Thirdly, I discuss how the film's themes are imbricated in a complex relationship between its primary authors, James Cameron and Kathryn Bigelow. Lastly, I explore its racial ideologies, especially as they relate to Bigelow's authorial influence. What does this film say about the epistemology of the hotly contested social categories of its historical moment and how does it bear the tracings of Kathryn Bigelow's authorship?

Fragmenting the Master Narrative

Strange Days has a postmodern look and attitude but, beyond that, the film also engages postmodern theory in its positioning of gendered and racial subjects and its understanding of history. By juxtaposing various modes of virtual reality and the historical real, the film explores what it means to know one's self, to relate to an 'other', and to exist in a world that proclaims to orbit 'beyond' the historical moment of contemporary feminist and civil rights movements. While postmodern theory has been problematised for glossing over power differences, some feminist theorists such as Barbara Creed have found it invaluable for understanding the multiplicity of subjective experience.

In an attempt to come to terms with the increasing technological proliferation and media saturation of contemporary Western culture, Jean Baudrillard argues that we live in a postmodern world governed by a superficial series of endless, schizophrenic networks where distinctions between inner and outer, self and other, and subject and object become blurry. Baudrillard laments, 'we will have to suffer this new state of things, this forced extroversion that the categorical imperative of communication literally signifies' (1983: 132). *Strange Days* challenges the existence of a universal 'master narrative' by blurring the lines between truth and fiction while also destabilising the notion of a centred subject through a breakdown of various subject/object dichotomies. Its digital drug of the future blurs such boundaries by enabling the subject to inhabit the experiences of others and incorporate their memories into his or her subjectivity. Hence, as Baudrillard puts it, a forced extroversion – and introversion – characterises this new site of communication. This site is governed by a disjunctive relation between the parts and the whole (Deleuze & Guattari 1977: 42). Within *Strange Days*' terms, the parts are represented by the memories and the whole by the subject, who, at least temporarily, owns them. The disjunctions between the two indicate the breakdown of identity and an inability to achieve some universalised experience.

The collapses theorised by postmodernism have provided strategies for feminists invested in deconstructing master narratives. For example, Barbara Creed suggests that postmodernism holds significant implications for feminism. For Creed, the 'cold universe of networks' described by Jean Baudrillard and the hodgepodge bricolage detailed by Gilles Deleuze and Feliz Guattari indicate a collapse of previously normalised Western master narratives which attempted to totalise experience and subjectivity (Baudrillard 1983: 134; Deleuze & Guattari 1977: 7). She defines this cultural moment of postmodernism most specifically as a crisis in the status of knowledge: how do we know things? How do we ascertain the true versus the inauthentic? How do we relate to our own experiences? Who has a claim to experience and knowledge? (Creed 1987: 51). Creed posits that as stories of the Other (represented in narratives by women, gays and lesbians, or people of colour) gain legitimacy, they chip away at the notion of a universal and 'neutral' white male narrative.

Strange Days delves into the complex relationship between these two different kinds of stories, providing numerous examples of male efforts to colonise the experiences of Others. In scene after scene, the film questions the status of knowledge and underscores the fragility of that universal narrative. The tension between these two kinds of narrative suggests that the film represents a response to a series of cultural crises, or symptoms of those crises, which shaped the historical moment in which it was made. 'Stories of the particular' had been playing out on the very public stages of film, television, and news media as had anxious responses on the part of individuals and institutions that, thirty years prior, would have been able to exercise more complete control over such stories by invoking white male privilege. The early-to-middle 1990s saw a string of controversial real-life but heavily mediated cultural events in the US including the trials of Lorena Bobbitt, O.J. Simpson, and the Los Angeles police who brutally attacked Rodney King, as well as the congressional hearings on Clarence Thomas. Each of these cases functioned as condensed representational forums in which the legitimacy of a marginalised perspective, or several marginalised perspectives, came into direct conflict with white, male hegemonic authority. At the same time, public debates ensued about highly visible and heavily circulating films such as *Thelma and Louise* and books such as Susan Faludi's 'Backlash' (1991) that articulated women's experiences of victimisation and their reasons for radical resistance. In this way, the middle 1990s socio-historical climate needs to be seen as a postmodern (which is not to say apolitical) extension of the 1960s civil rights and second-wave feminist movements.

Indeed, the year 1994 has been called the Year of the Angry White Male due to the massive congressional turnover to supposedly revolutionary Republicans who had been angered by President George Bush's defeat. As debates about multiculturalism, affirmative action, police brutality and violence against women became entrenched, a considerable backlash arose against the threat of political correctness and what was perceived as a 'cult of victimology' (which seeks to explain behaviour and support revenge tactics by re-inscribing the victim's point of view). The culmination of such defensiveness and the most extreme manifestation of the Angry White Male Congressional Revolution would be seen in the groundswell of support for the 1996 Defence of Marriage Act, in which heterosexuality was cast as a vulnerable and chaste character under militant attack from 'outside' forces.

This socio-historical context is extremely significant because the 'real-life' repetition of such competitions for the 'victim position' and battles over narrative authority clearly influenced *Strange Days*' representation of its male identity crisis. To a degree, Lenny Nero is best viewed as an extension of the Angry White Male Backlash whose only familiar response to the victim subject-position is fear of difference and desire for its re-territorialisation. He cannot regain confidence in his identity nor can he master his experience in any other way. Lenny cannot 'know' his story – indeed he does not have a story to tell – until he has repeatedly appropriated the narratives of Others and colonised their thoughts and memories. If the status of knowledge is at stake, then it is the knowledge of society's victims that poses the greatest threat to those in power.

Understanding *Strange Days*' relationship to its historical context does not undermine a focus on the authorship of Bigelow and Cameron, however. In fact, such an understanding helps to clarify authorship's influence (and Romi Stepovich's chapter in this collection also examines the role each played in the development of *Strange Days*, through the processes of scripting, financing and producing the film). To the extent that the film functions as a response to the cultural problems that were taking centre stage in the early-to-mid-1990s, Bigelow and Cameron apparently had different readings and reactions to the gendered and racialised questions raised by such problems. They engaged separate lines of political inquiry and different intellectual curiosities. They were, in other words, historically located subjects bringing different political viewpoints to the film and its mediation of current events.

While Bigelow and Cameron have similar styles, in some respects, they each bring a different vision of masculinity, feminism, subjectivity and spectacle to *Strange Days*. The film registers the impact of two authors who, at times, struggle over point of view. This struggle resonates with the film's own themes regarding the legitimacy of particularised (as opposed to universal) subject positions. Furthermore, because *Strange Days* embeds these themes into its visual structures, the film manifests various ways of seeing contradictory authorial impulses. *Strange Days* asks its characters who owns 'the look'? or more aptly, who has the right to own 'the look'?; but it asks these questions of its makers as well. Its major sequences call attention to the film's status as a doubly authored text and, in doing so, they converse with films of the past, such as *Peeping Tom* (Michael Powell, 1960) as well as paradigms of psychoanalytic theory, especially Jacques Lacan's understanding of the 'mirror stage' (1977a, 1977b).

Structures of Looking: Linking Two Gazes in a Reel Head Trip

On formal and thematic levels, *Strange Days* invokes Michael Powell's *Peeping Tom*, in which protagonist Mark Lewis (Carl Boehm) kills women with a stabbing device that holds a mirror up to their terrorised faces as they die. Steven Shaviro addresses the connections between the two films, and their indictment of their own audiences' voyeuristic complicity, in this collection (see chapter 9). *Peeping Tom* most specifically inspires *Strange Days'* structures of looking. Discussing Mark in the former, Carol Clover remarks that 'uniting with the victim position seems to be the point of his spectatorial enterprise' (1992: 179). Clover's reasoning is that Mark represents a divided self – a sadist and a masochist – which yokes together two kinds of gazes, projective and introjective. The projective gaze is more assaultive and voyeuristic, perhaps best exemplified in the stalking sequences of John Carpenter's *Halloween* (1979) in which spectators 'are invited to look not through a murderous camera, but with our own murderous eyes' (1992: 186).

Strange Days' wire trip sequences articulate just this mode of address whereby spectators, and the film's characters, assume a 'first-person' position in order to vicariously live out bank robberies, cross-gender masturbation, rape and murder. But, as Clover reminds us, this projective gaze never stands alone; instead, it is constantly undermined by a connection to its flipside, the introjective gaze. The former is often insecure: 'The "view" of the first-person killer is typically cloudy, unsteady and punctuated by dizzying swish-pans. Insofar as an unstable gaze suggests an unstable gazer, the credibility of the first-person killer-camera's omnipotence is undermined from the outset' (1992: 187).

The film makes this connection in the wire trip sequence involving the rape and murder of the prostitute, Iris. In the playback, the rapist not only records his attack on Iris, but he forces her to wear a wire that is jacked into his recorder. In effect, she sees what he sees – herself being raped – from his point of view, compounding the violence of his brutality. Because her fear only feeds his turn on further, she presumably also experiences the 'thrill' of the rapist simultaneously with her own victimisation. In a way, this scene encourages an empathetic identification with the introjective gaze, attending to Iris's subjective experience of her victimisation. This moment of identification is at best troubling though, from a feminist perspective, precisely because the rapist's pleasure cannot be extracted from the victim position. The visceral and violent way in which the camera interprets Iris's demise stands as an indictment of Hollywood codes that weave visual pleasure into conventional rape scenes; but it does so through a visual mediation that seems to encourage as much discomfort for critical-feminist spectators as for those accustomed to complying with masculinist ways of seeing.

Indeed, this scene's status as a mediation is crucial to understanding the film's gender politics. As the primary mediator, Lenny provides an anchoring point of view through which the victim's and the rapist's subjectivities are transmitted. At the level of metanarrative, the introjective gaze offered by Iris loses out – not to the projective gaze of the rapist but to Lenny's hysterical subject-position. Iris's rape scene continues to be interrupted by Lenny's overwhelming response to it, as his reaction shots in 'real' time and space are sprinkled throughout the playback. The effect of such editing creates another double layer. The reactions of Lenny show that he *is* identifying with Iris, as opposed to the rapist. They also have the effect, however, of privileging his experience of the rape over hers. Within the logic of the film, Lenny becomes as much of a victim as Iris has been, due to the fact that he is forced to re-live her experience.

The white male 'experience' of Iris's rape does not occur only in this instance. In fact, it is repeated, as Lenny screens it for two of his friends, Max and Tick. These characters' responses play even more directly on the tension between violent pain and voyeuristic pleasure because the sounds that accompany their reaction shots connote masturbatory participation as much as they do disgust. (Max, it should be noted, is faking whatever empathy he does demonstrate in an effort to cover up his own involvement.) The degree to which Max and Tick feel for Iris is in some way beside the point – their individual viewings reinforce Lenny's privileged subjective role, providing further distance from Iris's primary experience.

Lenny undergoes further victimisation at the climax of the film when he goes to the postmodern Bonaventura Hotel to rescue Faith, the ex-girlfriend whom he cannot seem to shake from his memory. A wiretrip is waiting for him in the hotel room and, upon playing it, he is led to believe that Faith has been raped in the same brutal manner as Iris. His torture is again revealed through reaction shots until the encounter ends and Faith tells the rapist 'I love you'. In one of the film's many blurs between fiction and reality, Faith has only been simulating her position as a victim of violence. So, in effect, Lenny is the one who has been victimised, having first thought he was re-living the rape of a woman he loves only to realise that he has just witnessed graphic evidence that his love-object has moved beyond their relationship. The focus on Lenny is even more accentuated here, compared to Iris's playback, in part because it contains more frequent and prolonged objective shots of him reacting to the playback, but mostly because he has become the true victim of a simulated rape. He has just been 'screwed' by his best friend, as literally as possible without the presence of Max's material body. In fact, the 'truth' of the female rape experience actually *de-materialises*, as Faith proves to be a weapon in the arsenal against Lenny.

It is during this sequence, however, that *Strange Days* most provocative discursive seeds about 'masculinity in crisis' begin to sprout and that, I will suggest later, Bigelow's high theory leanings make their mark. Lenny's awakening – his realisation about Max's complicity – functions as an internal critique of his behaviour and attitudes up to this point in the film. In keeping with *Strange Days'* engagement with postmodernism and post-structuralism, this awakening occurs during an all-important 'mirror stage'. Just after the 'rapist' has completed his act, but before Faith has voiced the words 'I love you' to him, he turns sideways to look at himself in the mirror. That mirror reflection reveals Max, hovered over Faith's quivering body, in an image that is doubled (because of the placement of the mirror panes). In addition to revealing Max as the culprit, this moment forces Lenny to see himself in relation to the villain, whom he has associated all along with sadism, brutality and perverse scopophilia.

Like all of the wire trips, this scene occurs in dual realities which means that Lenny must halfway expect to see himself in the mirror when he is caught off-guard by the villain's image. More to the point, this sequence is constructed in such a way that *Strange Days'* *spectators* are encouraged to experience this expectation. In the terms put forward by Christian Metz (1982), primary identification (denoting the cinematic apparatus) and secondary identification (denoting the protagonist's point of view) are suddenly disaligned just at the moment when the viewer probably expects them to coincide. The glance in the mirror functions as a temporary suspension of the action, a rehearsal of the mirror stage, during which Lenny's vision of an ideal 'imago' suddenly represents his worst fear, the threatening force that he has been hunting down throughout the film. Since the mirror stage serves as both a reminder and a denial of an individual's fragmented, incomplete ego, Lenny finally is forced to confront finally his desire to inhabit the 'other', that is, to enjoy and profit from the fragmented experiences of others.

A second 'mirror moment' occurs just after the murderer's identity is revealed. Once the wire trip is over, a long shot shows Lenny regaining his bearings. He sits on the bed, taking up the entire left side of the film's frame. Behind him is the same set of mirrors, whose separate panes form a vertical line down the centre of the frame. To the right of the frame – and therefore on the other side of the dividing line – is a brain dead Philo Gant, another one of Max's victims and the figure who has represented an extreme (very 'trippy') version of Lenny. The mirror suddenly reveals Max as he steps into the frame. Lenny turns toward the mirror as he spots Max's movement. The end result of all of these compositional elements is a cumulative shot in which Lenny sits as a spectator would on one side of the line gazing upon three men: Gant, Max and himself. He must confront his similarity to these two violent, pathological men. His image is literally wedged in between them and the question is whether or not he will be able to extricate himself from the grid of assaultive masculinity. He is, *Strange Days* suggests, one of them. Does he have, it asks, the ability to refrain from being one of them anymore?

In Lacanian terms, Lenny has passed from the Real world into the social world of the Symbolic, from the 'specular I into the social I' (Lacan 1977a: 5). Upon completing the mirror stage, one hypothetically understands the 'other' and has learned to compromise and cooperate with those outside the self. Lenny's contemplation of his own role in the villain's image – reflected back at him through the mirror – means that he momentarily sees those qualities of the murderer (the need to dominate, the moral shadiness, the colonisation of others' experiences) in himself. The implication is that he might shed that ideal imago and move beyond his previously self-centred identity.

In the traditional mirror stage, 'the child's recognition of its own image means that it has adopted the perspective of exteriority on itself' (Grosz 1990: 38). Here, perhaps Lenny has suddenly developed a critical awareness of his own complicity in these women's victimisation. He realises that he has been deluded to think that he could not only control what he looks at, but also the way in which the world returns his look in the form of a 'gaze'. According to Lacan, several responses to the mirror stage are possible, depending on the relation to power assumed by the individual. For the subject who disavows the presence of the gaze, part of the illusory quality of the mastering 'look' is that the subject supposes s/he can also control how s/he is being figured as an object, in other words, how that subjective look is reciprocated (Lacan 1977b: 80–2).

Once Lenny discovers how alienating it is to be gazed upon by the villain, he presumably recognises his technological complicity in alienating others. The notion that Lenny has learned a lesson about how to more fairly navigate the social world is certainly suggested by his final decision to release his voyeuristic obsession with Faith and start valuing the non-virtual reality world endorsed by Mace. In abandoning the playbacks, he has achieved moral and feminist development. Because of the severity of the image, Lenny's encounter with the villain's imago implies not only a leaving behind of the Real but also a realisation that he should relinquish the desire to master the images he sees. While, according to Lacan, the mirror stage typically leads to 'the assumption of the armour of an alienating identity' (Lacan 1977b: 81), the film implies that Lenny has gained insight into a different kind of ideal image – that is, a realignment of identification that will be less narcissistic and less alienating to others.

So *Strange Days'* conclusion offers a progressive theme about the reformation of aggressive masculinity: because Lenny's identity is divided into a split self, he has the potential to minimise his more voyeuristic, more defensive self and become more accepting of difference. This reading also suggests that Lenny, upon coming to terms with his identity's own fragmentation and vulnerability, can begin to respond to difference and, specifically, to victims' experiences in ways that do not involve mastery. He is more aware of his own inscription within looking relations, and now, not as inclined to take advantage of others in less powerful positions. One of the film's quandaries is how this message sits alongside the more voyeuristic qualities of the rape sequences. Is an ideological critique of a projective gaze enough to displace its sadistic impulse? Doesn't Lenny's co-optation of female rape still (narratively and visually) override the victims' experiences? The way that *Strange Days* interlocks and compounds projective and introjective gazes means that such questions can reach no answers – they simply loop around and fold in on one another. Perhaps it is unproductive to ask such questions about who owns the look in *Strange Days*. It is very productive, however, to apply this concept of the *loop*, rather than the look, as an appropriate metaphor for Bigelow and Cameron's authorial contributions to the film's gender politics. The film's various examples of doubling – whether occurring when the camera offers up both the perpetrator's and the victim's experiences simultaneously or when it repeatedly fragments Max's image into two – speaks to its own status as a doubly-authored text. It is working to accommodate the interests of both Bigelow and Cameron to such a degree that its heavy labour reveals itself. Written with two hands, the *camera stylo* of *Strange Days* amplifies the usual tension between projective and introjective gazes found in films such as *Peeping Tom* or *Halloween*. Two halves of a divided gaze; this divided gaze seen from two different points of view. If the kind of unstable camerawork described by Carol Clover is almost always a reminder of the instability of vision, here it also functions as a signature of the collision of two visions, each singular and auteurist yet also quite compatible.

Two 'Auteurs': One Film

Strange Days' complicated discourse on subjectivity needs to be contextualised in terms of two subjects who exist outside the film text, Bigelow and Cameron. While earlier in this analysis, I proposed that *Strange Days* constitutes a response to particular historical events, it is equally important to understand the film's institutional history and the divided investments that result in its ever-shifting meanings. To compare the authorial styles of Bigelow and Cameron makes for a loaded enterprise from the start. Given that Bigelow shared with the producer a two-year marriage (from 1989 to 1991) and worked with him professionally before, during and after their marriage, she has often been placed in the position of defending herself against subtly implied rumours that their sexual relationship benefited her career. They met on the set of *Blue Steel*, when Cameron was in talks with Jamie Lee Curtis about starring in *True Lies* (1994). At the time, he was in an estranged marriage to Gale Ann Hurd, with whom he had collaborated on *The Terminator* (1984) (Heard 1997: 138). It was during the early stages of their *Point Break* collaboration that Bigelow and Cameron become romantically involved, though by the time *Point Break* was wrapping up, their marriage was facing difficulties. Cameron divorced Bigelow and moved in with colleague Linda Hamilton. Bigelow has apparently taken the 'high road' when it comes to her divorce and Cameron's history of relationship-hopping, remaining cool and poised when questioned about him in the press. He approached her to make *Strange Days* when he realised he would not have time to direct it himself with the obvious release deadline of 1999 looming in the distance and his commitments to *True Lies* and *Spiderman* standing in the way (Cameron 1995: vii–viii). She put her other projects on hold, including her eventually diverted efforts to make *Company of Angels/Joan of Arc*, to facilitate the making of the film.

It is especially because Bigelow and Cameron were professional colleagues before they were spouses that she bristles at references to their personal relationship (Lane 2000: 102–3). And, I would argue, it is their professional relationship that engages more interesting issues. *Strange Days* begs to be contextualised in terms of the two film-makers' individual oeuvres. Is it 'a Kathryn Bigelow film' or 'a James Cameron film'? Though authorship is never more than an organising construct, a cluster of meanings that accrue around an individual whose identity and agency are heavily mediated (Wollen 1972), at what points do the 'Bigelow construct' and the 'Cameron construct' overlap? Where do they diverge?

Cameron's name has become synonymous with spectacle, with the ability to master special effects technology, expansive set pieces and narratives of epic proportions. In the early 1990s he was dubbed the 'king of the sequel' and, coming out of the Roger Corman tradition of film-making, Cameron has always had a penchant for borrowing from 1950s and 1960s genre films (Anon. 1991: 40–3; French 1996: 15–22). In films such as *Aliens* (1986), *Terminator 2: Judgment Day* (1991) and *True Lies*, his female characters have 'kicked butt', displaying muscular hard bodies, brandishing highly sophisticated weapons and devoting themselves to tough humanity-saving missions. As Alexandra Keller points out, these heroines embody an easily consumed feminism:

> Cameron's fierce women are always pressed back into the service of patriarchy, pleasantly reaffirming the way things are in a manner equally palatable to both women and men. Cameron's big fake-out, his ability to make these women do something on a par with a gender striptease, is that, time after time, his heroines use their spunk and force to maintain the status quo. (Keller 1999: 143–5)

One further sign of the director's style is his blockbuster ideology. As the texts and intertexts of Cameron's most successful film, *Titanic* (1998), reveal, his forte lies in creating a 'material object' that is both informed by and inviting of monetary excess, commodification and consumerist ideology.

Bigelow works in the same genres – thriller, science fiction, action films – as Cameron and, like him, she shows a versatility in and preoccupation with spectacle. Her features do not, however, fit into the blockbuster genre. Though a great deal of evidence suggests that she courts the commercial and professional accoutrements that come with blockbuster status, her previous work (such as *Blue Steel, Point Break*), have not done 'Cameron box office' nor do they speak to the same ideological concerns. Where he reaffirms consumer culture fed by a global, multinational economy, she critiques it. Where his narratives drive toward a return to status quo – and an individualistic, survivalist, Reaganite status quo at that – her films question and mock such a world order. Where he exploits the specular elements of *mise-en-scène* in an effort to satiate his audience, asking only that they return for multiple viewings of the same film, she exploits those elements in ways that provoke her audience to ask more complicated ideological questions than those encouraged by Cameron (see Keller 1999 for an insightful reading of *Titanic* as capital).

The two aforementioned concerns in relation to Cameron – his tendency toward homage and preference for tough heroines – provide significant sites for comparing the directors. Like Cameron, Bigelow weaves her knowledge of film culture and film history into her movies. Her body of work connotes a 'high art' sensibility that contrasts his. Bigelow's background as a painter, participant with the radical Art and Language Group, and theory student at Columbia University means that she draws on a different film culture than Cameron. She cites modernist directors such as Stanley Kubrick, Francois Truffaut and Martin Scorsese as having the strongest influence on her work. Film reviewers describe their surprise at how well-schooled she is in high theory and how adeptly she ties this cultural knowledge into the parameters of commercial film-making. (John Powers marvels, 'Bigelow's the only Hollywood director I've met who feels equally at home discussing Cy Twombly's paintings, Jacques Lacan's psychoanalytic theories and the charisma of Keanu Reeves' (1995: 196).) One fascinating illustration of the different low theory/high theory affiliations of Cameron and Bigelow surfaced in a 1991 *American Film* 'dinner conversation' between the two, who were married at the time. She takes the time to elucidate on the collaborative relationships between director/film and actor/film, stating, 'It's the same [whether director or actor]. The same trauma, the same precarious balance between ownership and authorship and a series of negotiations. Constant, perennial negotiations.' Cameron, on the other hand, attempts his own, less heavy-handed characterisation of the artistic process, claiming that it's a mixture of 'surprise and familiarity. It's like a Baked Alaska' (in Anon. 1991: 41). Such an example, not meant to pit the two against each other in an easy opposition, does place them at slightly opposite sides of a high culture/low culture, modernist/postmodernist spectrum. It also captures their different personas – she plays the mature professor to his succinct, childlike enthusiasm.

It would seem then that Bigelow and Cameron were approaching *Strange Days* from two separate places. While she was probably as interested as he in the high concept hook and technological innovations of the film, she was bringing her knowledge of Lacan and a deep immersion in the themes of Scorsese, and by extension Michael Powell, to the table – significant given the compositional and thematic choices made in the final mirror scene.

Bigelow also brought with her a more ambitious vision of the action-adventure heroine. While a number of scholars have debated whether or not her female characters in *Blue Steel* and *Point Break* are feminist, there is little question as to Bigelow's ability, in the case of *Blue Steel's* Megan (Jamie Lee Curtis), to deploy visual and editing techniques that ground spectators within an action heroine's subjectivity. In fact, Lornette 'Mace' Mason represents one of Bigelow's toughest 'bad-ass' heroines to date, despite the fact that she is not *Strange Days'* protagonist nor does she receive many of the film's point-of-view shots. As Lenny's limousine-driving confidante, Mace's impeccable instincts help her manoeuvre her armoured car out of constant danger (chases, bullets, fire) and her physical conditioning makes her a worthy opponent against Lenny's many adversaries. Her 'hard body' attributes (Jeffords 1994) become evident particularly in the film's final twenty minutes, as she glides through L.A.'s

New Year's Eve party wearing a tight black dress and a gun holstered in between her upper thighs (a phallic configuration to which Bigelow only dared allude in *Blue Steel*). Mace's relationship to feminist power seems much less ambivalent than those held by Megan, who sometimes held an itchy trigger finger, or *Point Break*'s Tyler (Lori Petty) who finds her hands literally tied.

According to *Strange Days* screenwriter Jay Cocks, who co-wrote the script with Cameron, he and Bigelow spent a good number of conversations fleshing out Mace's character. Cocks (*Last Temptation of Christ*, *Age of Innocence*, [uncredited] *Titanic*) entered into the writing process when Cameron finished his 131-page 'scriptment' and turned his attention to *True Lies*. His role was to serve as the instrument of Bigelow's vision – she guided him through the development of some dialogue and an overall visualisation of the film on the page (Cocks 2001). Cocks recalls in-depth conversations about two major facets of the film. One facet was developing Mace's characterisation. He remembers, 'We spent a good deal of time exploring Mace's inner subjectivity. What does she think about her job, her son, her life? What's going on in her mind?' The second major topic of conversation involved the complexity of the rape sequences. Cocks states:

> You see what stirs Kathryn in those emotional scenes. Lenny's crying a lot; he's getting hammered. His responses offer a corollary with Kathryn as a director. Shooting the rape scenes absorbed a great deal of time and concern, none of which diminished through the film's production, post-production and screening. But Kathryn didn't back down from those scenes. She's really great at digging her heels in. She went as far as I thought was possible, and then a bit further. (Cocks 2001)

From Cocks' account, it can be deduced that Bigelow knew just how troubling the scenes with Iris and Faith would be, but was motivated by what she could say about vision and power through those scenes. The fact that these two areas – Mace's characterisation and the execution of the rape sequences – drew most of her attention suggests that Mace's presence in the film represents a conscious effort to counterbalance the problematic moments of female victimisation. To have featured a less developed, less tough character in Mace alongside the troubling rape sequences would have been to disengage feminism almost entirely.

As realised on screen, Mace voices her critique of dominant ideology clearly and repeatedly. She despises Lenny's business of selling images and, in her criticisms of his SQUID involvement, articulates an unapologetic disparagement of capitalism. As a single, African-American mother she reminds him, 'I got a child. I got rent.

And I got an ex-husband doin' hard time who doesn't send me a dime of support.' Mace refuses Lenny's rationalisation that he is providing a healthy outlet ('safe sex') for his customers; she asserts, 'Porno. Face it. You sell porno to wireheads.' It's Lenny's hyper-capitalist, consumerist orientation that upsets her, as she makes clear when he tries to induce various favours from her for a 'cut of the deal'. Given the strong ambient presence of the transnational, hi-tech powers that be, Mace paves an important pathway toward resistance against the people, places and props that inhabit Lenny's universe and are fed by late monopoly, global capital. In other words, and in more Marxist terms, she provides a critical reading of Lenny's world on two levels – she challenges both the ideological superstructure of V-R's hedonism and its material base.

That Bigelow strengthened Mace's role as a 'voice of critique' in the film is supported by production documents. Cameron published his 'scriptment' for *Strange Days* soon after the film's release, embracing the fact that this published draft suffered rough spots and weak, undeveloped moments. In the introduction to the extended treatment, Cameron remarks that he had little involvement with the progression of the film after bequeathing it (as it now exists in its published state) to Bigelow and Cocks (Cameron 1995: ix–x). Cocks concurs, claiming that a comparison of the scriptment represents an accurate division between the producer and director's influence (Cocks 2001). He gives the credit for changes made from scriptment to film to Bigelow, insisting (with praise) that she exercised heavy authorial influence over the final draft of the screenplay. While deciding where to cast agency for production decisions always comes with its problems and hypotheticals, the circumstances surrounding this particular writing endeavour, and Cocks' readiness to attribute many of his own choices to Bigelow, help make this discussion of *Strange Days* a bit less confounding than most.

One of the most illuminating changes that Bigelow and Cocks effected was to re-write the scene in which Jeriko One's speech plays on a local newscast the day after his death. As written by Cameron, only Lenny and Max watch the speech and, once Max's monological response ends, Mace's limo pulls up outside the Coral Lounge (Cameron 1995). As Bigelow shaped the script, she has Mace enter in time to watch the rally speech and hear Max's diatribe. So all three characters, Lenny, Max and Mace are together for the telecast in which Jeriko One urges his audience toward an Afro-centric revolution:

'The mayor and the city council sit up in their offices with their social programs that don't work. These people are rearranging deck chairs on the Titanic. But a new day is coming; 2k is coming. The day of reckoning is upon us. History ends and begins again. Right here. Right now.'

At the end of the televised address, Max turns to Lenny and responds with his own (very Baudrialliardian) vision of the world: 'Every kind of music's been tried. Every government's been tried. I mean, fuckin' hairstyle. Fuckin' bubble gum. You know, breakfast cereal. Every fuckin' peanut. What the fuck we gonna do? How we gonna make another thousand years, for Christ's sake?' The juxtaposition of Max's speech next to that of Jeriko-One invokes a tension between a totalising, white, male perspective on history and a marginalised (hi)story of the 'Other'. The important history of racial oppression toward which Max is apparently oblivious is given weight by the film's intercuts, which highlight Mace's reaction to both Jeriko One and Max. Max's verbal rantings are interrupted continually by the mere visibility of her African American body in the frame. Her vision *of him* overrides his supposedly objective view on history. For Mace and Jeriko One, it is not that 'everything's been done already'; but rather that not enough has been done to secure the safety and livelihood of African-American communities. It would be very easy for them to 'make another thousand years' though not in any way that conforms to Max's worldview. The result of Bigelow and Cocks' re-write, then, is its demonstration that the stakes of Jeriko One's murder are higher for Mace than they are for the white, male characters. The change in the scene opens up a space for Max's point of view to be re-contextualised, not simply from Mace's perspective but from a broader ideological understanding of racialised histories, memories and futures.

It is in these two areas – the characterisation of Mace and a stronger linkage between the rape and rap plots – that *Strange Days* reveals itself to be a 'Kathryn Bigelow' film. Cameron suggests that it was Bigelow who saw the Jeriko-One assassination tape as a hinge that would intensify the 'crisis between [Lenny and Mace], with Lenny wanting to use it to save Faith while Mace demands that he do the right thing and bring Jeriko's killers to justice' (Cameron 1995: x). With this editorial move, Mace challenges Lenny's self-serving individualism with a more collective, politicised perspective about how the tape might bring increased access to knowledge. She becomes a crucial link in the Jeriko storyline and helps to elevate it above Lenny's romantic crisis.

As further evidence of Mace's increased importance in later screenplay drafts, she is granted a unique flashback in the film that did not appear in Cameron's scriptment. This flashback, which occurs as she strokes the hair of sleepy Lenny after a hard day of doing battle, replaces a scene written by Cameron in which she simply returns home to her sister and son after nurturing Lenny to sleep. In the film version, she remembers returning home to find the police carting off her husband to jail and her first-ever interaction with Lenny, who is caring for her son, Xander. By transforming a fairly superficial 'goodnight' scene into a memory event, Bigelow deepens the film's themes regarding knowledge, memory and experience. Mace's flashback is shot in warm, saturated colours, in stark contrast to the washed-out, cooler characteristics of the wiretrips. Though this scene plays out through subjective camerawork, the camera remains over her shoulder (and slows the film speed), differentiating it from the whirling dervish quality of the wire trips. These variations identify her visual field with authenticity and authority. They belie careful attention to Mace's way of seeing and the influence of her past experiences on her present-day actions (e.g. she negotiates her unrequited love for Lenny quite differently than he deals with Faith).

Mobilising Strange Days' Racial Discourses

In his article 'In Medias Race', David Crane (2000) discusses Mace's alignment with authenticity, especially given that she takes on the role of privileged spectator in relation to the Jeriko One assassination tape. She makes an exception and wears the SQUID apparatus after Lenny anxiously pleads: 'I know what you think about the wire – but you gotta see it – it's that important.' Several of Bigelow and Cocks's script changes worked to broaden the impact of this pivotal moment of spectatorship. Originally, it took Mace much less convincing to watch the tape. In their hands, the exchange evolved into a longer struggle, intensifying what would be at stake for Mace to 'see' in this way. Furthermore, the scene had been preceded initially by Mace's sister and her boyfriend transporting her sleeping son to the sister's house. It is a superficial interaction in which the boyfriend complains that he wants to enjoy 'the party of the century' (Cameron 1995: 125). By transforming this preceding scene into a South Central lawn party and giving Xander an excited presence at the party, Bigelow creates a reflective interlude in which Mace looks lovingly at her son. In doing so, the film's broader New Year's Eve/Armageddon themes open themselves up to a potentially positive future, a world that Mace wishes for Xander. And, for the specific purposes of this scene, given that she is about to view the assassination of a revolutionary leader, the visual framework provided by Xander reveals the very personal implications of Jeriko One's death for Mace.

When Mace finally does succumb to Lenny's plea to watch the tape, her decision has gained deeper dramatic significance. This is due in part to the fact that the experience is an initiation for her, but also because the film's audience is prevented from knowing the tape's content until we see it through her point of view. According to Crane, this sequence provides a 'doubly articulated' viewing experience from the point of view of the Other and forces Mace to confront her own principles regarding the technology (2000: 104). Crane writes, 'A few scenes later she chastises Lenny for his vicarious obsession with clips of Faith, signifying most clearly her role as "moral preservative" and how the unmediated real is at the heart of that moral preservative."

(2000: 104). Mace's claim that 'This tape is a lightning bolt from God – it's worth more than you, more than me, more than Faith, you understand? It can change things that need changin'' helps to forge the connection between Jeriko and Mace, 'a link grounded in their shared blackness and emphasised through their insistence on truth telling' (Crane 2000: 104–5). Given the problematic tradition in film and literature of locating 'authenticity' with women of colour, this connection comes with its own set of cultural baggage. To place the burden of the 'real' with Mace and Jeriko One is to free the white characters up to explore performativity, fantasy, and the world of hi-tech (see Abel 1993).

While these problems should not be dismissed – and they are read quite provocatively by Crane as participating in the film's ambivalence about technology and race – they have the interesting effect of furthering the critique of Lenny's troubled white, male vision and elevating a supposed subplot into the primary crux of the film (Crane 2000: 104–6). Mace takes the radical position that whatever violent responses the tape might spawn are justified and in fact necessary for social change. She tells Lenny: 'Do you know what this tape would do if it got out? … People findin' out. Seein'. That the LAPD flat out executed Jeriko One. Maybe they oughtta see.' And to Max, she says: 'Maybe it's time for a war.' These pieces of dialogue were not part of Cameron's draft, indicating that Bigelow had a stronger investment in pushing the radical racial politics of the film and advocating violence in the face of police brutality. All of this is to say that if extreme racial tensions served as *Strange Days'* backdrop when Lenny first acquaints us with his millennial milieu, they prove to be the ultimate source of conflict in this world of virtuality, violence and paranoia. If Cameron initially envisioned the Jeriko One storyline as a fortunate plot point and a rather obvious allusion to the Rodney King beating, Bigelow shaped it into a central conflict for her two main characters and an opportunity to politicise police corruption, the everyday lived experience of racism, and racialised conventions of seeing and specularity.

This influence is also suggested by the fact that Bigelow and Cocks changed the Jeriko One wiretrip chain of command. In Cameron's draft, it is Lenny who approaches Deputy Director Palmer Strickland in the bathroom and provides him with the assassination tape (Cameron 1995: 159–61). Bigelow and Cocks made this Mace's scene, giving her the opportunity not only to transgress the male space of a men's restroom but also to take the destiny of the tape and its possible cultural effects into her own hands. If Lenny had delivered the tape to Strickland, the role of the white patriarch that the Director already assumes would have been further reinforced and Lenny's centralisation as a white, male subjectivity would have been given more authority than the film suggests it deserves.

This decision helps position Mace as a main character; but it is not until the finale when the villainous LAPD officers chase her that her narrative and thematic importance truly crystallises. She boomerangs on Steckler and Engelman, making a citizen's arrest by commandeering Steckler's baton, tazer, handcuffs and gun. Then, as LAPD riot cops descend upon her and beat her into submission, her body becomes overdetermined with multiple image histories, including those of slavery, the 1968 Watts Riots, and most obviously the LAPD's brutality against Rodney King. The image of white policemen beating her bare, black body as she lies helplessly in handcuffs stands in as a spectre of a much larger and deeply embedded representational history of institutionalised white-on-black violence. In a moment that looks to re-envision and revise the events of the King beating, a crowd of African Americans gather to 'bear witness' to the violence. This particular beating, then, is made immediately public rather than being publicised later through the private documentation of an amateur camcorder. And, as though the 'lightning bolt from God' that Mace has spoken of prior has suddenly literalised, an African-American, teenage boy, emerges from the crowd and attacks the officers. While it takes the (highly problematic) entrance of Deputy Director Strickland to finally quash the brutality, the sequence has been carefully constructed so as to encourage spectatorial identification *with* the rioters whose goal is upheaval and civic unrest rather than with the officials who seek to restore nation-state order.

Given the nature of Bigelow's changes to Cameron's draft, it seems that part of her major contribution to *Strange Days* was the visual links she made between the film's universe and the media images surrounding the Rodney King beating, and the subsequent rioting and looting that occurred in April 1992 when three of the four officers were acquitted. Its mise en scene is shaped by the violent outbursts and expressions of racial conflict that were occurring in Southern California and many other US urban centres during the film's development and pre-production. This visual influence and the narrative climax of Mace's beating are important because of the relationship they bear to the film's themes of vision, experience and power. As Michael Renov (1993) points out, the events surrounding King's beating and the officers' verdict call into question 'authentic' visual evidence of trauma as much as they stabilise it. Renov claims, 'For despite the very real loss of life and destruction, the furore that has enveloped Los Angeles since the original King arrest in March 1991 has been largely fuelled by images and their interpretation: of King's beating, of the shooting of an African American teenager, Latasha Harlins, by a Korean American merchant; of the attack of white truck driver Reginald O. Denny during the postverdict arrest' (1995: 8). He argues that the ability on the part of the defence attorneys representing the LAPD officers to re-contextualise the incriminating videotape – a strategy that led to the initial acquittal – points to the complicated status of the recording as 'real'. Renov continues, 'These images were understood to be inviolably "real" even when their meanings came to be vehemently contested. In many quarters, it was assumed that these images "spoke for themselves." We have learned the contrary only through much tragedy' (Ibid.).

Like Renov, Bigelow seems to understand the tragedy of the contested meanings encoding King's obviously traumatic experience. Her strategy is to place the Jeriko One shooting and Mace's radical response to it within a long-standing historical continuum of black resistance and civil rights activism. Because this historical context was written out of most news coverage and media narratives of the looting and rioting in Los Angeles, the 1992 acts of resistance were framed as individual raids and random, self-serving outbursts (see *The Nation Erupts*, 1992). So by making visual connections between contemporary riot officers and those who restrained 1960s civil rights protesters, and by supporting Mace's suggestion that a revolutionary war is in order, Bigelow codes the rioters as energetic, political agents. One should not underestimate the significance of the placement of her vanity title card in the closing credits: the words 'A Film by Kathryn Bigelow' overlay the image of a looter raising his arms in victory toward a street fire as military policemen look on. This shot bears a much stronger relation to photo-journalistic codes of 1960s civil unrest than they do to the futuristic aesthetic of the film.

This is not to say that the more radical elements of *Strange Days* erase its problems, nor is to say that Bigelow should be immune from criticism for its ideological contradictions. The film's decision to resolve Mace's beating and the ensuing riot with the intervention of the white patriarchal figure embodied by the Deputy Director superficially glosses over the political problems and perspectives raised by riot. This moment provides perhaps the most obtrusive and easily recognisable example of *Strange Days'* status as a problematic and inconsistent text; however it would be easy to locate other such instances throughout. They point to both the contradictory structures of Hollywood studio cinema and the problematic politics that tend to characterize Bigelow's work in general. Another possible conundrum posed by the film's resolution concerns Mace's final acceptance of Lenny, in their climactic kiss, which might appear to obfuscate the critique of him as voyeuristic and self-centered. (This is especially true when considered in conjunction with Megan's puzzling desire for the condescending Nick Mann in *Blue Steel* (1990).) In this analysis of *Strange Days*, I have suggested that Mace unites with Lenny only once he has proven that he affirms cultural otherness and difference. Yet their union might be perceived as an attempt to sweep ideological issues under the finale's confetti-strewn carpet, just the kind of valuation of romance over politics that Mace has argued against throughout the narrative. Nevertheless, their coupling, in an inter-racial kiss that went nearly unprecedented in commercial Hollywood in 1995, presents a progressive avenue toward moral awakening and political dialogue.

To the degree that a director's influence can be determined, *Strange Days* is 'a Kathryn Bigelow film' most at those moments when the concerns of an Other's vision are made the most clear. By drawing out the implications of *seeing* Jeriko One's murder and looking for opportunities for Mace to struggle for that vision to be legitimated, Bigelow makes valuable connections between female victimisation and racial oppression. She capitalises on the fact that his murder is seen only through the eyes of two women, Iris and Mace, searching out visual and dramatic moments that intensify the conflict between dominant and non-dominant ways of seeing. Through her direction and her contribution to the screenplay, Bigelow takes the film's discourse on voyeurism and rape one step beyond its initial framework by illuminating voyeurism's racialised dimension. She pushes its relationship to contemporaneous events such as the King videotape as far as it can go, using it to interrogate visual modes of police surveillance and localised 'street' footage. Without this influence, particularly without her attention to Mace, the film's strength would simply be its critique of white masculinity (like so many other 'paranoid male films' of the 1990s). With this influence, *Strange Days* became an alternative vision of feminist and black power – not merely a destabilising displacement of normative male visuality but a radical replacement of an aesthetic governed by a 'maybe they oughtta see', 'maybe there oughtta be a war' victim subject-position.[1]

Notes

1   I would like to thank Susan Murray and Michael DeAngelis for their insightful suggestions during the early stages of this chapter. I also appreciate Deborah Jermyn and Sean Redmond's helpful comments. Additionally, I wish to thank Jay Cocks for his generosity of time and spirit.

CHAPTER ELEVEN

Rescuing Strange Days: Fan Reaction to a Critical and Commercial Failure

Will Brooker

From future fiction to alternate earth

Like *2001* (Stanley Kubrick, 1968), *Strange Days* (1995) is no longer a film about the future. Neither is it a film about the past, any more than Michael Radford's film adaptation of Orwell's *Nineteen Eighty-Four* (1984) is a historical piece about the 1980s; for a reminder of our popular culture fifteen years ago we are more likely to rent a John Hughes movie, just as we turn to *Reality Bites* (Ben Stiller, 1994), not *RoboCop* (Paul Verhoeven, 1987), for a nostalgic glimpse of the mid-1990s. All these future fictions have, in the year that their predictions failed to come true, performed a sidestep in popular consciousness and become visions of an alternate world; the way things could have been, rather than the way they might be.

Strange Days is a particularly interesting example of this phenomenon because, unlike *Nineteen Eighty-Four*, its future has only just passed; and unlike *2001*, its attempt to visualise society at the turn of the third millennium represents a modest jump of five years, rather than the thirty-two which separate *2001*, with its dream of graceful space stations, from 2001 as a date on bus passes and tabloid newspapers.

Strange Days only asks us to believe in one major technological change between 1995 and 1999 – the development of the SQUID hardware which offers direct experience of another person's memories – the rest is just minor tweaking of fashion and household gadgets. As such, the film offers a far more direct social commentary on mid-1990s society than, say, *Blade Runner* (Ridley Scott, 1982) does on the world in 1982. Most notably, while *Blade Runner's* Los Angeles of 2019 only refers obliquely to racial tension through the replicant-human relationship – Deckard draws a parallel between the terms 'skinjob' and 'nigger', but this voiceover commentary is lost in the director's cut – *Strange Days* depicts LA as a pressure-cooker of racial tension where one African-American character is executed and another beaten by white police. At least five contemporary reviews of the film linked the latter scene to Rodney King's beating by the LAPD in 1991 and the subsequent LA riots of 1992, while two more saw a parallel with the O.J. Simpson's acquittal for murder in 1995.[1]

Unlike the other films noted above, however, *Strange Days* slipped sideways very quietly. The start of 2001 saw the British media making ironic comparisons between Kubrick's vision and the mundane reality, just as commentators in 1984 had done with Orwell's novel; but despite *Strange Days'* dramatic focus on 1999's millennium celebrations and its attempts at direct social comment through the science fiction genre, there were not to my knowledge any newspaper features which set out Bigelow and Cameron's predictions against the reality of Los Angeles in 2000. A mere five years after its attempt to depict the near future, *Strange Days* had apparently been forgotten.

The initial critical reaction to *Strange Days* was unenthusiastic, and the film performed badly at the box office in the year of its release, making $7.9 million in the United States. To provide some context from the same genre, *The Fifth Element* (Besson, 1996) took $63.5 million and *Twelve Monkeys* (Gilliam, 1995) $53.9 million, while *Independence Day* (Emmerich, 1996) scooped $306.2 million domestically. Even *Blade Runner*, notoriously overlooked on its theatrical release, made $27 million.[2]

Strange Days, then, occupies an overlooked parallel universe. My research turned up only two websites dedicated to the film – run by Rhlannon and Chris – both of which are admirably designed and informative but relatively limited in size. A fan site for the director at kathrynbigelow.com has a page of information and articles, but the links to related pages simply leads back to Rhlannon and Chris.[3] The webring of *Strange Days* devotees is apparently made up of three people.

However, a larger core of *Strange Days* fans does exist online, gathered around the forum at the Internet Movie Database (imdb.com). The main site here is an online encyclopaedia of film and television, with discussion boards attached to each entry so that visitors can submit their own reviews and in turn debate them with others, posting up a message and responding to existing opinions. Many of these discussion boards are deserted. When I visited in January 2001, the *Strange Days* forum had 79 entries, indicating some need on the part of fans to register their enthusiasm, debate specific aspects of the film and join a community based around a neglected text. These discussion board posts became my primary archive for this research. I used a hard copy, categorised the responses according to their content – authorship, stardom, comparison to other films – and attempted to reconstruct this audience's engagement with *Strange Days* through the textual evidence they had left behind.

In describing the contributors to these pages as fans I may be stretching the term a little; though the word 'viewers' would fail to convey their strength of feeling, none of them seems to have built a webpage around their enthusiasm for the film, and it seems unlikely that they engage in *Strange Days* filk songs, fanfic, slash, erotic art or any of the other activities through which fans of *Star Wars*, *Star Trek* and *Xena* celebrate their favoured text (See Jenkins 1992; Bacon-Smith 1992; Tulloch & Jenkins 1995; Penley 1997; Gwenllian Jones 2000; Brooker, forthcoming 2002). I use the term here for convenience, but we should bear in mind that *Strange Days* does not seem to have inspired a level of active creativity among its audience to the point where it continues to live in home-made folk art, and that these 'fans' seem far more casual in their loyalty than those who keep the faith for, say, *Star Trek: The Original Series*.

In a sense, my research here is unusual within the wider context of academic work on fandom, as it deals with the traces left after the fact, the online imprints of people rather than the people themselves (compare, for instance, with the face-to-face ethnography of Bacon-Smith, 2000). The *Twin Peaks* fans of Jenkins' article 'Do You Enjoy Making The Rest of Us Feel Stupid?' (1992), who debated the series on text-based newsgroups, or the online *Xena* fans of Sara Gwenllian-Jones' recent study (2000), were also analysed at a distance, questioned in text rather than in person and mediated through the internet, but these were fans engaging with a current TV series as it unfolded rather than a half-forgotten film text from six years previously. Even the *Alien* (Ridley Scott, 1979) and *Blade Runner* fans who formed the subject of my chapter on Internet fandom (Brooker 1999) were anticipating possible sequels, and roamed a wide online network of webrings devoted to their favoured texts. In this case, though, while the archive may seem small and isolated, we have to assume that there is no vibrant and active fan community based around *Strange Days*, and that this corner of the web may constitute the only available evidence of online fan response to the film.

Based on a textual analysis of those seventy-nine posts on the *Strange Days* boards at imdb.com,[4] this chapter examines the ways in which a small group of *Strange Days* fans attempts to 'rescue' the film from its position as a critical disappointment and commercial disaster. Firstly, I look at the explanations offered for the film's perceived failure. I go on to categorise the response in terms of the aspects of the film that fans highlight to support their own positive opinion, arguing that these short critiques, with their discussion of cinematography and generic context, serve to establish the reviewer's credentials almost as much as they encourage a reassessment of the movie. I go on to consider the forum's approach to authorship around *Strange Days* – noting that, for a significant number of these fans, the film's main focus is neither writer-producer nor director but the star and supporting cast – and ask whether the characteristic denial of Bigelow's contribution in these responses can be explained in terms of a specifically male reaction to a female director.

Finally, I explore the fan argument that *Strange Days* needs to be re-viewed multiple times on video and DVD, and the suggestion that it has continued relevance as a vision of 'potential' American society even when its predictions have, strictly speaking, become outdated. In conclusion, I note that while these fans seek to re-evaluate the film and bring its qualities to public notice, there is also an underlying pleasure in its relative unpopularity; while they want to rescue *Strange Days*, they also enjoy keeping it to themselves.

First discovery and reassessment

A common feature to many of these discussion board reviews is the narrative of discovery; of finding *Strange Days* by accident, or experiencing it alone. The forum therefore serves as a medium for explaining the pleasure of that first surprising viewing, and as a link to a small community of like-minded souls who feel the same way about a relatively little-known and neglected text.[5]

> I first watched this movie the day it premiered on Cinemax. I had never heard of it before and I thought I would give it a try. I was thrown into one of the best and the most shocking movies I have ever seen![6]

> I caught this film almost by accident on TV this week. I was staggered by how agood it was, because I just hadn't heard of *Strange Days* at all. How can such a good film have passed me by when it was only released five years ago?[7]

> I had never even heard of this movie called *Strange Days* when I first watched it on Cinemax one late night. But after the opening sequence that felt like I was 'inside' the movie, I couldn't even get up for a glass of water.[8]

This movie aired a few times on the SciFi channel and HBO in later 96/97 and I stayed up to 5:00am eager to find out how the weaving plot would go.[9]

The reviews were more or less indifferent … still, I was determined to see the movie on opening night, which I did in a nearly empty theatre. True to the movie's graphic nature, some members of that viewing's sparse audience even walked out at the midway point. I, however, was spellbound.[10]

Having established the film as a forgotten gem, many of the commentaries go on to ask why it met with such a disappointing critical and commercial reception. As one reviewer puts it, 'how the HELL did this movie tank?'[11] Others echo this bafflement: 'I'll never understand how this movie went ignored',[12] 'Why wasn't this movie such a big success? I really don't know.'[13]

At the simplest level, the explanation given is a lack of publicity – 'who knew? I didn't. Apparently no one else knew, or else it would have been a bigger hit.'[14] – while more than one commentator blames the teaser trailer which featured Ralph Fiennes as Lenny performing a hard sell of the SQUID experience direct to camera, as if the viewer were a potential buyer.

I was so annoyed with the trailer … just Ralph Fiennes face uttering questioning sentences and sentences and wondering what is all this hubbub about bub?[15]

I remember seeing the teaser trailer … the one with the bright colors and then simply a head shot of Ralph Fiennes yapping about 'wiring in' and all of that kind of stuff with text flying around his head … that trailer turned me off to the film in the theatre because it was extremely lame for someone not familiar with the film. This movie is an example of how horrid advertising leads to negative buzz that sinks a movie.[16]

Further comments place the film in the context of surrounding and subsequent releases, arguing that it was swamped by more obvious blockbusters. 'Sadly this film was lost behind the *Bravehearts, Apollo 13s* and *Se7ens* of 1995.'[17] 'It's a shame that *Titanic* looms so large … *Strange Days* is Cameron's true masterpiece of the decade, but in the public eye it will always be obscured by the big boat.[18] 'It should be a classic, but unfortunately will probably go down as an underdog that barks in the shadow of *Titanic*.'[19]

Finally, these fan reviewers blame the prejudices and limitations of audiences and film critics alike for the film's lukewarm reception.

The critics gave this movie a hard time because they were probably turned away at the sex and the rape scene.[20]

Despite its flirtation with the mainstream, *Strange Days* is a film that dares to pervert the traditional course of Hollywood into a future that is worth seeing. Perhaps predictably, it made little impact at the box office.[21]

I can only guess that because it came out after the O.J. verdict, it was doomed to fail at the theatres. Strange days, indeed.[22]

How this film missed out on getting its due is still a mystery to me. Perhaps it's just too dark in the portrayal of its themes to appeal to the mainstream, or maybe it was just too smart when it was released for audiences on mass [sic] to 'get it' at the time.[23]

The critics have given this movie a hard time, saying that the film can't decide what it wants to be; Sci-Fi, Action or Romance. The very fact that you can't put this film in one category is what makes it all the more interesting for me.[24]

It should be noted that these theories do tally with the film's critical reception in the American press. The *San Francisco Examiner* criticised the SQUID clips as 'a sex-and-violence overload' (Rosenberg 1995), while the *Deseret News* was dismayed by the 'muddled' plot and the 'parade of senses-assaulting indignities' (Hicks 1995). The *San Francisco Chronicle*, in turn, described the film as 'overwhelming, chaotic and sometimes disturbing' (Guthman 1995), and the *Sacramento Bee* concluded that *Strange Days* was 'irresponsible', 'gruesomely violent' and 'wildly messed-up' (Baltake 1995). The fan reading of this response simply inverts 'chaotic', 'disturbing' and 'muddled' into 'smart', 'dark' and 'interesting', laying the blame on the reviewers' inability to deal with a complex and demanding narrative.[25]

Having established themselves as a minority group based around a criminally neglected film, then, the fans go on to define themselves implicitly as intelligent, discriminating and open-minded viewers by contrast to those critics and audiences whose preconceptions blinded them to the film's challenges and ambiguities. 'A true "thinking person's" action movie', writes JDWalley,

which doesn't center around a big man (Arnold, Sly or Bruce) with an even bigger gun blowing his way through the bad guys. Instead we have characters with complexity ... compared to this, a recent success like *The Matrix* (which some might compare it to) seems merely a rehash of the tired old shoot-em-up papered over with a gimmicky sci-fi plot premise.[26]

'I would recommend that anyone with any type of brain see the movie', Eli concludes,[27] while Tim Gerchmez suggests 'here's a film you not only don't have to turn your brain off to enjoy, but will enjoy more with your brain turned ON.'[28]

Fandom and film theory

This construction of the film – and by implication its fans – as unusually thoughtful and perceptive is supported by a discourse on the discussion boards which seeks to establish *Strange Days'* credentials through an appeal to theoretical concepts such as cinematography and generic context; even, in odd instances, the notions of the 'Other' and the 'gaze'. Again, I would suggest that these comments have a dual purpose; while reassessing the film's merits, they also serve as a showcase for the reviewer's knowledge and critical abilities, a form of class presentation before a jury of peers. Richard At The Flicks, who opens this sample, is perhaps the model student.

> This is a panicky, nervous film … with a few exceptions, no one and nothing seem to stand still. Either the camera is on the move, or the editing dices and chops the scene, creating in the viewer an unsettled anxiousness. […] Given … the overwhelming nature of episode of [sic] first-person cinematography, quibbles about the plot seem almost irrelevant.[29]

> From its superb cinematography (by Matthew F. Leonetti) to the terrific editing job by Howard Smith (and an unaccredited James Cameron), and even down to the production and costume design (by Lilly Kilvert and Ellen Mirojnick respectively) this is a film where, for me at least, everything works…[30]

> [Bigelow] is THE single best director running around in Hollywood when it comes to the technical…she also manages to slip in unusual angles for her shots and quite simply unusual techniques.[31]

> From its tour-de-force first-person perspective opening sequence until its poetically beautiful final image, the film never ceases to … remain visually inventive and interesting throughout.[32]

These assessments of the film's visual style are relatively unusual; most of these fans situate *Strange Days* within its genre, rather than discussing technical detail. Some, of course, do both: the first comment below is again courtesy of Richard At The Flicks.

> This reviewer was reminded at times of Blade Runner, such is the care taken over a presentation of a futuristic society and detailed environment.[33]

> *Alien* and *Blade Runner* envision a gloomy future but have redeeming qualities, such as the symbolism of the 'other' in the alien organism or the Biblical undertones in the Tyrell Corporation.[34]

> Ralph Fiennes ... is the absolute bottom-feeder in the Gibsonian world ... this is what *Johnny Neumonic* [sic] should have been.[35]

> Had it been released now, there's no question that it would be a smash hit, and *The Matrix* may very well have fallen by the wayside along with the other virtual-reality flicks, *The 13th Floor* and *Existenz*.[36]

> James Cameron's script takes a science fiction premise we've seen before (*Brainstorm*, *Lawnmower Man*) and gives it a bit of a dark twist.[37]

While *Strange Days* is most commonly positioned by these reviewers in the generic context of virtual reality/cyberpunk – William Gibson novels, *Blade Runner* (Ridley Scott, 1982), *The Lawnmower Man* (Brett Leonard, 1992), *Johnny Mnemonic* (Robert Longo, 1995), *The Matrix* (Andy and Larry Wachowski, 1999), *The 13th Floor* (Josef Rusnak, 1999) – there are also references to a wider film history which draw comparisons between *Strange Days* and non-generic, widely-respected classics on the basis of technical skill or common theme. Some of these parallels are convincing, others more tenuous; all of them emphasise the perceived status of *Strange Days* as a sophisticated and underestimated film, both by drawing out what they see as its knowing intertextuality and by grouping it with more established favourites of film criticism.

> Rather like the killings in Powell's *Peeping Tom* (another reflection on the nature of the cinematic 'gaze'), victims are made to watch their own death agonies.[38]

> *Strange Days* is like a perfect choreography of film. Every part stands in perfect

relation to another. Be it the acting, directing, music ... the link with *Citizen Kane* isn't that hard to make, because in the same respect as *Strange Days*, *Kane* was far ahead of its time ... I believe it was finally surpassed as a complete film by *Strange Days*, which managed to do everything *Kane* did, only better...[39]

The LA of the future...is quite dystopian in nature, and *Strange Days* manages to present all aspects of that using *Taxi Driver*-influenced car rides through the city.[40]

As I suggested above, by praising the film in these terms the fan-reviewer is in part establishing his or her own credentials as an intelligent and knowledgeable commentator. Richard at the Flicks in particular, from his name to his carefully-crafted prose and airy reference to 'this reviewer', seems to imagine himself as a professional critic, while Adec's mention of 'an unaccredited James Cameron' is surely slipped in as a nugget of trivia to impress other readers. The nods to similar texts also involve a degree of knowingness – 'Gibsonian', 'a premise we've seen before' – and the comparisons with films that fall outside the science fiction genre almost seem an excuse to casually namedrop *Kane* and Powell. Note that the films cross-referenced in these latter examples constitute an auteurist cinema of widely-acknowledged classics; again, the reviewer displays his own awareness and sophisticated taste through the comparison. One commentator on the boards even challenges the reader to match his knowledge, albeit with a healthy degree of self-deprecation:

The inspiration comes from one of the colour *Twilight Zone* episodes which had even less viewers than *Strange Days* and so the movie can rest assured it is safe in obscurity. (Give up? Okay, it was episode 23, season three, 1989, 'The Mind of Simon Foster.' I'm an anorak, I know these things).[41]

The sense of mild showing-off and pretension that runs through many of the posts – 'it's one of the few sci-fi films that is deeply poetic. Not only that, it is visually stunning, and hyperkinetic'[42] – reaches its peak in the assessment from Michael Neal which, subconsciously or not, lifts directly from Roger Ebert's 1995 review. Neal points out that *Strange Days* 'invents its own vocabulary (tapehead, jack-in and playback are the most popular words)'.[43] Ebert, four years earlier, had written that the film 'provides a vocabulary. Look for "tapehead", "jacking in" and the movie's spin on "playback" to appear in the vernacular.' (Ebert 1995)

While there are exceptions – those contributors content to argue that "Juliette Lewis is just plain sexy, and shown off to great effect"[44] or, more disturbingly, that "watching and feeling yourself get raped are pretty cool"[45] – there is a general air of self-consciousness about the forum. These are not, for the most part, dashed-off first impressions, but careful, sometimes extensive reviews presented to a group of evidently critical and in many ways expert fellow fans.

Fandom and authorship

In addition to the discussion of cinematography and generic context, the discussion board comments frequently locate *Strange Days* in terms of authorship. Intriguingly, this fan discourse – echoing decades of scholarly debate around the *auteur* – identifies *Strange Days* through James Cameron's 'personal stamp' as writer and producer at least as often as it relates the film to Katherine Bigelow's work as director. In fact, credit is sometimes shared out equally between Cameron, Bigelow and the main performers, as in this review:

> Kathryn Bigelow, James Cameron, Ralph Fiennes and Angela Bassett
> et all [sic] were bold enough to break down certain film stereotypes and
> they should be proud of that fact.[46]

While this approach to mainstream cinema as a jointly-authored group project is fairly unusual on the forum, it is important to note that for a number of these fan-critics, *Strange Days* is defined by its stars, rather than its director or screenwriter. Sydney's review, for instance, is titled 'Ralph Fiennes at his best!' and goes on to celebrate "my favorite role of Ralph Fiennes's. He's absolutely enchanting as Lenny Nero'; not once in the three-paragraph comment is there a mention of Cameron or Bigelow.[47] Sebastian Faught also reviews the film in relation to its principal actor, moving on to discuss the other performers but again, seeing no reason to acknowledge anyone outside the main cast:

> I approached this film with caution in the time I was doing back-research for
> 'Films with Fiennes' for my English Patient dissertation … Fiennes was good
> (but isn't he always?) and Angela Bassett was alright. It's just Juliette Lewis who
> managed to screw things up.[48]

Andrew Hobson's brief celebration of the film is based entirely on the fact that 'Ralph Fiennes is one of my favourite actors', with the afterthought that 'Juliette Lewis is a fox, too'.[49] Scoop-6 announces that 'this film has all the ingredients an exiting [sic] movie should have' but mentions none of these ingredients beside the fact that

'Ralph Fiennes has never looked or played better'.[50] Lastly, Johnbee-2 confesses that 'I had no idea that it was produced and directed by James Cameron until the credits rolled'.[51] These fans are clearly drawing on a more fluid notion of 'authorship' than is common in most film criticism, based – perhaps not surprisingly – on the more visible contributors to the film rather than on those whose face never appears on-screen and whose name may only be recognised in the end credits.

That said, most of these commentators highlight either Bigelow or Cameron's role in the production, primarily to establish *Strange Days'* position in a wider oeuvre. Like the discussion of generic links, these comments encourage a broader perspective on the film; rather than allow *Strange Days* to be left in isolation as a messy and overlong sci-fi thriller, the fans begin to raise questions about its relation to Bigelow's treatment of 'male' genres, or to Cameron's recurrent themes. As the sample below indicates, the credit for 'authorship' is split fairly evenly between writer/producer and director.

Kathryn Bigelow puts more action in this than ten male directors…[52]

James Cameron may not have directed this one, but his influence is all over it … the industrial blue tinting and presence of aggressive females.[53]

Bigelow shows she can do a lot more than make vampire movies in this one.[54]

The final scene of this movie … let's say it is trademark Cameron, and leave it at that.[55]

Kathryn Bigelow (*Near Dark, Point Break*) does a bang-up job keeping the pace moving steadily forward in James Cameron's view of where we were headed…[56]

Kathryn Bigelow provides direction that is slick, assured and stylish. This should be enough to bury the notion that action films are 'guy things' which need a male at the helm.[57]

Cameron wrote and it shows … yep, it sure shows that Cameron has laid his hand on this film. It has a superb plot, great timing and a spectacular ending.[58]

The script, and James Cameron's directing, and the music make this movie wild, fun and intriguing.[59]

Note, however, that the last review – by Peter Milkman – goes beyond merely neglecting Bigelow's role as author-director, and seems to give Cameron responsibility for the whole production. That he is not alone in writing Bigelow out of the creative process – recall John-Bee above, who realised at the end of the film that it was 'directed by James Cameron', and Keith Petit, who saw *Strange Days* as 'Cameron's true masterpiece' – might lead us to suspect an impulse among these reviewers to play down or ignore the director's contribution.

It could in turn be argued that some of those who mention Bigelow, like Efua, tend to list her as one of a group, and that those few who single her out for praise almost invariably foreground her gender in terms of the male-dominated action genre. These latter comments could feasibly be read as patronising; there is a sense of novelty in the praise for Bigelow's successful handling of a 'guy thing', and the fact that she can do more than direct vampire films is deemed worthy of comment. Cameron's ability to shift from the grubby future-war of *Aliens* (1986) to the doomed historical romance of *Titanic* (1997) is, by contrast, never mentioned. Even TripperM's praise for Bigelow's 'bang-up job' is based on a hierarchy of authorship with Cameron at its apex – her 'job' is apparently to keep things moving in accordance to his vision 'of where we were headed.'

Given that the forum seems overwhelmingly to be made up of male contributors – so far as we can tell from the names given – it seems plausible that some members of this group may assume that an action film must be directed by a man, and even feel uneasy about the notion of a woman directing their favourite science fiction thriller; significant credit is therefore passed on to the producer, relegating Bigelow to a position of visionary's assistant, or writing her out completely. Bearing in mind the tendency of scholars, critics and professional reviewers to privilege the director as the most important creative figure in film production, the mistaken attribution on the part of John-Bee, Keith Petit and Peter Milkman is an interesting case of generic expectation and gender stereotyping overriding auteurist convention.

By extension, this small online community could be accused of operating as a boy's club, with a specifically male approach to the film – two contributors remark on Juliette Lewis' sex appeal, and it seems unlikely that a woman would offer the comment "watching and feeling yourself get raped are pretty cool.'[60] On the other hand, note Sydney's description of Ralph Fiennes as 'absolutely enchanting', Scoop-6's assertion that the actor 'has never looked or played better' and Sebastian's comment 'Fiennes was good (but isn't he always?) … it's just Juliette Lewis who managed to screw things up'. The latter comment clearly implies a condemnation of Lewis for her acting, rather than a focus on her looks, while the first two suggest that Fiennes' appearance and manner are, for these reviewers, a primary source of pleasure.

Despite a couple of inane remarks – and the unconscious sexism that seems to lie behind the frequent denial of Bigelow's contribution – this is not simply a narrow-minded group of young men whose main pleasure in a film extends no further than gawping at the actresses and getting off on sexual violence. There is clearly evidence of traditionally patriarchal assumptions, and some examples of male fans treating Lewis as pure spectacle; but just as the SQUID shifts between subject and object by allowing its users, and the film's viewers, to see through the eyes of the opposite sex, so the comments from Scoop-6, Sydney and Sebastian disrupt any conclusions that the forum is governed by a conventionally male gaze.

Re-viewing Strange Days

The recommendation that *Strange Days* is best viewed multiple times recurs throughout the discussion board entries. Again, this argument positions the film as a complex object whose details and implications have been overlooked by a casual mass audience and misguided critics, and enhances its status as a cult text that repays close study. Many commentators stress that they bought the film on DVD – which of course enables closer, step-by-step analysis, but in this case also includes Bigelow's discussion of the opening p.o.v. shot and two cut scenes.[61]

Strange Days is one film I like better every time I see (I own it on DVD).[62]

I have seen the movie five times now, and I have noticed small details which, before, I had missed every time. [63]

I finally bought the DVD (had to get an import for that) and it just went to show how great this film is … to really enjoy it, it needs multiple viewings. I have so far seen it 3 times on a big screen, and about 3 or four times since I bought it on DVD, and I always manage to discover new things hidden away.[64]

Just look in the background. There is always something going on, someone getting arrested or stealing something or burning something … all of it enhances the doomsday feeling you get when watching.[65]

There were many parts where I had to rewind and watch them again to actually understand what was going on.[66]

These comments – as was the case in the discussion of genre – seem to be positioning

Strange Days in the same category as *Blade Runner*; films which construct a coherent future world and fit it out with intricate background detail for the benefit of the careful viewer and dedicated fan. *Blade Runner*'s internal clues and puzzles are widely-known – the ambiguity over the number of escaped replicants, the significance of Gaff's origami models, the slight alterations in Leon's dialogue between the actual interview and the playback in Deckard's car – while *Strange Days* has received nothing like the same attention. Clearly, the comparison benefits *Strange Days*, and in common with the suggested parallels to *Peeping Tom* (Michael Powell, 1960), *Citizen Kane* (Orson Welles, 1941) and *Taxi Driver* (Martin Scorsese, 1976), seeks to elevate it to the status of richly intricate but under-appreciated cult film.

From my own repeat viewings, I would argue that *Strange Days* simply does not offer the same level of significant detail or hidden implications. The *mise-en-scène* contains a few interesting background visuals, such as the '2000 Worldwide' campaign which appears as an illuminated poster during Iris' subway chase and crops up again as a giant billboard at the car pound. The slogan is finally revealed as a teaser for Channel 2's millennium broadcast when we see it displayed on the giant view screens at the film's finale. Channel 2's shots of Madrid and London, accompanied by glimpses of Arabic and Japanese text, convincingly suggest an international celebration marshalled by global media, and the sense of cultural mixing is emphasised by the amateurish 'Feliz Navidad, Feliz 2000' lettering on a shop façade and the choice of African drummers and Scottish bagpipes for the Bonaventure Hotel band.

Similarly, the radio phone-in during Lenny's drive to his first job gives the viewer almost subliminal suggestions about the city's racial tension, as an African-American called Duane offers 'a new year's resolution for the police … hey yo, 5-0, better get down with the 2k … we gonna take it, make it new, make it our own'. A white Christian woman, Laurie, follows his call with her own warning that 'you only have to look at the signs, there are wars, and rumors of wars…'

The film's vision of 1999 is a combination of standard-issue dystopia – repeated shots of a burning car – and exaggerated early 1990s pop culture. Lenny, a dedicated follower of millennial fashion, has the bobbed hair and goatee of a Gen-Y slacker, far more similar to Ethan Hawke's look in *Reality Bites* than the cropped masculine styles of the late 1990s. Faith bawls out covers from a 1993 P.J. Harvey album in a club packed out with bondage and boiler suit fashions; a grunge singer beats his bare chest, punks cling to metal cages, sluts strut in leopard skin.

In contrast to this faintly clichéd notion of a 'futuristic' society which merely takes contemporary fashion to wild extremes, it is worth looking at the African-American neighbourhood we visit when Mace takes Lenny home; no silver jackets or leather trousers, just sleeveless t-shirts, jeans, chains, bandannas and check gilets. The film suggests, at least, that different communities might have different approaches towards the dominant millennial trends; while the young hedonists at the Retinal Fetish have the disposable income for the latest fad, and a hustler like Lenny can afford Armani's 1999 collection, the African-American characters who celebrate in their own homes are apparently wearing mid-1990s clothes in slightly unfamiliar combinations. Unusually for a near-future film, the production designers seem to have remembered that single mothers and their friends on similar budgets may wear the same item for at least five years.

Intriguingly, a close re-viewing of *Strange Days* does suggest that Bigelow or Cameron – perhaps under the influence of co-writer Jay Cocks, who came close to optioning Phillip Dick's *Do Androids Dream of Electric Sheep* in 1969 (Sammon 1996: 23) – may have been attempting a pastiche of or homage to *Blade Runner*. Lenny and Deckard could almost be neighbours; one an ex-cop, one semi-retired from the LAPD, both holed up in the same city; both caught up against their best intentions in detective stories which will make them question what they see and what they remember. Both men have to suffer red neon flashing through the blinds into their cramped apartments as they retire with a drink – neat Penguin vodka for Lenny, Tsing-tao for Deckard – and stare at images of women on their home viewers. Ironically, the 1999 vintage SQUID headset through which Lenny relives his days with Faith is technically more advanced than Deckard's circa-2019 ESPER machine, which only produces a still, albeit three-dimensional, image of Zhora.

Blade Runner's riff on the theme of vision is picked up in Bigelow's first shot of Lenny's eye – immediately echoing *Blade Runner*'s opening close-up of Leon's pupil – and developed in Faith's 'I love your eyes, Lenny – I love the way they see', which strikes a chord with Roy Batty's 'Chew, if only you could see what I've seen with your eyes.' *Blade Runner*'s doomed showgirl on the run from the cops is called Zhora; in *Strange Days*, the camera-eye theme is further emphasised by naming the equivalent character Iris.

The parallels extend to soundtrack: a variant on *Blade Runner*'s eerie chorus of 'Oriental' singing, used whenever Deckard makes a new discovery, is playing when Iris drops the clip of Jeriko-One's murder into Lenny's car. Most trivial, but perhaps the most plausible case for deliberate cross-reference, is the scene where Faith, stripping off her silver outfit backstage, throws a towel at Lenny and orders 'dry me'; an identical exchange occurs between Deckard and Zhora as he watches her change in the club dressing-room.

Of course, this is simply one interpretation, and I could be accused of drawing a handful of coincidences into a theory of self-conscious pastiche. However, it seems entirely possible that a writer and director who decided to base their tech-*noir* sf thriller in a near-future Los Angeles would have *Blade Runner* very much in mind throughout the production, especially given that Cameron's co-writer had always shown an interest in the source novel. *Strange Days* may even have been intended as a mid-1990s equivalent of *Blade Runner* – whose original title, lest we forget, was *Dangerous Days* – and the parallels noted above could be considered postmodern nods of acknowledgement to the earlier film.

Whatever the authorial intention, this is how the discussion board fans tend to respond to *Strange Days*, to the extent that one commentator – having compared the film to *Blade Runner* – asks not for a theatrical re-release, but a director's cut.[67] Just as *Blade Runner* was largely overlooked on its first appearance in 1982 and earned a critical reappraisal in its revised form ten years later, so these fans maintain that '*Strange Days* was a movie made before its time.'[68]

Relevance and revelations

As 2000 approached, many of the fans on this forum discussed *Strange Days* as a vision of the near future, which, in their opinion, was only too likely to come true. The film's relative failure in 1995 only added to their sense of it as a wake-up call that was in danger of going unheeded. Many of the comments on this theme take a tone of doomy soothsaying:

> There are scenes I think you better watch with an open mind for the future – cause I imagine it to become sort of what Kathryn Bigelow shows us here.[69]

> *Strange Days* is too right on target, too plausible, too believable for a lot of people right now. Looking at what man is able to do RIGHT NOW with computers and other technology is enough to scare anyone ... society better brace itself for any technology that even resembles this movie.

> This movie is a 'wonderful' slap in the face that our worse times are ahead ... virtual addiction will have NO boundaries, NO prejudices and NO respect for its victims. If you want to be enlightened as well as awakened about our future, you need to see this movie.[70]

> A grim look at life: a dirty, sexy, lustful, repulsive view of what we could easily become.[71]

In the lead-up to New Year's Eve 1999, some commentators even suggested ways of bringing the film's vision in line with reality:

Forget Times Square and its big glowing ball. I know what I'll be watching when the millennium hits.[72]

5 days till the Millennium … this movie captures the spirit … should I say, the madness and mood of the period, that will be upon us, in just a few days. Go to la2000celebration.com. That site will tell of a party at Hope and Grand, between 1ˢᵗ and 5ᵗʰ streets, in downtown LA – and watch the end of this movie … for a taste of how it will be! The movie itself gives a great sense of how things will be in the immediate future, and an excitement of the streets, that I hope I feel in myself, partying with my friends … 5 days from now.[73]

Both fans' plan to make New Year's Eve 1999 a simulation of the *Strange Days* finale, the first by immersing himself in the movie's world at the stroke of midnight, and the second by effectively recreating *Strange Days'* Y2K party on the streets of Los Angeles. In the latter case, the film serves as a blueprint for celebration, a prediction to be acted out in real life. In the former, it provides an alternative, virtual 31 December, better than reality; in a fitting twist, this fan is treating *Strange Days* as a SQUID, a conduit for living other people's (fictional) lives at the turn of the millennium rather than creating his own experience and memories.

Of course, by the stroke of midnight the film was technically outdated, a parallel view of how things could have been rather than a prediction. The fans are well aware of this sideways shift, but significantly this has no effect on their enthusiasm: as can be seen from the endnotes, the forum contributions run well into 2000. There is a noticeable reassessment of *Strange Days'* relation to the 'future', though, and a swift rhetorical move to defend the film's continued relevance by comparing it to *Nineteen Eighty-Four* and *2001*. Note the way this first contributor checks himself when referring to the film's historical position, and that the second includes a (possibly unconscious) nod to *Blade Runner*; the replicants have a 'built-in sell-by date' of four years from inception.

The LA of the future (well, future back when it was released in 1995) is quite dystopian in nature…[74]

One of the two greatest science fiction films of the 90s – the other being *Twelve Monkeys* – both have built-in sell-by dates by fixing their time period in a very near locale. Hence while the supposed date of *Monkeys* is long past at 98, this film now becomes a historical document as of New Year's Eve 1999. But then does it follow that we will stop watching *2001* in 2002? Hopefully not, and *Strange Days* is one that too deserves to be revisited in years to come.[75]

I can easily imagine some people seeing this film in 2000 or later and dismissing it as the prediction of a future that didn't, in fact, occur. But, if we can still appreciate Orwell's *1984* some fifteen years after the supposed time of that novel, there seems to be no reason not to enjoy *Strange Days* well into the next millennium.[76]

Indeed, the fact that *Strange Days*' 'future' had been overtaken by real time proved no hindrance to those fans wanting to proclaim its relevance. On the contrary, it gave them the opportunity to match up the film's predictions with the state of the world in 2000, and suggest that its dystopian vision, having been proved accurate in several respects, was still in the process of coming to pass.

In 1995 I could see the direction the world was going in the same downward spiral as the world in *Strange Days*. High tech getting higher (along with the population) and morals getting lower. Kids carrying guns to school, cops taking matters into their own hands, people getting self-obsessed and paranoid.[77]

The future it depicted is just a characterisation of what it really is now. Kids shooting kids. High gas prices. All said in the movie. Kind of creepy.[78]

Strange Days' world is still being born and therefore the dread of what is to come more acute. But ultimately…this is a masterpiece of futuristic urban prediction, a flamboyant and daring vision of mankind whose reputation is growing as time passes.[79]

Sharing has its limits

There is, finally, a paradox running through this celebration of *Strange Days*. As I have discussed, the comments usually begin from the premise that the film has been neglected, tell the story of the writer's first discovery and multiple re-viewings, and highlight the film's overlooked qualities with reference to genre, film form, authorship and social relevance. Many of them express disbelief that *Strange Days* failed, and urge the reader to try it for him or herself; some advocate a theatrical re-release. The main point of the commentaries is to encourage a reassessment of a neglected film, and promote its merits more widely.

However, there is also a sense that these fans are, on one level, quite happy with the way things are. *Strange Days* has been publicly overlooked as a confusing sci-fi thriller, but the fans show that they can engage with its challenges and unearth its hidden detail through repeated viewings. The professional critics found it too dark, too unrealistic, but the fans can face up to the disturbing elements, recognising them as portents of a still-evolving future society. There is, as I have noted, a mild air of self-congratulation about the boards, coupled with a subtle competition; contributors feel some need to prove their credentials and critical abilities when joining the online community. This feeling of knowing superiority depends entirely on the film remaining a minority taste. Accordingly, despite all the talk of the film deserving a worldwide re-release, it seems that what these fans really want *Strange Days* to be is a cult, with themselves as members.

> *Strange Days* is an instant cult classic ... Juliette Lewis is magnificent in this cult classic.[80]

> I agree that this one is destined to become a cult classic.[81]

> *Strange Days* is one of the great neglected classics of the nineties.[82]

> This little gem is a fabulous cult classic.[83]

> Has become a cult classic ... I was originally going to type that this movie WILL become a cult classic, but it's darn near six years old and I think it already has.[84]

This is the contradiction, then, in 'rescuing' a failure; the pleasure comes partly from the discovery in a half-empty cinema or during late-night Cinemax, from finding a forgotten treasure. Along with the urge to tell others, there is a feeling of possessiveness, even caution; if *Strange Days* did get that theatrical re-release in 2002, was reappraised by critics who now saw its social relevance and gained a far wider mainstream audience on its second outing, the nature of the discussion boards would surely change. I would argue that these fans actually enjoy the film's minority status, much as they bemoan it. There is no complaint behind the 'cult classic' labelling above, rather a tone of satisfaction or pride. By concluding that *Strange Days* has become a cult, these fans are keeping the film where they want it; they have lifted it out of failure, but – equally importantly – they are implying that their favoured text will never be lost to mass popularity.

Notes

1   See for instance the reviewer's comment in the *Sacramento Bee*: 'Her film approximates the feelings that permeated the Rodney King tape and tries to expound on and expand it' Joe Baltake (13 Oct 1995). 'The daring use of the race card is easiest to criticise – insert your own O.J. comment here', writes Michael J. Legeros in another 1995 review (www.moviehell.com/1995/strangedays.html).

2   Figures are taken from www.boxofficeworldwide.com. *Independence Day* is ranked at 9 in terms of the most financially successful films of the last century, while *Strange Days* limps in at 2140.

3   Rhlannon is based at www.geocities.com/sunsetstrip/balcony/3948favsstranged.html; Chris at www.geocities.com/hollywood/lot/8220/index.html.

4   There is no way of assessing the gender of these contributors by their nicknames alone, although the majority seem to be male. From the locations given, almost all are based in the USA and Europe.

5   It should be pointed out that the discussion board is not simply a fan community. By far the majority of the comments are positive, but there are also reviews which condemn *Strange Days* as 'pathetic … an utter waste of film' (chomsky-2), and 'amazingly horrible' (Paladin-27). The film is rated at 7.9 overall out of 10, from an average of visitors' scores.

6   Dwill4 (10 May 2000). All discussion board comments are taken from the *Strange Days* page at http://us.imdb.com.

7   Pebble-2 (1 Jan 2000).

8   Todd Witek (13 Oct 1998).

9   SciFly (21 Oct 1999).

10   J.D. (31 Oct 1999).

11   Flick-18 (12 Jul 1999).

12   Dmolitn Man (16 Nov 1999).

13   Amigard (7 Sept 1998).

14   Pfha (11 Jun 1999).

15   Munyeca (30 Apr 1999).

16   Coorswhite12 (1 Jun 2000).

17   The Greenflash (20 May 2000).

18   Keith Petit (5 Oct 1999).

19   JohnBee-2 (3 Jul 1999).

20   Keith Petit.

21   Richard Callaghan (12 Jan 2000)/

22   Jeen (25 Feb 1999)/

23   Adec (8 Sept 1999)/

24   Efua (7 Jan 2000)/

25   One commentator refers explicitly to the reviews in his 'hometown paper', which 'condemned the movie's excessive violence', before offering his own, more positive assessment. See J.D. op. cit.

26   JDWalley (8 Dec 1999).

27   Eli (29 Apr 1999).

28   Tim Gerchmez (8 Aug 2000).

29   Richard at the Flicks (4 Oct 2000).

30   Adec, op. cit

31   Joep Moens (22 Feb 2000).

32 Keith Petit (5 Oct 1999).

33 Richard at the Flicks, op. cit.

34 teeveeke (6 Aug 1999).

35 Mrgumbopants (20 Nov 2000).

36 Gazzer-2 (5 Sept 1999).

37 Craig Delahoy (6 Dec 1999).

38 Richard at the Flicks (op. cit.).

39 Joep Moens, (22 Feb 2000).

40 diffusionx (3 Jul 2000).

41 Richard Callaghan, op. cit.

42 Efua, op. cit.

43 Michael Neel (5 Aug 1999).

44 Craig Delahoy (6 Dec 1999).

45 Aman Verjee (7 Apr 1999).

46 Efua, op. cit.

47 Sydney (10 Jul 2000).

48 Sebastian Faught (13 Sept 1998).

49 Andrew Hobson (21 Mar 1999).

50 Scoop-6 (13 Jan 1999).

51 Johnbee-2, op. cit.

52 Jeen (25 Feb 1999).

53 Stephen E. Currence (14 Feb 1999).

54 Jayman_30339, op. cit.

55 Lioness (23 Dec 1998).

56 TripperM (11 Dec 2000).

57 JDWalley, op. cit.

58 Anders Aslund (24 Jan 2000).

59 Peter Milkman (29 Feb 2000).

60 While this remark may seem crass at best, sickening and twisted at worst, we should remember that this presumably male viewer is not commenting that he enjoyed the spectacle of a woman on screen being raped. Rather, he is expressing enthusiasm about the masochistic experience the film offered him of 'being' a woman subject to sexual violation, and seeing through her eyes rather than watching her as an object. However alarming and unappealing this view may seem, it offers a direct parallel with the film's SQUID addicts – like them, this viewer finds an attraction lies in vicariously living out violent fantasies through the immediacy of a first-person point of view.

61 Bigelow's explanation of the opening shot is apparently lifted from her appearance at the BFI, and inserted as voiceover; the two deleted scenes feature Lenny almost frying his brain while trying to see the killer in the blackjack clip, and his entrance to the Bonaventure Hotel on New Year's Eve.

62 Tim Gerchmez (8 Aug 2000).

63 Joep Moens (10 Dec 1998).

64 Joep Moens (22 Feb 2000).

65 Anders Aslund (24 Jan 2000).

66 Kektokio (10 Dec 1999).

67 Pebble-2 (1 Jan 2000).

68 William Shelton (2 Jul 1999).

69 Stefan Leuthold (4 Apr 1999).

70 William Shelton (2 Jul 1999).

71 Craig Delahoy (6 Dec 1999).

72 Flick-18 (12 Jul 1999).

73 Paul A. Cook (27 Dec 1999).

74 diffusionx (3 Jul 2000).

75 Richard Callaghan, op. cit.

76 JDWalley, op.cit.

77 TripperM (11 Dec 2000).

78 Sydney (10 Jul 2000).

79 Richard at the Flicks, op. cit.

80 Medusalith (26 Nov 1999).

81 Tim Gerchmez (15 Oct 1999).

82 Adec, op. cit.

83 TripperM, op.cit.

84 Jayman_30339 (26 Oct 2000).

FILMOGRAPHY

d: director; *w*: writer; *ph*: principal photogropher; *p*: producer; *c*: cast

The Set-Up
US 1978 20 min
w & d: Kathryn Bigelow
c: Gary Busey

The Loveless
US 1982 82 min Pioneer/Atlantic
d: Kathryn Bigelow, Monty Montgomery
w: Kathryn Bigelow, Monty Montgomery
ph: Doyle Smith
p: Grafton Nunes, A. Kitman Ho
c: Willem Defoe, Robert Gordon, Marin Kanter

Near Dark
US 1987 94 min Entertinment/Scotti Brothers/International VideoEntertainment
d: Kathryn Bigelow

w: Eric Red, Kathryn Bigelow

ph: Adam Grenberg

p: Steven-Charles Jaffe

c: Adrian Pasder, Jenny Wright, Lance Henriksen

Blue Steel

US 1990 102 min Vestron/Lightning Pictures/PrecisionFilms

d: Kathryn Bigelow

w: Kathryn Bigelow, Eric Red

ph: Amir Mokri

p: Edward R. Pressman, Oliver Stone

c: Jamie Lee Curtis, Ron Silver

Point Break

US 1991 122 min TCF/Largo/Tapestry

d: Kathryn Bigelow

w: W. Peter Iliff

ph: Donald Peteman

p: Peter Abrams, Robert L. Levey

c: Patrick Swayze, Keanu Reeves, Lori Petty

Strange Days

US 1995 145 min UIP/Lightstorm

d: Kathryn Bigelow

w: Jay Cocks, Kathryn Bigelow, James Cameron

ph: Mathew F. Leonetti

p: Steven-Charles Jaffe, James Cameron

c: Ralph Fiennes, Angela Bassett, Juliette Lewis

The Weight of Water

US 2000 113 min Le Studio Canal+/Miracle Pictures

d: Kathryn Bigelow

w: Alice Arlen, Christopher Kyle

ph: Adrian Biddle

p: A. Kitman Ho, Janet Yang

c: Sean Penn, Elizabeth Hurley, Catherine McCormack

K-19: The Widowmaker

US 2002 138 min First Light Productions/20th Century Fox/Paramount Pictures

d: Kahryn Bigelow

w: Christopher Kyle, Louis Nowra

ph: Jeff Crovenweth

p: Kathryn Bigelow

c: Harison Ford, Liam Neeson

Television

Wild Palms, Episode 3 'Rising Sons', May 1993

d: Kathryn Bigelow

Homicide: Life in the Streets: 'Fallen Heroes, parts 1 and 2', 'Lines of Fire', 1997–98

d: Kathryn Bigelow

BIBLIOGRAPHY

Abel, Elizabeth (1993) 'Black Writing/White Reading: Race and the Politics of Feminist Interpretation', *Critical Inquiry*, 19, 3, Spring, 470–98.

Abrams, M. H. (1981) 'Literature as a revelation of personality', in John Caughie (ed.) *Theories of Authorship*. London, Routledge, 17–21.

Allen, R. (1999) 'Psychoanalytic Film Theory', in Robert Stam & Toby Miller (eds) *A Companion to Film Theory*. Oxford: Blackwell, 123–45.

Althusser, Louis (1971) *Lenin and Philosophy*. New York: Monthly Review Press.

Anon. (1988) *Near Dark. Cinefantastique*, March. Available at: http://www.kathrynbigelow.com/articles/cinef.htm.

Anon. (1991) *American Film*, July, 40–3.

Anon. (1994) 'Buzz' Column, *Weekly Variety*, 10 January, 4–10.

Anon. (1995a), 'Strange Days Press Notes', 20th Century Fox, *Strange Days Clipping File*. Margaret Herrick Library, Academy of Motion Picture Arts and Sciences, Beverly Hills, CA, 6.

Anon. (1995b) 'Keanu's Excellent Adventure', *Maclean's*, 108, 4, 52–6.

Anon. (1999) 'Joan of Arc', *US Premiere*, September, 13, 1, 64.

Arched, Amy (1994), *Daily Variety*, 3 March, 4.

Bacon-Smith, Camille (1992) *Enterprising Women: Television Fandom and the Creation of Popular Myth*. Philadelphia: University of Pennsylvania Press.

_____ (2000) *Science Fiction Culture*. Philadelphia: University of Pennsylvania Press.

Bahiana, Ana Maria (1992) Interview with Kathryn Bigelow, *Cinema Papers*, January, 86, 32–4.

_____ (1994) 'Lightstorm Spins Out Fantasy Slate', *Screen International*, 18 March, 4.

Baltake, Joe (1995) *Strange Days* review, *Sacramento Bee*, 13 October.

Barthes, Roland (1968) 'The Death of the Author', in John Caughie (ed.) *Theories of Authorship*. London: Routledge, 208–13.

_____ (1977) *Image-Music-Text*. Glasgow: Fontana.

Baudrillard, Jean (1983) 'The Ecstasy of Communication', in Hal Foster (ed.) *The Anti-Aesthetic: Essays on Postmodern Culture*. Washington: Seattle Bay Press, 126–34.

Bazin, André (1971a) 'The Western, or the American Film *par excellence*' and (1971b) 'The Evolution of the Western', in Hugh Gray (ed. and trans.) *What is Cinema?* Vol. 2. Berkeley: University of California Press, 140–8.

_____ (1989) *What is Cinema?* Vol. 1. Berkeley: University of California Press.

Benjamin, Walter (1969) 'The Work of Art in the Age of Mechanical Reproduction', *Illuminations*. Hannah Arendt (ed.) New York: Schocken, 217–51.

Benshoff, Harry M. (1997) *Monsters in the Closet: Homosexuality and the Horror Film*. Manchester and New York: Manchester University Press.

Bigelow, Kathryn (2001) Letter to the *LA Times*, 18 March. Available at: http:// www. kathrynbigelow.com/articles

Bordwell, David (1989) *Making Meaning: Inference and Rhetoric in the Interpretation of Cinema*. Cambridge, MA: Harvard University Press.

Brennan, Judy and Suzan Aysough (1993) 'New Lightstorm Prez; Former Carolco Exec. Sachini Joins Cameron', *Daily Variety*, 9 July, 1.

Brooker, Will (1999) 'Internet Fandom and the Continuing Narratives of *Blade Runner*, *Alien* and *Star Wars*', in Annette Kuhn (ed.) *Alien Zone 2*. London: Verso, 50–72.

_____ (forthcoming) *Using The Force: Creativity, Community and Star Wars Audiences*. London: Continuum.

Bukatman, Scott (1993) *Terminal Identity*. Durham: Duke University Press, 1993.

Busch, Anita (1992) 'Cameron to Fox: I'll Be Back', *Hollywood Reporter*, 22 April, 1–6.

Buscombe, Ed (1981) 'Ideas of Authorship', in John Caughie (ed.) *Theories of Authorship*. London, Routledge, 22–34.

_____ (1988) *The BFI Companion to the Western*. London: André Deutsch/BFI.

Cameron, James (1995) *Strange Days*. New York: Plume.

Carroll, Noël (2002) 'Psychoanalysis and the Horror Film', in Steven Jay Schneider (ed.) *Freud's Worst Nightmares: Psychoanalysis and the Horror Film*. Cambridge: Cambridge University Press.

Chion, Michel (1994) *Audio+Vision: Sound on Screen*. Claudia Gorbman (ed. and trans) New York: Columbia University Press.

Citron, Alan (1993) 'Dark Clouds Over Carolco' Lightstorm', *Los Angeles Times* Business Section, 11 June, 4.

Clover, Carol J. (1992) *Men, Women, and Chainsaws: Gender in the Modern Horror Film*. New Jersey: Princeton University Press.

Coburn, M. (1987) 'Revamping vampires', *Chicago Tribune*, 11 October. Available at: http://www.kathrynbigelow.com/articles/chi1.html.

Cocks, Jay (2001) Conversation with the author, June 22.

Corrigan, Timothy (1991) *A Cinema Without Walls: Movies and Culture After Vietnam*. New York: Routledge.

Crane, David (2000) 'In Medias Race: Filmic Representation, Networked Communication, and Racial Intermediation', in Beth E. Kolko, Lisa Nakamura, and Gilbert B. Rodman (eds) *Race in Cyberspace*. New York and London: Routledge, 87–115.

Creed, Barbara (1987) 'From Here to Modernity: Feminism and Postmodernism', *Screen*, 28, 2, February, 47–67.

D'Silva, Beverly (1996) 'A Woman of Substance', *The Sunday Times*, 25 February, 10.

Deleuze, Gilles and Feliz Guattari (1977) *Anti-Oedipus: Capitalism and Schizophrenia*. New York: Viking Press.

Deleuze, Gilles (1990) *The Logic of Sense*. New York: Columbia University Press.

Diamond, Jamie (1995) 'Kathryn Bigelow Pushes the Potentiality Envelope', in *New York Times*, 22 October, H1, H20.

Doty, Alexander (1993) *Making Things Perfectly Queer: Interpreting Mass Culture*. Minneapolis and London: University of Minnesota Press.

Dyer, Richard (1994) 'Action!', *Sight and Sound*, 4, 10, 6–10.

Ebert, Roger (1995) *Strange Days* review, *Chicago Sun-Times*, 13 October.

Ehrenstein, David (1991) 'Class Action', *L.A. Style*, July, 80.

Faludi, Susan (1991) *Backlash: The Undeclared War against American Women*. New York: Anchor Books.

Flynn, Peter (n.d.) 'The Silent Western as Mythmaker', *Images*, Issue 6. Available at: http://www.imagesjournal.com/issue06/infocus/silentwesterns.htm

Foucault, Michel (1977) 'A Preface to Transgression', in Donald F. Bouchard (ed. and trans.) & Sherry Simon (trans.) *Language, Counter-Memory, Practice*. Oxford: Basil Blackwell.

____ (1979) *Discipline and Punish*. London: Peregrine.

____ (1980) *Power/Knowledge*. Brighton: Harvester.

Fox, David J. (1992), 'Fox Signs Cameron to $500-Million Deal', *Los Angeles Times* Calendar Section, 22 April, 1.

Francke, Lizzie (1995) 'Virtual Fears', *Sight and Sound*, 5, 12, 6–9.

French, Sean (1996) *The Terminator*. London: BFI.

Freud, Sigmund (1959) 'Family romances' (1908), in J Strachey (ed.) *The Standard Edition of the Complete Psychological Works of Sigmund Freud, volume 9*. London: Hogarth Press, 237–41.

Fuller, Graham (1995) 'Big, Bad Bigelow', *Interview*, November, 25, 11, 42–5.

Gorbman, Claudia (1987) *Unheard Melodies: Narrative Film Music*. London: BFI.

Greene, Ray (1995) 'Rich and Strange', *Boxoffice*, 22 October, 10–12.

Grosz, Elizabeth (1990) *Jacques Lacan: A Feminist Introduction*. New York and London: Routledge.

Guthman, Edward (1995) 'Virtual Reality Run Amok in "Strange" Thriller', *San Francisco Chronicle*, 13 October.

Gwenllian Jones, Sara (2000) 'Histories, Fictions, and *Xena: Warrior Princess*', *Television and New Media*, 1, 4, 403–18.

Hall, Stuart (1997) 'The Centrality of Culture: Notes on the Cultural Revolutions of Our Time', in Kenneth Thompson (ed.) *Media and Cultural Regulation*. London: Sage, 207–38.

Hamburg, Victoria (1989) 'Dark by Design', *Interview*, August, 19, 8, 85.

Heard, Christopher (1997) *Dreaming Aloud: The Films of James Cameron*. New York: Bantam Books.

Hicks, Chris (1995) *Strange Days* review, *Deseret News*, 13 October.

Hillier, Jim (1992) *The New Hollywood*. New York: Continuum.

Hinson, Hal (1988) *Near Dark*, *Washington Post*, 5 May.

Honeycutt, Kirk (2000) Review of *The Weight of Water*. Available at: www.hollywoodreporter.com/reviews.

Hoberman, J. (1995) 'Sunset on Sunset', *Village Voice*, 17 October, 1.

Hopkins, Jim (1991) 'The Interpretation of Dreams', in Jerome Neu (ed.) *The Cambridge Companion to Freud*. Cambridge: Cambridge University Press, 86–135.

Hultkrans, Andrew (1995) 'Reality bytes (interview with Hollywood director Kathryn Bigelow)', *Artforum International*, 34, 3, 78.

Internet Movie Database user comments on *The Weight of Water*. Available at: http://uk.imdb.com/CommentsShow?0210382.

Islam, Needeya (1995) '"I Wanted to Shoot People": Genre, Gender and Action in the Films of Kathryn Bigelow', in Laleen Jayamanne (ed.) *Kiss Me Deadly: Feminism and Cinema for the Moment*. Sydney: Power Publications, 91–125.

Jackson, Rosemary (1981) *Fantasy: the Literature of Subversion*. London: Methuen.

Jeffords, Susan (1993) 'The Big Switch: Hollywood Masculinity in the Nineties', in Jim Collins, Hilary Radner and Ava Preacher Collins (eds) *Film Theory Goes to the Movies*. London: Routledge, 196–208.

_____ (1994) *Hard Bodies: Hollywood Masculinity in the Reagan Era*. New Brunswick, NJ: Rutgers University Press.

Jenkins, Henry (1992) *Textual Poachers: Television Fans and Participatory Culture*. London: Routledge.

_____ (1994) 'Do You Enjoy Making The Rest Of Us Feel Stupid? alt.tv.twinpeaks, the Trickster Author and Viewer Mastery', in David Lavery (ed.) *Full of Secrets: Critical Approaches to Twin Peaks*. Detroit: Wayne State University Press, 51–69.

Jones, Ernest (1971) *On The Nightmare*. New York: Liverwright Publications.

Johnston, Claire (1975) *The Work of Dorothy Arzner*. London: BFI.

_____ (2000) 'Women's Cinema as Counter-Cinema', in E. Ann Kaplan (ed.) *Feminism and Film*. Oxford: Oxford University Press, 22–33.

Jordan, Cattherine (1995) 'CD-ROM Opens "Strange" Doors', *The Hollywood Reporter*, 6–8 October, 37.

Karnicky, J. (1998) 'George Bataille and the Visceral Cinema of Kathryn Bigelow', *Enculturation: a Journal for Writing, Rhetoric and Culture*, 2, 1, Fall. Available at: http://www.uta.edu/huma/enculturation/2_1/karnicky.html.

Keane, Colleen (1997) 'Director as "Adrenaline Junkie"', *Metro*, 109, 22–7.

Keller, Alexandra (1999) '"Size Does Matter": Notes on Titanic and James Cameron as Blockbuster Auteur', in Kevin S. Sandler & Gaylyn Sandler (eds) *Titanic: Anatomy of a Blockbuster*. New Brunswick, NJ: Rutgers University Press, 132–54.

Kellner, Douglas (1995) *Media Culture*. London: Routledge.

Kitses, James (1969) *Horizons West*. London: Thames and Hudson/BFI.

Lacan, Jacques (1977a) *Ecrits. A Selection*. London: Tavistock.

_____ (1977b) *The Four Fundamental Concepts of Psycho-analysis*. London: Hogarth Press.

Lane, Christina (1998) 'From *The Loveless* to *Point Break*; Kathryn Bigelow's Trajectory in Action', *Cinema Journal*, 37, 4, 59–81.

_____ (2000) *Feminist Hollywood: From Born in Flames to Point Break*. Detroit: Wayne State University Press.

LeDoux, Joseph (1998) *The Emotional Brain*. New York: Touchstone.

Levy, Emanuel (2000) Review of *The Weight of Water*, *Variety*, September, 18–24, 32.

Lippman, John (1992) 'It May Be A Classic', *Los Angeles Times* Business Section, 23 April, 1.

McLuhan, Marshall (1994) *Understanding Media*. Cambridge: MIT Press.

Mag.Coll (1995) 'Keanu's Excellent Adventure', *Maclean's*, 108, 4.

Maio, Kathi (1996), 'Strange Days and Your Average Psycho Killers', *Fantasy and Science Fiction*, May, 1–6.

Massumi, Brian (2002) *Parables for the Virtual*. Durham: Duke University Press.

Mayne, Judith (1994) *Directed by Dorothy Arzner*. Bloomington and Indianapolis: Indiana University Press.

Metz, Christian (1982) *The Imaginary Signifier: Psychoanalysis and the Cinema*. Bloomington: Indiana University Press.

Mills, Nancy (1989) '*Blue Steel*: Kathryn Bigelow in Action', *American Film*, 14, 10, 59.

Mizejewski, Linda (1993) 'Picturing the female dick: *The Silence of the Lambs* and *Blue Steel*', *Journal of Film and Video*, 45, 2–3, 6–23.

Mulvey, Laura (1999) 'Visual Pleasure and Narrative Cinema', reprinted in Leo Braudy & Marshall Cohen (eds) *Film Theory and Criticism: Introductory Readings*. Oxford: Oxford University Press, 833–44.

Murphy, Kathleen (1995) 'Black arts (the films of Kathryn Bigelow)', *Film Comment*, 31, 5, 51–3.

Nathan, Ian (1996) 'No retreat, no surrender', *Empire*, February, 82, 78.

Neale, Steve (1981) 'Art Cinema as Institution', *Screen*, 22, 1, 11–39.

_____ (2000) *Genre and Hollywood*. London and New York: Routledge.

Not Channel Zero Collective (1992) *Nation Erupts, Parts I and II*, PBS.

Nowell-Smith, Geoffrey (1987) 'Minnelli and Melodrama', in Christine Gledhill (ed.) *Home Is Where The Heart Is*, London: BFI, 70–4.

Osgerby, Bill (2002) 'Full Throttle on the Highway to Hell: Mavericks, Machismo and Mayhem in the American Biker Movie', in Xavier Mendik & Steven Jay Schneider (eds) *Underground U.S.A.: Filmmaking Beyond the Hollywood Canon*. London: Wallflower Press, 123–39.

Parisi, Paula (1995) '*Strange Days* and Rockin' Nights', *The Hollywood Reporter: Film and TV Music Special Issue*, 29 August, S9-S64.

Penley, Constance (1991) 'Time Travel, Primal Scene, and the Critical Dystopia', reprinted in Janet Bergstrom, Constance Penley & Lynne Spiegel (eds) *Close Encounters: Film, Feminism, and Science Fiction*. Minneapolis: University of Minnesota Press, 62–81.

Powell, Anna (1994) 'Blood on the Borders: *Near Dark* and *Blue Steel*', Screen, 35, 2, 136–56.

Powers, John (1995) 'The Director Wore Black', *Vogue*, October, 195–6.

Puig, Claudia & Richard Natalie (1995) 'A Scary Time at the Box Office', *Los Angeles Times*, Calendar Section, 20 October, F1-F28.

Ransley, Hannah (2002) 'Kathryn Bigelow', in Yoram Allon, Del Cullen & Hannah Patterson (eds) *Contemporary North American Film Directors: A Wallflower Critical Guide* (second edition). London: Wallflower Press, 50–1.

Rascaroli, Laura (1997) 'Steel in the Gaze: on POV and the discourse of vision in Kathryn Bigelo's cinema', *Screen*, 38, 3, 232–46.

_____ (2001) 'Scopic Drive, Time Travel and Film Spectatorship in Gilliam's *Twelve Monkeys* and Bigelow's *Strange Days*', *Kinema: A Journal for Film and Audiovisual Media*, Spring. Available at: http://www.arts.uwaterloo.ca/FINE/juhde/rasca011.htm.

Renov, Michael (1993) 'Introduction: The Truth About Non-Fiction', in Michael Renov (ed.) *Theorizing Documentary*. New York and London: Routledge, 1–11.

Ressner, Jeffrey (1999) 'A Maiden's Vision', *Time*, 154, 19. Available at: http://www.time.com/time/magazine/intl/article.

Rosenberg, Scott (1995) 'SQUID Junkies Make "Strange" Bedfellows', *San Francisco Examiner*, 13 October.

Rynning, Roald (1996) 'Happy New Millennium', *Film Review*, May, 14, 22–4.

Salisbury, Mark (1991) 'Hollywood's Macho Woman? Kathryn Bigelow talks to Mark Salisbury', *The Guardian*, 21 November, 27.

Sammon, Paul M. (1996) *Future Noir: The Making of Blade Runner*. London: Orion Media.

Sarris, Andrew (1981) 'Notes on the auteur theory in 1962', in John Caughie (ed.) *Theories of Authorship*. London: Routledge, 62–7.

Schmitz, Greg (2000) Preview of *The Weight of Water*. Available at: www.upcomingmovies.com/weightof water.htm.

Schneider, Steven Jay (2002) 'Psychoanalysis in/and/of the horror film', *Projections: a Publication of the Forum for the Psychoanalytic Study of Film*, 15, 1, 3–20.

Self, Robert T. (1994) 'Redressing the law in Kathryn Bigelow's *Blue Steel*', *Journal of Film and Video*, 46, 2, 31–43 (extract reprinted in this collection).

Sharrett, C. (1996) 'The Horror Film in Neoconservative Culture' (1993), reprinted in Barry Keith Grant (ed.) *The Dread of Difference: Gender and the Horror Film*. Austin: University of Texas Press, 253–76.

Shaviro, Steven (1993) *The Cinematic Body*. Minneapolis: University of Minnesota Press.

Shreve, Anita (1997) *The Weight of Water*. London: Abacus.

Silverman, Kaja (1988) *The Acoustic Mirror*. Bloomington: Indiana University Press.

Smith, Gavin (1995) 'Momentum and Design', *Film Comment*, 31, 5, 46–60 (extract reprinted in this collection).

Stilwell, Robynn J. (2000) '*Sense & Sensibility*: Form, Function, and Genre in the Film Score',

Acta Musicologica, 72, 2, 25–46.

_____ (2001) 'Sound and Empathy: Gender, Subjectivity, and the Cinematic Soundscape', in Kevin J. Donnelly (ed.) *Film Music: Critical Approaches*. Edinburgh: Edinburgh University Press, 167–87.

_____ (forthcoming) '"The Sound is Out There": Score, Sound Design and Exoticism in *The X-Files*', in Allan Moore (ed.) *The Sound of Popular Music*. Cambridge: Cambridge University Press.

Stringer, Julian (1997) '"Your tender smiles give me strength": paradigms of masculinity in John Woo's *A Better Tomorrow* and *The Killer*', *Screen*, 38, 1, 26–41.

Svitil, Torene (1997) 'Kathryn Bigelow – Director', *US Premiere*, February, 88.

Tasker, Yvonne (1999) 'Bigger Than Life', *Sight and Sound*, 9, 5, 12–15.

_____ (2002) *Fifty Key Contemporary Filmmakers*, London: Routledge, 59–65.

Todorov, Tzvetan (1975) *The Fantastic: A Structural Approach to a Literary Genre*. Ithaca and New York: Cornell University Press.

Tudor, Andrew (1974) *Image and Influence: Studies in the Sociology of Film*. London: Allen and Unwin.

Tulloch, John & Henry Jenkins (1995) *Science Fiction Audiences: Watching Doctor Who and Star Trek*. London: Routledge.

Twitchell, James B. (1985) *Dreadful Pleasures: An Anatomy of Modern Horror*. New York: Oxford University Press.

Ulmer, James & Robert Marich (1993) 'Lightstorm Deal with Fox Changes Direction', *The Hollywood Reporter*, 9 July, 1–25.

'Vassar Girl' (2000) Review of *The Weight of Water*. Available at: www.insideout.co.uk/films/w/weight_of_water.shtml.

Vertov, Dziga (1984) *Kino-Eye: The Writings of Dziga Vertov*. Berkeley: University of California Press.

Vincendeau, Ginette (1998) 'Issues in European cinema', in John Hill & Pamela Church Gibson (eds) *The Oxford Guide to Film Studies*. Oxford: Oxford University Press, 440–8.

Waldman, Diane (1990) 'There's More to a Positive Image than Meets the Eye', in Patricia Erens (ed.) *Issues in Feminist Film Criticism*, Bloomington and Indiana: Indiana University Press, 13–18.

Weis, Elisabeth (1982) *The Silent Scream: Alfred Hitchcock's Sound Track*, Rutherford, NJ: Fairleigh Dickinson University Press.

Williams, Linda (2000) 'Film Bodies: Gender, Genre and Excess', in Robert Stam & Toby Miller (eds) *Film and Theory: An Anthology*. Oxford: Blackwell, 207–21.

Wollen, Peter (1971) 'The *auteur* theory', in John Caughie (ed.) *Theories of Authorship*. London: Routledge, 138–51.

_____ (1972) *Signs and Meaning in the Cinema*. Bloomington: Indiana University Press.

Wood, Robin (1979) 'Introduction', in Andrew Britton, Richard Lippe, Tony Williams & Robin Wood (eds) *American Nightmare: Essays on the Horror Film*. Toronto: Festival of Festivals.

_____ (1986) *Hollywood from Vietnam to Reagan*. New York: Columbia University Press.

Wyatt, Justin (1994) *High Concept: Movies and Marketing in Hollywood*. Texas: University of Texas Press.

Zahedi, Firooz (1995) 'Movies', *Vogue*, October, 194–6.

Zizek, Slavoj (1999) *The Ticklish Subject: The Absent Centre of Political Ontology*. London: Verso.

INDEX